Functional Future for Bibliographic Control

The quest to evolve bibliographic control to an equal or greater standing within the current information environment is on-going. As information organizers we are working in a time where information and communication technology (ICT) has pushed our status quo to its limits and where innovation often needs the pressure of do or die in order to get started. The year 2010 was designated as the Year of Cataloging Research and we made progress on studying the challenges facing metadata and information organization practices. However, one year of research is merely a drop in the bucket, especially given the results of the Resource and Description and Access (RDA) National Test and the Library of Congress' decision to investigate the possibility of transitioning the MARC21 format. This book addresses how information professionals can create a functional environment in which we move beyond just representing information resources and into an environment that both represents and connects at a deeper level. Most importantly, it offers insight on transitioning into new communities of practice and awareness by reassessing our purpose, re-charting our efforts, reasserting our expertise in the areas that information organizer have traditionally claimed but are losing due to stagnation and lack of vision.

This book was published as a double special issue of the *Journal of Library Metadata*.

Shawne D. Miksa is an Associate Professor in the Department of Library and Information Sciences and Associate Director of the Interdisciplinary Information Science PhD Program in the College of Information (COI), University of North Texas, USA. She has published and taught in the areas of Information Organization, Cataloging and Classification.

Functional Future for Bibliographic Control

Transitioning into new communities of practice and awareness

Edited by
Shawne D. Miksa

LONDON AND NEW YORK

First published 2014 by Routledge

2 Park Square, Milton Park, Abingdon, Oxfordshire OX14 4RN
711 Third Avenue, New York, NY 10017

Routledge is an imprint of the Taylor & Francis Group, an informa business

First issued in paperback 2018

Copyright © 2014 Taylor & Francis

All rights reserved. No part of this book may be reprinted or reproduced or utilised in any form or by any electronic, mechanical, or other means, now known or hereafter invented, including photocopying and recording, or in any information storage or retrieval system, without permission in writing from the publishers.

Notice:
Product or corporate names may be trademarks or registered trademarks, and are used only for identification and explanation without intent to infringe.

British Library Cataloguing in Publication Data
A catalogue record for this book is available from the British Library

ISBN 13: 978-0-415-71602-4 (hbk)
ISBN 13: 978-1-138-37747-9 (pbk)

Typeset in Sabon
by Taylor & Francis Books

Publisher's Note
The publisher accepts responsibility for any inconsistencies that may have arisen during the conversion of this book from journal articles to book chapters, namely the possible inclusion of journal terminology.

Disclaimer
Every effort has been made to contact copyright holders for their permission to reprint material in this book. The publishers would be grateful to hear from any copyright holder who is not here acknowledged and will undertake to rectify any errors or omissions in future editions of this book.

Contents

Citation Information   vii

1. Introduction
   Shawne D. Miksa   1

2. Authority Control for Scientific Data: The Case of Molecular Biology
   Shuheng Wu, Besiki Stvilia, and Dong Joon Lee   9

3. The Intersection of Standards and Professional Knowledge, Skills, and Service: One Road to Ensuring a Functional Future of Bibliographic Control for Serials Acquisition, Management, and Access
   Nadine P. Ellero and Dean E. Cody   31

4. Could the Functional Future of Bibliographic Control Change Cataloging Work? An Exploration Using Abbott
   Gretchen L. Hoffman   59

5. The Ship Has Sailed and We Aren't On It: How Catalogers Could Support User Tasks and Why We Won't
   Mary Z. Rose   75

6. Subject Access: Conceptual Models, Functional Requirements, and Empirical Data
   Oksana L. Zavalina   88

7. Reconsidering Universal Bibliographic Control in Light of the Semantic Web
   Gordon Dunsire, Diane Hillmann, and Jon Phipps   112

8. Serials, FRBR, and Library Linked Data: A Way Forward
   Laura Krier   125

9. Effective Learning and Teaching of RDA: Applying Adult Learning Theory
   Naomi Kietzke Young   136

10. Charting a Course With NOMAP: Integrating Metadata Workflows Into a Traditional Cataloging Unit
    Teressa M. Keenan   147

CONTENTS

11. Preliminary Training for RDA: A Survey of Cataloging Department Heads
    Elyssa M. Sanner — 161

12. "Mind the [Trans-Atlantic] Gap, Please": Awareness and Training Needs of UK Catalogers
    Anne Welsh, Celine Carty, and Helen Williams — 190

13. Inadvertent RDA: New Catalogers' Errors in AACR2
    Jean Harden — 212

14. What Language Death and Language Planning Tell Us About MARC and RDA
    Sarah Theimer — 227

15. The Possibility of the Infinite Library: Exploring the Conceptual Boundaries of Works and Texts of Bibliographic Description
    Stacy Allison-Cassin — 242

    Index — 259

Citation Information

The chapters in this book were originally published in the *Journal of Library Metadata*, volume 12, issue 2–3 (2012). When citing this material, please use the original page numbering for each article, as follows:

Chapter 1
Introduction
Shawne D. Miksa
Journal of Library Metadata, volume 12, issue 2–3
(2012) pp. 53–60

Chapter 2
Authority Control for Scientific Data: The Case of Molecular Biology
Shuheng Wu, Besiki Stvilia, and Dong Joon Lee
Journal of Library Metadata, volume 12, issue 2–3
(2012) pp. 61–82

Chapter 3
The Intersection of Standards and Professional Knowledge, Skills, and Service: One Road to Ensuring a Functional Future of Bibliographic Control for Serials Acquisition, Management, and Access
Nadine P. Ellero and Dean E. Cody
Journal of Library Metadata, volume 12, issue 2–3
(2012) pp. 83–110

Chapter 4
Could the Functional Future of Bibliographic Control Change Cataloging Work? An Exploration Using Abbott
Gretchen L. Hoffman
Journal of Library Metadata, volume 12, issue 2–3
(2012) pp. 111–126

Chapter 5
The Ship Has Sailed and We Aren't On It: How Catalogers Could Support User Tasks and Why We Won't
Mary Z. Rose
Journal of Library Metadata, volume 12, issue 2–3 (2012) pp. 127–139

Chapter 6
Subject Access: Conceptual Models, Functional Requirements, and Empirical Data
Oksana L. Zavalina
Journal of Library Metadata, volume 12, issue 2–3 (2012) pp. 140–163

Chapter 7
Reconsidering Universal Bibliographic Control in Light of the Semantic Web
Gordon Dunsire, Diane Hillmann, and Jon Phipps
Journal of Library Metadata, volume 12, issue 2–3 (2012) pp. 164–176

Chapter 8
Serials, FRBR, and Library Linked Data: A Way Forward
Laura Krier
Journal of Library Metadata, volume 12, issue 2–3 (2012) pp. 177–187

Chapter 9
Effective Learning and Teaching of RDA: Applying Adult Learning Theory
Naomi Kietzke Young
Journal of Library Metadata, volume 12, issue 2–3 (2012) pp. 188–198

Chapter 10
Charting a Course With NOMAP: Integrating Metadata Workflows Into a Traditional Cataloging Unit
Teressa M. Keenan
Journal of Library Metadata, volume 12, issue 2–3 (2012) pp. 199–212

Chapter 11
Preliminary Training for RDA: A Survey of Cataloging Department Heads
Elyssa M. Sanner
Journal of Library Metadata, volume 12, issue 2–3 (2012) pp. 213–241

Chapter 12
"Mind the [Trans-Atlantic] Gap, Please": Awareness and Training Needs of UK Catalogers
Anne Welsh, Celine Carty, and Helen Williams
Journal of Library Metadata, volume 12, issue 2–3 (2012) pp. 242–263

Chapter 13
Inadvertent RDA: New Catalogers' Errors in AACR2
Jean Harden
Journal of Library Metadata, volume 12, issue 2–3 (2012) pp. 264–278

Chapter 14
What Language Death and Language Planning Tell Us About MARC and RDA
Sarah Theimer
Journal of Library Metadata, volume 12, issue 2–3 (2012) pp. 279–293

Chapter 15
The Possibility of the Infinite Library: Exploring the Conceptual Boundaries of Works and Texts of Bibliographic Description
Stacy Allison-Cassin
Journal of Library Metadata, volume 12, issue 2–3 (2012) pp. 294–309

Please direct any queries you may have about the citations to clsuk.permissions@cengage.com

Introduction

SHAWNE D. MIKSA

Department of Library and Information Sciences, College of Information, University of North Texas, Denton, Texas, USA

The quest to evolve bibliographic control to an equal or greater standing within the current information environment is ongoing. The pace is often uneven, peppered with furious starts and stops, but it is moving; the price of inactivity, of not moving at all, is too great. This special issue of the *Journal of Library Metadata* focuses on the functional future of bibliographic control and was intended to substantiate the need for a decade of research in our profession (Carlyle, 2009). In hindsight it seems childish to ask for a mere decade, especially when compared to the large number of paper proposals received for this issue. We need a good 20 years' research just to accommodate the study of the shifts in thinking and in practice that our field is currently undergoing, then another 20 to evaluate the impact of that shift. The articles in this issue show that we are perched at the top of the big events coming our way—we are leaning over—and gravity is starting to pull us in a new direction. It is how we react to these events that will be a deciding factor.

The 14 articles comprising this issue are divided into two parts (for convenience) and are ordered in such a way as to give the reader a road map of sorts through some of the common themes and ideas expressed in each one individually and collectively as a whole. The more prominent themes revolve around (1) our taking a step back in order to contemplate and reconsider what we do within the broader context of the current and future information environment; (2) how we need to rechart or redirect our efforts within that context; (3) how we need to reassert our expertise of the processes and practices through learning/relearning and through retraining, exploring, and integration, and perhaps even giving ourselves permission to do all of it in a way that is comfortable and nonthreatening; and (4) the transitioning into new communities of practice and awareness. Several papers address specific issues such as subject access, authority control, serials management, and philosophical foundations in light of Functional Requirements for

Bibliographic Records (FRBR) and Resource Description and Access (RDA), while others address more general issues such as education, awareness of trends and issues, and metadata creation, control, and use.

On one hand, it is all very exciting. We are working in a time when information and communication technology (ICT) has pushed our status quo to its limits and where innovation often needs the pressure of do or die in order to get started. On the other hand, it is terrifying, depressing, and has many experienced professionals thinking of an early retirement. (The Clash's anthem "Should I stay or should I go?" has been rolling around in my mind for a while now).

This issue starts with an article on authority control in molecular biology. Why? Sometimes it's good to pull our minds out of our collective professional and academic environments in order to see how processes that we know so well work somewhere else. Wu, Stvilia, and Lee provide an opportunity to see a different kind of metadata and the processes used to organize it for access by biologists and bioinformatics professionals. The authors write that "providing open access to data and integrating data from different contexts also highlight the need for better reasoning about the quality and interoperability of identifier and reference/knowledge organization systems use for data referencing and entity resolution." The conceptual similarities (named entity recognition, disambiguation, and unification in molecular biology, and name and subject heading identification, validation, justification, and contextualization in descriptive cataloging) are quite evident and the authors make a good case for how bioinformatics professionals and information professionals can inform the other, especially "with academic libraries increasingly involved with scientific-data curation through institutional data repositories." It also provides a good opportunity to emphasize the value of looking with new eyes at the kinds of data we work with every day. Data in need of control for access and use should be familiar to us, regardless of its origin, its carrier, and its eventual "context." Furthermore, we mitigate that data with structure and standards. Ellero and Cody "strongly contend that continued and deepening participation in the review and creation of standards by librarians will significantly add to building a functional future of bibliographic control that is vibrant and flexible." One of the most important components of bibliographic control is "control" itself—where and when it is needed, or not—and a crucial part of ensuring that control is reliant upon what goes on behind the scenes. Ellero and Cody relate their collective professional experience of reviewing NISO standards through their participation on the Medical Library Association's Technical Services Standards Committee (MLA/TSSC) and in doing so provide a strong example of the importance of professional participation and responsibility for what goes on behind the scenes.

It is not surprising at this stage in the development of RDA and its implementation that many of the papers focus on training, retraining, and overall changes in cataloging practices. It isn't just "change," this shouldn't be in question, but rather how fundamental the change.[1] Several authors employ theories to address issues such as adult learning and how technology changes a profession, as well as to explore conceptual boundaries of works and texts. Hoffman uses Abbott's "System of Professions" to show "how technology can both destroy and create professional work". There is no doubt that the future will entail new tasks and new work jurisdictions. We have already seen it in play. As a profession we will need to decide how competitive we want to be and how much territory we will claim. There will be no easy pathway, with new models (FRBR, FRAD, etc.), new rules, and new information environments to navigate. As shown in the past with the implementation of AACR2, there was a period of craziness, criticism, and resistance and, as we are seeing with the change to RDA, a tendency to sit back and wait to see who makes the first move. Hoffman states that "professional work can be given away, taken away, or simply abandoned." New work needs to be claimed. This will be difficult because much of it has already been given away (i.e., to vendors, paraprofessionals) or claimed by other professionals (e.g., metadata librarian vs. catalogers). As to the latter, including both types of work in a name many show library administrators that cataloging units want to do the work. Furthermore, Hoffman feels that cataloging could be put in a tenuous position if catalogers give up or abandon tasks without claiming new ones. She argues that RDA, FRBR, and Functional Requirements for Authority Data (FRAD) provide new work, especially authority work, but only if there are enough catalogers to claim it, or reclaim it, from library vendors. This also puts much great emphasis on educating and training new catalogers. It would be beneficial to come to terms with the similarities and the differences of metadata work and cataloging work as neither has to be mutually exclusive. In many ways, Hoffman echoes what Jesse Shera wrote about the library profession exactly 40 years ago: "The profession cannot go on as it has in the past; it must either remold itself into a true profession or it must surrender its age-old responsibilities to others" (Shera, 1972, p. 498).

But how can a profession claim work if the right tools (i.e. the catalog) are not there to help convey the results of that work to the users? Through an examination of the interface characteristics of an ideal "FRBR-ized" catalog and a conventional catalog, Rose concludes that "it isn't possible for catalogers to catalog for a future FRBR-based catalog and simultaneously modify cataloging practices to promote the effectiveness of current interface design." Unfortunately, there are few FRBR-based catalogs populated with MARC-encoded and RDA-based records currently on hand to provide an environment in which this modification can take place. Rose rightly points out that collaborating with the interface designers and "changing cataloging practices to optimize the effectiveness of the catalog interfaces being developed" is the only way to move forward. Just as put forward by Hoffman, catalogers have to make a choice about in which direction to move and the work that is to be done. Rose offers some practical suggestions for going about enhancing a key component of our future bibliographic control.

Another of these key features, especially in the proper functioning of the catalog information system, is subject access by way of quality subject metadata. Zavalina provides a discussion of the treatment of subject entities, attributes, and relationships in FRBR, FRAD, and FRSAD models as well as empirical evidence of users search queries in a large-scale digital library in order to inform how subject access, subject entities, and representation are addressed in RDA. While it is true that there are placeholder chapters in RDA intended to address subject access and control, it is apparent to Zavalina that "subject access is not currently sufficiently addressed by any of these documents" and that is has long been a inadequacy in bibliographic control. She concludes that priority should be given to providing more detail about the "relationships of *objects* to other entities, in particular to other FRBR Group 3 entities of *event*, *concept*, and *place*." This study is a good example of the type of research involving the FR models and RDA that should take place now and in the future.

The issue of richer entity relationship representation is bringing to the forefront the possibility of bibliographic control moving to new domains, or evolving into something radically different. In particular, linked data and the Semantic Web have become popular discussion points of late in the cataloging arena. This falls squarely within the theme of looking at what we do within the broader context of the current and future information environment and how we need to rechart or redirect our efforts within that context. Dunsire, Hillmann, and Phipps present an argument for placing metadata statements within Resource-Description-Framework-based environment so that "individual metadata statements represented by three-part data triples in the form subject-predicate-object statements", instead of a traditional catalog record, are created and linked. They write:

> RDF [Resource Description Framework] "records" represent arbitrary collections of statements. These statements may be defined and validated by any number of metadata "formats" and a collection of such statements can be composed of properties selected by the publisher of the metadata. Systems aggregating this published data are free to choose the properties from this record that the system "understands." Properties defined by MARC21 can be freely mixed with properties defined by RDA, or any other vocabularies. RDF "records" can vary widely in terms of overall content and there are no constraints on what a system may publish.

If we are to remain relevant within new and emerging information infrastructures then we need to consider best methods and best practices for working within and across multiple metadata schemas and in systems that may not necessarily use the traditional "record" unit as the vessel for containing data. As suggested by Dunsire, Hillmann, and Phipps, shifting our focus from a top-down approach of controlling data to a bottom-up approach hinged on semantic mappings is developing as one of these possible futures.

Moving away from a records-based system certainly would bring about a radical shift in what we do and how we do it. Krier's article takes the idea of linked data in an RDF-based framework and applies it to serials cataloging. Krier contends,

> [that the] separation between the journal and the articles it contains has been deeply embedded in cataloging practices for over a century, and current ideas about bibliographic relationships haven't adequately addressed the issue of trying to bring these two work-level resources together.

If the model were to be expanded then it would be possible to effectively use RDF as "the engine that drives collocation and discovery." This greatly hinges on both the journal and the article being considered a "work" as defined in FRBR. Krier's article makes a strong argument for what really comes down to the bibliographic-control community making the decision to accept new definitions and new models. This includes modifying the FRBR model to better reflect the variations of attributes and relationships between entities when dealing with different information resources. FRBR gives us a good starting place, but there are still changes that could be made (Zhang & Salaba, 2009).

The articles in Part 2 reflect and reinforce the themes from Part 1 by examining issues such as education, training, integration, awareness, planning, and exploration, some within specific scenarios or environments. The first two articles focus on new and changing communities of practice and how they will greatly inform changes in practice as the profession moves forward. Young addresses the need to change our teaching and learning habits during this time of upheaval by viewing the profession through the lens of adult learning theory. She advocates that as a profession we can "bring about long-term understanding and fluency to the profession" by exploring new types of education and training practices, instead of limiting them to the traditional workshops and seminars. Young also highlights the emotional side of learning to show how our personality type is closely tied to how we do our job, and that we need to create learning environments that take personalities into account.[2] She concludes by stating that "this time of upheaval will lead to the ascendancy of new experts and the decline of former ones, and the re-forming of alliances of various kinds." Keenan also discusses some of the more personal aspects of transition in the workplace by relating the steps involved and lessons learned about changes in cataloging workflow while working on digital projects. Keenan echoes Hoffman's earlier conclusions about new work tasks and new jurisdictions by relating how at each stage of the NOMAP project "workflows have been evaluated and redesigned to better integrate metadata creation into the general workflow of traditional cataloging." Overall, the lessons learned from the project brought about changes in philosophies and procedures.

The next three articles highlight specific issues of training and educating of new and experienced catalogers. Through a survey of cataloging department managers in U.S. academic libraries, Sanner provides evidence of the kind of preliminary training taking place, training that should occur in the future, and perceptions of the usefulness and effectiveness of the training as the implementation of new standards and new cataloging rules comes closer to realization. The data suggest a positive move toward the successful implementation of RDA, but Sanner also found gaps that need to be addressed. In particular, she found that willful ignorance with regard to some of the changes coming down the pipeline could be harmful to all. She writes that "the cataloging community cannot remain ignorant and must begin learning about RDA in order to avoid being left behind." This echoes Hoffman's sentiments that a profession has to claim its territory. If we want to move forward, then we adapt.

Welsh, Carty, and Williams also study awareness and training needs via action research in which they characterize two days of email exchange in an online forum in the United Kingdom. The e-forum focused on current awareness of RDA, in addition to the issue of from where and from whom the training would come. What is most interesting about this piece is the emotional perspective of the catalogers in the United Kingdom. The authors write,

> The issues we identify are the same on both sides of the Atlantic, but without the culture of the annual ALA conference and the structured training provided by the US RDA Test (which can now be cascaded from test institutions to other cataloguing agencies), UK cataloguers in these emails express themselves less confidently about their actions and observations so far.

Participants also expressed concern about the possible demise of the MARC standard, which had just been made known to both the United Kingdom and, in truth, much of the global cataloging community.[3] The thought of having to work with records created using AACR2 and RDA in a sort of "hybrid" catalog was a prominent concern on its own. (In the United States there was almost instantaneous protest of RDA records mixed in with AACR2 records during the national testing.) The possibility of a new or radically changed encoding standard served only to heighten the level of tension.

Harden's study, however, offers an interesting spin on future education and training, especially as it concerns new catalogers, paraprofessionals, and student workers. The professional music catalogers at the University of

North Texas were part of a subgroup of music catalogers who participated in the national RDA test. In addition to the professional catalogers, student workers were also used in the construction of AACR2-based records. Harden feels that the project "produced the ideal situation for making a preliminary determination of how easy it would be to train catalogers to use the new cataloging code" and that it "provided a treasure trove of errors from which it was possible to deduce how readily new catalogers were apt to accept the new rules." Harden found that beginning catalogers creating AACR2-based records, and without ever having read RDA, very often produced RDA-compliant cataloging. In terms of training, this would shift the burden of more elemental cataloging away from experienced catalogers and allow them to concentrate more on the harder aspects of cataloging such as "challenges of clarifying the links among the applicable FRBR entities." At the very least, Harden's study illuminates a future area of research that looks at how RDA may support more instinctive cataloging judgment.

Theimer's essay on language death and language planning and Allison-Cassin's essay on the possibility of an infinite library brings this special issue to a close. Both authors delve into the more philosophical aspects of bibliographic control and both offer food for thought as we lean forward into what will surely be a terribly terrifying and exciting time. Instead of the brutish and mocking attacks on MARC found throughout the literature, Theimer presents one of the finer and more scholarly examples of a thoughtful essay on MARC by examining "environmental and cultural factors that typically accompany language death to determine if those traits are exhibited in MARC." Is MARC really a language? We cataloger's often joke that we "speak MARC" or that we engage in "MARC-speak." (Our secret language. The purity of the numerical tag has long had universal appeal; the 245 designates the title regardless of where in the world the record originates.) Theimer's essay is timely. Library of Congress (LC) made the announcement in 2011 to investigate how to transition to a new bibliographic framework in order to better support the type of bibliographic control that is relevant for the current and future information environments. MARC will surely make a long, slow shuffle out the door. Hopefully it will be with the respect that it deserves and in a way that Henriette Avram would approve.[4]

Whatever that future is for MARC and for bibliographic control overall, Allison-Cassin contends that "radical re-thinking of traditional conceptions of the bibliographic universe, work, text and information is required if we are to truly have a new vision of "the library," one that truly approaches and approximates a "universe of knowledge." She asked how we might create a more performative form of bibliographic control. Like Hoffman, Allison-Cassin echoes Shera (and so too Margaret Egan) and the idea of a social epistemological foundation for librarianship—social activity interacting with knowledge.[5] How can we create a functional environment in which we move beyond just recording attributes of information resources as a mechanism for matching query to resources and support what Allison-Cassin describes as social connections and "the messy, serendipitous ways in which our everyday interactions with information build human culture." While this isn't an unfamiliar goal, it is something we have consistently neglected for the desire of making a good descriptive record. We need "to connect" and not just "represent."

While this collection of articles in no way covers all the issues as it concerns the functional future, it does address some of the more important issues that we should take note of as we move forward. As a profession we consist of many communities of practice and as happens again and again over time we need to reassess and reorient ourselves in order to keep moving in the right direction. Perhaps the more important action for us is to keep the larger picture in mind; to look overall at what we do, how we do it, and, most importantly, why we do it.

NOTES

1. For example, instead of bibliographic control, why not multigraphic control?
2. Young cites a study of library personality types using the Myers-Briggs Type Inventory (MBTI) and not surprisingly most technical service librarians were classified as 'introverts'. Interestingly, at the time of my reading Young's paper CNN's news website was running a story by Susan Cain in which she discusses how introverts quietly run the world. See http://www.cnn.com/2012/03/18/opinion/cain-introverts-power/index.html?iref=allsearch for a video clip and article. In the article Cain writes "... the more freedom we give introverts to be themselves, the more they'll dream up their own unique solutions to the problems that bedevil us" (para 17). Cain's book is entitled *Quiet: The power of introverts in a world that can't stop talking*.
3. I doubt it came as a big shock, though, considering the volume of literature advocating for MARC's retirement.
4. In January 2012 at the ALA Midwinter meeting, Dr. Deanna Marcum, only recently retired as Associate Director of Library Services at LC, fittingly asked how Henriette Avram (primary developer of MARC in the 1960s) would view MARC in the age of Google. See http://www.loc.gov/marc/transition/news/minutes-alamw-2012.html.
5. Shera wrote that "the new discipline that is envisaged here (and for which, for want of a better name, Margaret E. Egan originated the phrase, *social epistemology*) should provide a framework for the investigation of the complex problem of the nature of the intellectual process in society—a study of the ways in which society as a whole achieves a perceptive relation to its total environment." (Shera, 1972, p. 112)

REFERENCES

Cain, S. (2012, March). Introverts run the world—quietly. *CNN Opinion*. Retrieved from http://www.cnn.com/2012/03/18/opinion/cain-introverts-power/index.html?iref = allsearch

Carlyle, A. (2009). Invited editorial: Announcing 2010, year of cataloging research. *Cataloging & Classification Quarterly, 47*(8), 687–690.

Shera, J. H. (1972). *Foundation of education for librarianship*. New York, NY: Wiley-Becker & Hayes.

Zhang, Y., & Salaba, A. (2009). Implementing FRBR in libraries: Key issues and future directions. New York, NY: Neal Schuman.

Authority Control for Scientific Data: The Case of Molecular Biology

SHUHENG WU, BESIKI STVILIA, and DONG JOON LEE
School of Library and Information Studies, Florida State University, Tallahassee, Florida, USA

This article analyzes the authority control practices in molecular biology using literature review and scenario analysis and makes a comparison with bibliographic authority control. The analysis indicates the absence of conceptual authority control model in molecular bioinformatics. In addition to traditional knowledge organization tools, authority control in molecular biology requires the use of reference sequences and version numbers to identify entities and keep track of entity changes. The identified authority control issues are conceptualized as quality problems caused by four sources. This study can inform librarians and educators of the need for and approaches to authority control in molecular biology.

INTRODUCTION

Research processes have become increasingly data driven, and there are growing needs as well as opportunities to share, reuse, and aggregate data from different contexts. The Institute for Museum and Library Services (IMLS, 2011), the National Endowment for the Humanities (NEH, 2011), the National Science Foundation (NSF, 2010), and the National Institutes of Health (NIH, 2010) now require applicants to submit data management plans, including plans for disseminating and providing access to research data and related metadata. To maintain data in a usable/reusable state for ongoing research, education, reporting, verification, and evaluation, it is essential to ensure the quality of related metadata, including entity metadata (i.e., entity profiles). Effective reuse and aggregation of data may require knowledge of community, disciplinary and cultural differences in metadata quality requirements, rules, norms, and references sources (Atkins et al., 2003; National Science Board, 2005; National Science Foundation, 2007; Stvilia, Gasser, Twidale, & Smith, 2007).

Entities are distinguishable objects that can be concrete or abstract (Elmasri & Navathe, 2000). Examples of entities are books, authors, proteins, or genes. A set of important attributes that characterize a particular entity constitutes the entity's metadata profile, which can be included in reference databases (e.g., authority databases) and used for entity determination and disambiguation. Effective management of entity metadata, the ability of entity resolution and disambiguation, are essential for scientific research processes, as well as for scientist productivity and impact evaluation. In biology, taxonomists may need to determine whether a particular specimen belongs to an established taxon, or if it represents a new taxon. Genomics researchers may need to distinguish the sample's identity in order to identify genotype-phenotype relationships at the individual or population level. Librarians, and in particular catalogers, need to resolve different entities in bibliographic databases in order to link and collocate related works. Likewise, administrators and bibliometrics/scientometrics researchers may need to resolve author names to evaluate the productivity and impact of individual scientists, groups, or institutions.

There have been distinct domain-specific approaches to entity metadata management. Libraries have managed entity metadata through authority databases and controlled vocabularies. Similarly, life sciences rely on elaborate manually constructed and manually maintained taxonomies, keys, and ontologies to make entity determination. In addition, there have been efforts to automate entity resolution and disambiguation in large-scale text collections (see Smalheiser & Torvik, 2009, for a recent review). Different communities have proposed different conceptual frameworks, metadata schemas, and data structures for entity identifiers and metadata profiles (e.g., FRAD, URI, ISBN, DOI, LSID, PURL, MARC21 for Authority). As Semantic Web technologies become more widely accepted, libraries, institutions, governments, and communities are starting to disseminate their data and the reference sources used in entity resolution as linked data for open access and use (e.g., DBpedia,[1] LinkingOpenData[2]).

The efforts of providing open access to data and integrating data from different contexts also highlight the need for better reasoning about the quality and interoperability of identifier and reference/knowledge organization systems used for data referencing and entity resolution. Needs and requirements for entity metadata control, and their operationalizations—what entities are controlled, what sets of attributes are used for each entity—may change in time and space. Different domains may control for different entities using different sets of attributes. Furthermore, these sets may evolve and change over time as the amount of data grows and more attributes are needed for entity resolution. Finally, entities and their instances are dynamic in that they move in space and time. Authors may change names, affiliations, disciplines, and residences. Data, too, are often "works in progress." Old knowledge becomes obsolete as new knowledge becomes available, and can be reused and updated by different actors (e.g., genome annotation data).

PROBLEM STATEMENT

Most biology journals now require submission of newly sequenced DNA to one of the public nucleotide repositories (e.g., GenBank[3]) before publication. This policy has led to great success in the progress of biology, and exponential increase in the size and usage of nucleotide sequences. Since the publication of the human genome in 2001, the world has entered into the "post-genome age" (Higgs & Attwood, 2005, p. 4). With advances in sequencing technologies, high-throughput experimental techniques have been developed to study large numbers of genes or proteins simultaneously. Microarrays, proteomics, and structural genomics are examples of high-throughput techniques. The exponential increase in the size of nucleotide sequences, the availability of whole genome sequencing, and the large amount of data generated from high-throughput experiments—data encoded in different formats using different vocabularies and stored in different databases—pose challenges for organizing, storing, retrieving, analyzing, and managing data in biological repositories. Furthermore, the increasingly-data-driven science, along with funding agencies and publications requiring scientists to provide access to research data, puts pressure on scientists' home institutions and their libraries to provide appropriate infrastructure and expand the scope of their traditional services to meet the changing data management and dissemination needs of their constituents.

Metadata management for entity and instance determination, disambiguation, and referencing, referred to in libraries as authority control, is an essential part of data management in any domain. Libraries need to have better understanding of the data practices of different disciplines to be effective in assisting their faculty with the management and dissemination of research data. Although there is significant prior research of the disciplinary practices of authority control in Library and Information Science (LIS) and other disciplines, there has been relatively little examination of the similarities and differences of authority control, and the reusability of authority models, tools, and data across different domains.

This paper analyzes the authority control practices in the area of molecular biology, and compares those to the authority control practices in libraries. This can inform librarians and library educators about the requirements for authority data in molecular biology, and help align library authority models, vocabularies, and data with the needs of scientific-data curation and research tasks.

OVERVIEW OF RESEARCH QUESTIONS AND METHODOLOGY

This paper explores the needs and requirements for data referencing, entity resolution, and authority control in molecular biology. It helps illuminate the following research questions: What are the needs and requirements for data referencing and authority control in molecular biology? How is authority control currently implemented in molecular biology? What are some of the frameworks, models, controlled vocabularies and schemas used? What are some of the issues and problems with the current practices of authority control in molecular biology? What solutions have been sought? How do the models and practices of authority control from molecular biology compare to bibliographic authority control and how can one field inform the other? A detailed examination of the literature and entity resolution and authority control frameworks, models, and systems is provided.

In addition to literature analysis, the study's methodology includes the use of specific data-use scenarios to illustrate the needs for and issues surrounding data referencing, entity determination, and disambiguation at different levels and in different activities within molecular bioinformatics. Scenarios and scenario-based task analysis (Go & Carroll, 2004a, 2004b) are particularly helpful when there is a need to identify and develop an inquiry into nonroutine or future possible uses of technology and, thus, nicely complement the analysis of established frameworks, models, and standards from the literature that are tailored to the routine tasks of a particular domain. The scenario development in this study was informed by an examination of the data sets generated from three NSF funded research projects at the Florida State University and were collected from the American Chemistry Society Publications Database[4] and the Web of Knowledge.[5]

AUTHORITY CONTROL IN MOLECULAR BIOLOGY

Molecular biology is a branch of biology that seeks to explain the structure, function, and interaction of biological molecules, primarily nucleic acids (i.e., DNA, RNA) and proteins (MacMullen & Denn, 2005; Turner, McLennan, Bates, & White, 2005). Molecular bioinformatics is concerned with developing and applying computer-information technologies for studying and organizing data and knowledge about these entities and relationships. The concept of authority control in molecular biology is associated with three tasks: *named entity recognition*, *disambiguation*, and *unification*. The named entities in molecular biology include RNA, DNA (e.g., genes, gene clusters, genomes), proteins, species, organisms, and others (Blaschke, Hirschman, & Valencia, 2002; de Bruijn & Martin, 2002; Krallinger, Erhardt, Valencia, 2005; Krallinger, Valencia, & Hirschman, 2008). Biological scientists usually report newly found entities in the literature, and deposit their information to related databases as required by scholarly journals. Each record of these databases usually provides references to the publications that discuss the data in the record. Biological scientists search these databases for information about biological entities using their names and alternates, which are usually incomplete with respect to those found in the literature (Cohen & Hersh, 2005).

The purpose of named entity *recognition* in biology is to identify all the instances of a name for a specific type of biological object within a collection of text (Cohen & Hersh, 2005). Due to the dynamic properties of biological objects, biological terminology constantly changes. Hence many biological entities have multiple names and abbreviations used and referenced interchangeably in databases and the literature. In addition, names can sometimes refer to different concepts dependent on context. The purpose of name entity *disambiguation* is to link a recognized named entity to a correct concept in a taxonomy, controlled vocabulary, thesaurus, or ontology (Ananiadou, Friedman, & Tsujii, 2004). Overall, the purpose of named entity recognition and disambiguation is to identify key concepts of interest in literature or data, and represent these concepts in a consistent, formalized, and related form. However, there does not exist a complete dictionary for the standardized use of most types of named entities (Cohen & Hersh, 2005). The purpose of named entity *unification* is to produce a unification of biological entities to conceptualize the shared biological objects among communities, standardize the nomenclature and use of these entities, and enable interoperability of biological databases (Gene Ontology Consortium, 2000).

Entities and Relationships: Central Dogma of Molecular Biology

The main theoretical model that conceptualizes relationships among entities in molecular biology is a principle known as central dogma theory. It states that genetic information passes from DNA to RNA to proteins (Crick, 1970). Transcription refers to the process from DNA to RNA, where synthesis of RNA involves rewriting or transcribing the DNA sequences in the same language of nucleotides. Translation refers to the process from RNA to proteins, where synthesis of proteins involves translating the language of nucleotides to the language of amino acids. In addition to DNA (e.g., genes, gene clusters, genomes), RNA, amino acids, proteins, and traditional entities of authority control (such as persons and organizations), some of the other entities that are important to knowledge organization in molecular biology are cells, tissues, species, populations, organisms, drugs, and diseases (Blaschke et al., 2002; Krallinger et al., 2005; Krallinger et al., 2008). Based on these entities, the properties of (e.g., protein functions, cellular locations) and relationships between (e.g., protein-protein interactions, protein-drug interactions) these entities are also recognized and extracted from the literature and used to construct thesauri, controlled vocabularies, and ontologies (Blaschke et al., 2002).

Authority Control Tools in Molecular Biology

The authority control infrastructure of molecular biology consists of several kinds of metadata and knowledge organization systems, such as nomenclatures, ontologies, reference sequence databases, and metadata and identifier schemas.

NOMENCLATURES

Nomenclature is concerned with the scientific naming of objects and establishing principles on which scientific names are based. Through the standardized and unique naming of biological objects, nomenclature is essential for the literature search, entity representation and retrieval, and scientific communication among different communities. In the domain of molecular biology, a number of conventions have been developed to standardize gene and protein nomenclatures. The HUGO Human Gene Nomenclature Committee is the only authority to assign and approve unique and meaningful human gene names and symbols (Wain et al., 2002). The Committee published the Guidelines for Human Gene Nomenclature as early as 1979, with later updates to evolve with new technology (e.g., high-throughput techniques). The Guidelines recommend that gene names be brief, specific, use American spelling, and convey the function of the gene. The Committee stores all approved human gene nomenclature in a publicly accessible database, genenames.org[6] (Seal, Gordon, Lush, Wright, & Bruford, 2011). Each gene in the database has a symbol report that contains approved nomenclature: previous symbols, names, and aliases; and a unique identifier that remains stable even if the nomenclature changes. Manually curated and reviewed by the Committee editors, the genenames.org web site serves as an authority file for approved human gene nomenclature. Responding to the need to report and describe changes (mutations) in DNA and protein sequences, the Human Genome Variation Society developed the nomenclature for sequence variants, suggesting, for example, that the description should be at the most basic level (i.e., DNA) and be related to a reference sequence (den Dunnen & Antonarakis, 2000).

Many species-specific communities have also established gene nomenclature committees to assign and approve gene names and symbols, such as the International Committee on Standardized Genetic Nomenclature for Mice. In addition, some model organism databases provide guidelines for establishing gene names and symbols, such as FlyBase[7] and WormBase.[8] However, there are no specialized organizations establishing protein-naming rules and standardizing protein names across species. Some protein repositories, such as UniProt,[9] have developed local naming guidelines to standardize the nomenclature for a given protein across related organisms (UniProt Consortium, 2011). This is accomplished through ongoing efforts to assign a recommended name to existing proteins with a list of alternative names as references in the repository based on the UniProt guidelines.

REFERENCE SEQUENCES

As any scientist can submit data to GenBank or other sequence databases, there are cases that several entries in these databases are representing the same sequence or presenting alternate views of protein or entity names. To resolve the data redundancy problem in GenBank, the National Center for Biotechnology Information (NCBI)[10] established a publicly accessible nucleotide and protein sequence database—Reference Sequence (RefSeq)[11]—by collocating, synthesizing, validating, and summarizing the sequence data available in GenBank (Pruitt, Tatusova, & Maglott, 2005). The goal of RefSeq is to provide a nonredundant collection of genomic and protein sequence data for any given species. In addition to the annotation propagated and validated from GenBank records, NCBI staff may provide supplementary annotation to each record in RefSeq with support from collaborative nomenclature committees, model organism databases, user feedback, and other scientific communities (Pruitt et al., 2005; Pruitt, Tatusova, Klimke, & Maglott, 2009). In particular, RefSeq assigns current entity names and symbols approved by collaborative nomenclature committees to represent the current view of entities. Scientists use RefSeq as an international authority for genome annotation and a stable genomic-sequence standard for reporting sequence variants that might be of clinical significance (Pruitt et al., 2009). Likewise, NCBI built RefSeqGene[12] to store reference sequences for well-characterized individual genes, which is used as the gold standard for determining and describing gene variants (Gulley et al., 2007, p. 862).

BIO-ONTOLOGIES

Recently, there has been a trend towards the development and adoption of bio-ontologies in the biomedical and biological communities, attempting to:

(a) represent current biological knowledge, (b) annotate and organize biological data, (c) improve interoperability across biological databases, (d) turn new biological data into knowledge, and (e) assist users in analyzing data across different domains (Bard & Rhee, 2004; Gene Ontology Consortium, 2000). Bard and Rhee (2004) define bio-ontologies as "formal representations of areas of knowledge in which the essential terms are combined with structuring rules that describe the relationship between the terms" (p. 213). Unlike thesauri and taxonomies, ontologies are more flexible. The relationships among terms in a thesaurus are loosely specified and usually include broader terms (BT), narrower terms (NT), related terms (RT), and synonymous terms (ST) (Allen, 2011; Hodge, 2000). However, the relationship between two concepts in an ontology can be of any type, not limited to those BT, NT, RT, and ST relationships in thesauri or the "is-a" relationship in taxonomies (Lambe, 2007). For example, the Gene Ontology[13] uses three types of relationship between terms ("is-a," "part of," and "regulates") to encode knowledge about genes and gene products related to biological processes, molecular functions, and cellular components (Gene Ontology, 2011).

Among many bio-ontologies that have been developed, the Gene Ontology and the Unified Medical Language System (UMLS)[14] are the most influential in molecular biology and biomedicine, and they have been widely used for text mining and information extraction (Blaschke et al., 2002). The UMLS is a large-scale repository of biomedical vocabularies developed by the U.S. National Library of Medicine, aiming to enhance access to biomedical literature and improve interoperability of biomedical databases by solving the problem of a variety of names being used for the same concept (Bodenreider, 2004). The UMLS consists of three knowledge sources: Metathesaurus, Semantic Network, and SPECIALIST Lexicon. Metathesaurus is a repository integrating more than 2.6 million concepts and their relationships from 135 source vocabularies, including the Medical Subject Headings (MeSH),[15] NCBI Taxonomy,[16] Gene Ontology, and HUGO Gene Nomenclature (Bodenreider, 2004; Unified Medical Language System, 2011). Besides relationships inherited from source vocabularies, Metathesaurus editors assign one or more semantic categories to each concept in the Metathesaurus from the Semantic Network, which is a catalog of 133 semantic categories linked by 54 relationships. Most of the relationships in the Semantic Network are hierarchical (e.g., "is a," "part of"), but some of them are associative (e.g., "spatially related to," "temporally related to," "functionally related to"). Independent of the structure of source vocabularies, the Semantic Network serves as an authority of semantic categories and relationships for concepts in the Metathesaurus, and enables cross-references of biomedical concepts from different source vocabularies. Therefore, the UMLS may be viewed as a large-scale biomedical ontology (Bard & Rhee, 2004).

Entity Identification System

In order to promote a consistent identification mechanism for assigning and recognizing identifiers in the scientific community, the Interoperable Informatics Infrastructure Consortium published the life science identifier (LSID) specification (Martin, Hohman, & Liefeld, 2005). The LSID is a special form of universal resource name and has six components delimited by colon, including an authority ID (e.g., "ncbi.nlm.nih.gov") that identifies an authority that assigned the LSID, an authority namespace ID (e.g., "GenBank.accession") that identifies an authority-specific namespace within which the LSID lives, a unique object ID, and an optional revision ID (Clark, Martin, & Liefeld, 2004). The LSID specification requires any LSID to be location independent, globally unique, and permanent; it can specify only one object at a time and can never be reassigned. A change of even a single bit to the object identified by an LSID should result in a new LSID. This is known as the byte-identity contract (Martin et al., 2005). It is recommended that the new LSID be based on the original one, but with an increment to the revision ID. The use of the revision ID allows users to retrieve different versions of the data object, and indicates the number of times the object has been changed (Dalgleish et al., 2010).

Compared with other identifiers, the LSID can provide semantics or context to make it recognizable to machines, and easier to parse (Clark et al., 2004). For example, the LSID "URN:LSID:ncbi.nlm.nih.gov:GenBank.accession:NC_003428.1" is an identifier for a GenBank record stored at the NCBI database. The existing identifiers can be wrapped into or included within LSIDs (as the GenBank example above, where "NC_003428.1" is a current GenBank identifier), and thus data providers do not need to create new identifiers and discard their current ones. Furthermore, as location-independent and globally unique identifiers, LSIDs can be associated with concepts in ontologies, taxonomies, and controlled vocabularies and serve as the foundation for the biological Semantic Web.

Metadata Schemas

Previous studies (e.g., MacMullen & Denn, 2005; San Gil, Hutchison, Frame, & Palanisamy, 2010) have identified the need for metadata standardization to support interoperability among disparate biological databases. There is also a need for added metadata in existing biological databases to fulfill different users' needs. For example, contextual metadata describing the environment from which a gene or an organism was collected (in terms of space, time, and habitat characteristics) is a prerequisite to understanding the function of unknown genes and organisms (Yilmaz, Gilbert et al., 2011; Yilmaz, Kottmann et al., 2011). However, contextual metadata, usually found in the literature, is missing in sequence databases (Field et al., 2008; Yilmaz,

Kottmann et al., 2011). With the exponential increase in the quantity of genome sequences, it is imperative to provide adequate contextual metadata in a standardized format to extend the existing sequence databases and support genomic analysis. In response to the need to enhance the classic GenBank metadata, the Genomic Standards Consortium (GSC) published the Minimum Information about a Genome Sequence (MIGS) specification to define a set of core (required) metadata for genomes, including information about the environment from which the sample was collected (contextual metadata), taxonomic groups of the sequence, and the experimental process (Field et al., 2008). The GSC implements MIGS in extensible markup language (XML)[17] as Genomic Contextual Data Markup Language, specifying the use of particular identifier systems (e.g., PubMed identifier, digital object identifier), controlled vocabularies, and ontologies (e.g., the Environment Ontology[18]) for most genomic metadata in the standard.

More recently, the GSC published the Minimum Information about a Metagenome Sequence (MIMS), which is an extension of MIGS to include habitat contextual metadata to describe metagenome sequences (Genomic Standards Consortium, 2011). Based on the results of community-led surveys about marker gene descriptors and analysis of contextual data in published rRNA gene studies, the GSC proposed the Minimum Information about a Marker Gene Sequence (MIMARKS) and the environmental packages to standardize descriptions for a more comprehensive range of environmental parameters (Yilmaz, Kottmann et al., 2011). The primary reason for introducing the environmental packages is that the existing keyword search in sequence databases cannot retrieve sequences originated from certain environments or particular locations (e.g., freshwater lakes). The environmental packages can be combined with any GSC standard to enhance sequence description. In order to have a single entry for all the GSC standards, the GSC created the Minimum Information about Any (x) Sequence (MIxS) specifications as an overarching framework to include MIGS, MIMS, MIMARKS, and the environmental packages (Yilmaz, Kottmann et al., 2011).

Authority Control Issues in Molecular Biology

The issues and problems of authority control can be conceptualized as data and metadata quality problems rather than unexpected phenomena. In general, quality is defined as "fitness for use," and it is contextual (Juran, 1992; Wang & Strong, 1996). The issues of authority control in molecular biology can be analyzed under four facets or categories of quality problem sources: (a) problems of inaccurate, inconsistent, or incomplete mapping; dynamic quality problems such as (b) problems caused by context changes; (c) problems caused by changes in the entity; and (d) problems caused by changes in the entity's metadata (Stvilia et al., 2007; Wand & Wang, 1996).

INCONSISTENT MAPPING

Biological researchers usually need to consult or collect data from multiple sources to conduct experiments, interpret results, and make predictions. For example, in order to study the structure of an unknown protein, researchers need to take into account several types of data, ranging from gene sequences to protein structures. However, most publicly accessible databases curate only one type of data, and no resources are available to provide one-stop shopping for all information (Khatri et al., 2005). In order to gain a complete picture of the problem under study, researchers need to navigate from one resource to another. Therefore, it is necessary to create cross-references among related databases: A gene database needs to link to a genome database to signify the location of a gene on its genome; an mRNA database needs to link to a gene database and a protein database to indicate a gene from which an mRNA is transcribed and a protein to which an mRNA translates; and a protein database needs to link to a gene database and a protein structure database. Even though many public databases now provide cross-references to related databases, each of them has its own metadata schema and identifier system. Most of the time, users have to manually convert an identifier from one database to another or use the online converters (e.g., X-REF Converter[19]).

Scenario 1. Biomedical researchers want to analyze proteins in Androgen-repressed human prostate cancer (ARCaP) cells. They have the names and International Protein Index (IPI) accession numbers (identifiers) of these proteins, and want to identify their cellular locations, functions, and pathways by searching the NCBI databases and the Pathway Interaction Database.[20] However, these databases do not identify proteins by the IPI accession number. Considering various names used for these proteins in the databases, researchers have to use an identifier converter to convert the IPI accession numbers to the GenBank protein accession numbers and UniProt protein accession numbers that are recognized in these databases.

SOLUTIONS TO INCONSISTENT MAPPING

The biological text-mining community has created dictionaries to aggregate and resolve various gene and protein names to improve entity recognition and retrieval in the literature (Goll et al., 2010). For example, Liu, Hu, Zhang, and Wu (2006) constructed a BioThesaurus by collecting gene and protein names from 13 databases and mapping them to protein entries in UniProt. The synonymous protein names in the Thesaurus can be used for query expansion when doing database or literature searches. For each protein, the Thesaurus also includes information about protein classifications and source organisms that can help disambiguate homonymous protein names used for different organisms. Fundel and Zimmer (2006) demonstrated that combining different gene and protein databases could result in a broader coverage of the dictionary, which considerably increased the number of terms and decreased the ambiguities of gene and protein names in different databases and with common English words.

The other approach to dealing with mapping problems is to construct a single new bio-ontology by combining terms and relationships from multiple orthogonal ontologies. However, the difficulties of this approach are in determining which overlapping terms should be eliminated and analyzing new concepts generated by the combination of related terms. Although the UMLS covers concepts from a variety of domains (e.g., anatomy, clinical genetics, nursing, psychiatry), it still preserves views and architecture from diverse source vocabularies (National Library of Medicine, 2009). Instead of constructing a general new bio-ontology, the UMLS combined terms from source vocabularies through identifying and mapping synonymy relationships among the terms (Smith et al., 2007).

INCOMPLETE MAPPING

Biologists may have difficulty finding and reusing data underlying published research due to incomplete metadata (Greenberg, 2009). Missing the metadata necessary for discovering, interpreting, using, and reusing existing data—such as spatial and temporal coverage, revision ID, specimen identity information, or contextual metadata—may hamper the research process. Publication without mentioning the version number (revision ID) of sequences can result in ambiguous interpretations and inconsistent descriptions of the data (Dalgleish et al., 2010). Geneticists and clinicians may find current reference sequences are missing annotations of clinically relevant transcripts (i.e., RNA sequences produced from transcription) that are essential for reporting sequence variants. Bioinformaticians doing phylogenetic analysis (studying evolutionary relatedness among groups of organisms) or phylogeographic analysis (studying geographic distributions of organisms) may spend longer than expected collecting and identifying samples from existing sequence databases due to the lack of geographic or contextual metadata describing organisms.

Scenario 2. A graduate student is doing a bioinformatics course project to determine the taxonomy of the giant panda from the phylogenetic perspective. The student wants to collect the ND2 gene sequence of the giant panda and six different kinds of bears from the GenBank to do phylogenetic analysis. In particular, the student is trying to determine whether the giant panda belongs to Ursidae as true bears or is an independent species. To answer this question, the student wants to collect the ND2 gene sequence from multiple individuals within a species. Even though they have their own identifiers, several records retrieved from the GenBank are representing the same sequence. As no identity information about the specimen (individual) is provided in the GenBank, the student has to examine the publication information in each record or read the publications that discuss the data to determine if the sequence was collected from the same individual or not.

SOLUTIONS TO INCOMPLETE MAPPING

In order to extend current sequence databases, the International Nucleotide Sequence Database Collaboration (INSDC)[21] has recently adopted the MIxS specifications to include contextual metadata in the sequence records (Yilmaz, Kottmann et al., 2011). Additionally, the GSC recommends that authors of genome and metagenome publications submit a MIGS report (about contextual metadata) after depositing sequence data in the INSDC databases (Field et al., 2008). To enrich data service and enhance metadata in biological databases, Patterson et al. (2010) proposed a taxon name-based infrastructure: a linked data cloud consisting of taxon names interconnected to an array of data including nomenclature and taxonomies, publication data, georeferences, and social network data. For example, the latitude-longitude metadata in a sequence record of a rare spider allows access to maps that display where the spider was found; nomenclature and taxonomies enable reconciliation and disambiguation of the spider and access to worldwide distributional data of the spider in the Global Biodiversity Information Facility;[22] publication data (e.g., keywords) enables retrieving more publications about the spider in digital libraries; and author's social network data can provide access to all the publications by the author and the author's collaborators and colleagues.

Greenberg (2009) proposed and demonstrated the applicability of automatic metadata propagation, inheritance, and adoption from outside (non-biology) standardized value systems (e.g., the Library of Congress Subject Headings, the Library of Congress Name Authority File) to enhance biological repositories. For example, a data object in a repository can inherit keywords from its original research article, which can be used as seeds to harvest more keywords for the data object from outside controlled vocabularies. The author of an article is usually the creator of or contributor to the data object represented in the article, and therefore the author metadata can be automatically propagated as the creator metadata of the data object.

DYNAMIC QUALITY PROBLEMS

As stated previously, proteins and genes are recommended to be named based on their functions and homology to known proteins (Goll et al., 2010; Wain et al., 2002). Scientists, however, are still learning more about protein functions, and thus protein names need to be changed frequently to reflect newly found or revised knowledge of functions. With the large scale of data generated by high-throughput techniques, the manual correction of existing problematic names is not feasible (Goll et al., 2010). As a consequence, several names (synonyms) are in use for the same genes and their corresponding proteins across databases and the literature. Researchers should consider all available gene or protein names when doing database or literature searches; otherwise they risk missing information. Furthermore, the number of cross-references among databases has increased significantly since many of them began to collaborate and share data (Fundel & Zimmer, 2006). Cross-referencing, however, may lead to data redundancy and inconsistency since some data are stored in multiple databases and might be updated or changed asynchronously (Khatri et al., 2005).

Scenario 3. Biomedical researchers are interested in the function of a protein named FAM20C in humans. They want to know about previous research on this protein by doing database and literature searches. Since protein names are usually based on their functions, this protein might have various names if different researchers have identified different functions over time. Researchers use the protein name "FAM20C" to find related articles from databases and analyze the reference list of these articles to know about other names (e.g., dentin matrix protein 4) for this protein. They then use these names to find more related articles.

SOLUTIONS TO DYNAMIC QUALITY PROBLEMS

The difficulties of maintaining bio-ontologies lie in gaining community acceptance and integrating new knowledge. One solution to these problems is to create forums (Bard & Rhee, 2004) or Wikis for bio-ontologies, allowing those with specialized domain knowledge or interested in ontology development to provide feedback and contribute new concepts. Community involvement in the maintenance of ontologies can, not only help gain public support and facilitate public ownership, but also ensure that only a single ontology is used in any particular domain. Because of the proliferation of bio-ontologies, the Open Biological and Biomedical Ontologies (OBO) consortium was founded in 2001 to establish principles to standardize the format of bio-ontologies, foster interoperability, and ensure a reference ontology for any particular domain (Smith et al., 2007). Built on the success of the Gene Ontology, the OBO principles specify that ontologies must be open access without any constraint; be expressed in a shared syntax, either the OBO syntax or OWL[23]; possess a unique identifier space; be receptive to community feedback and modification; and be orthogonal without overlap in content (Open Biological and Biomedical Ontologies, 2011; Smith et al., 2007).

DISCUSSION

The literature analysis indicates that molecular bioinformatics does not define a high level conceptual model of information systems with relationships among tasks and entities. Although the Central Dogma theory defines the relationships among DNA, RNA, and proteins, there is no overall community-agreed model that defines relationships among entity metadata and information tasks. Entity databases have their own data models, nomenclatures, and identifier schemas. Users are often forced to do complex mapping and translation of entity names and identifiers to search and aggregate data from these databases. In contrast, libraries have already developed and to some extent adopted clear conceptual models for organizing and providing access to library materials. The International Federation of Library Associations and Institutions (IFLA) developed the Functional Requirements for Bibliographic Records (FRBR), which uses the Entity-Relationship Diagram (ERD) conceptual modeling technique and language to conceptualize main bibliographic entities and relationships. First, FRBR defines a data model for library catalogs, which consists of three groups of entities: products of intellectual or artistic endeavor (Group 1); those responsible for the content, production, or custodianship of the products (Group 2); and entities that may serve as subjects of the entities (Group 3; International Federation of Library Associations and Institutions, 2009). Next, FRBR links these entities to four user tasks that "are defined in relation to the elementary uses that are made of the data by the user": (a) *Find* entities using entity attributes or relationships; (b) *Identify* entities, or distinguish entities with similar attributes; (c) *Select* entities corresponding to the user's needs; and (d) *Obtain* access to online electronic entities, or acquire physical entities (International Federation of Library Associations, 2009, p. 79).

IFLA has also developed a conceptual model for authority records, the Functional Requirements for Authority Data (FRAD), which specifies attributes of and relationships between entities (e.g., subject headings, personal names, etc.), and the authority records for those entities are based on another set of four user tasks: (a) *Find* entities using stated criteria or explore using entity attributes or relationships; (b) *Identify* the attributes of an entity to be used as an access point, or validate the attributes; (c) *Contextualize* or clarify the relationship between entities used as access points; and (d) *Justify* or document the reasons for the choices made by the authority data creator (Patton, 2009, p. 83). The three tasks associated with the concept of authority control in molecular biology—*named entity recognition, disambiguation*, and *unification*—have parallels to the users' tasks in FRAD. Similar to *named entity recognition* and *disambiguation* in molecular biology, bibliographic-authority–data creators *identify* versions of entity names and *validate* or *establish* authorized versions of entity names. Similar to *named entity unification* in molecular biology, bibliographic-authority–data creators *justify* the choice of authorized versions of entity names, and *contextualize* entity names, collocating and relating access points where relationships exist. The bibliographic conceptual models and the best practices of model implementations in libraries could benefit the molecular biology communities and help them develop their own aggregate data and authority control models.

The absence of overall conceptual data and task models in molecular bioinformatics could be attributed to the complexity of the field and the data. Molecular bioinformatics is a relatively new field developing computational methods to study the structure, functions, and relationships of multiple entities, such as RNA, genes, and proteins (Higgs & Attwood, 2005). The curators of molecular biology databases and knowledge organization tools have to collect data about entities and standardize the descriptions of these entities that are independent from each other and stored in different databases maintained by different communities. In contrast, libraries, until recently, have been organizing and providing access to mostly one entity: the item entity from Group 1 of the FRBR model (books, serial publications, maps, etc.). Catalogers are responsible for describing these materials and creating access points. Cataloging also includes authority control to ensure the consistency of access points through terminological control (Gorman, 2004; Svenonius, 1986; Tillett, 2004). These access points—typically name and subject terms and phrases—are then used to help the user find, identify, select, and obtain relevant resources via the library catalog. Although librarians create a separate authority record for each entity serving as a controlled access point, the creation of the authority record is triggered by creation of the information resource and/or its introduction into a collection. Most importantly, the completeness of the data model for an entity (i.e., the set of attributes) is determined by how the user tasks of finding, identifying, and selecting a publication in a library catalog need to be supported. This limits the use or reuse of bibliographic entity data for the data tasks (e.g., annotation) or for research focused on an access point entity rather than on publication (see Scenario 4).

Scenario 4. Researchers want to determine whether team demographic characteristics (e.g., affiliation, discipline, gender, and seniority) are correlated with team publication productivity and impact in a community of scientists gathered around a specialized national scientific laboratory. The researchers use the Web of Knowledge[24] to identify the number of publications produced by each team in the community and the number of citations received by those publications within a fixed time window. However, the Web of Knowledge provides little authority control and presents no demographic information about authors beyond providing institutional affiliation for only some of the publications. Hence, the researchers have to resort to manual search, collection, disambiguation, and triangulation of author identities and their demographic information from other sources on the Web, such as institutional and lab web sites.

Interestingly, the successor to the Anglo American Cataloguing Rules, 2nd edition (AACR2), the Resource Description and Access (RDA) standard, allows catalogers to extend the scope of attributes, relationships, and access-point–control data associated with the entities of FRBR and FRAD (Joint Steering Committee for Development of RDA, 2009). Through the extension of entity descriptions, not only may more detailed entity profiles and a larger number of access points for bibliographic resources be produced, but library entity metadata may become more usable for nonlibrary tasks and for different communities.

Entity metadata in molecular biology is different from traditional library metadata in that biological entities and their attributes are dynamic and can change or mutate with time and space (e.g., exposure to radiation). In addition to linguistic description of an entity, researchers and curators need a "data" representation—a reference sequence—to determine the entity and variants of the entity (e.g., mutated genes). Hence, authority control in molecular biology requires, not only the knowledge of naming standards (i.e., nomenclatures), metadata schemas, and ontologies, but also significant subject knowledge and the knowledge of sequencing techniques and alignment tools to identify identical or similar sequences. Different from creating a single accumulative authority record for the entity (e.g., person, corporate body) in library catalogs, the biology community uses version number (revision ID) to keep track of sequence changes to the entities, creates separate records for each version of the entity linked by identifiers, and enables retrieving metadata associated with each version of the entity. Hindered by the semantic ambiguities in terminology, the biology community resorts to natural language processing techniques, such as text-mining and information extraction, to perform named entity recognition and disambiguation in the literature. Furthermore, the complexity of biological entities and their relationships leads to the development and adoption of bio-ontologies to represent, disambiguate, and unify entities and to manage biological knowledge.

CONCLUSION

This paper examined the authority control practices for scientific data in the area of molecular biology and made a comparison with bibliographic authority control. The literature analysis and data use scenarios were used to illustrate the types of authority data quality problems and issues in molecular biology as well as the solutions sought. Similarly, a data use scenario was also used to illustrate the limited use of library metadata as data in research and nonlibrary tasks. Comparing the two practices of authority control suggests that managers and curators of molecular biology data repositories could benefit by following cataloging librarians' approach of developing systematic conceptualizations of authority metadata and task-based relationships within bibliographic databases. Likewise, the analysis of data management practices in molecular biology can inform libraries how they could extend their existing authority data model and systems to enable more effective reuse of library metadata outside of the traditional library context, as well as develop new models and services for authority control for scientific data.

With academic libraries increasingly involved with scientific data curation through institutional data repositories, understanding authority control needs and practices in different disciplines becomes important. By improving our understanding of the needs for data referencing, entity determination, and disambiguation across different domains, we can better understand how to support the development of more effective data management systems as well as to enable more effective reasoning about the interoperability of these systems, and reuse of entity metadata across different domains. Future research could include examining concepts, entities, and relationships of and needs for authority control in other scientific disciplines, such as condensed-matter physics.

ACKNOWLEDGMENTS

We express our gratitude to Paul Stewart and Dr. Qingxiang Sang for providing datasets. We thank Debbie Paul, Adam Worrall, and Jianzhong Wen and Hong Huang for helpful conversations. We also thank the reviewer for helpful comments and feedback.

NOTES

1. DBpedia. http://dbpedia.org/About
2. LinkingOpenData. http://www.w3.org/wiki/SweoIG/TaskForces/CommunityProjects/LinkingOpenData
3. GenBank. http://www.ncbi.nlm.nih.gov/genbank/
4. American Chemistry Society Publications Database. http://pubs.acs.org/doi/suppl/10.1021/pr2000144
5. Web of Knowledge. http://wokinfo.com/
6. http://www.genenames.org/
7. FlyBase. http://flybase.org/
8. WormBase. http://www.wormbase.org/
9. UniProt. Universal Protein Resource. http://www.uniprot.org/
10. National Center for Biotechnology Information (NCBI). http://www.ncbi.nlm.nih.gov/
11. NCBI Reference Sequence (RefSeq). http://www.ncbi.nlm.nih.gov/RefSeq/
12. RefSeqGene. http://www.ncbi.nlm.nih.gov/refseq/rsg/
13. Gene Ontology. http://www.geneontology.org/
14. Unified Medical Language System (UMLS). http://www.nlm.nih.gov/research/umls/
15. Medical Subject Headings (MeSH). http://www.nlm.nih.gov/mesh/
16. NCBI Taxonomy. http://www.ncbi.nlm.nih.gov/Taxonomy/
17. Extensible Markup Language (XML). http://www.w3.org/XML/
18. Environment Ontology. http://environmentontology.org/
19. X-REF Converter. http://refdic.rcai.riken.jp/tools/xrefconv.cgi

20. Pathway Interaction Database. http://pid.nci.nih.gov/
21. International Nucleotide Sequence Database Collaboration (INSDC). http://www.ncbi.nlm.nih.gov/projects/collab/
22. Global Biodiversity Information Facility. http://www.gbif.org/
23. OWL. http://www.w3.org/TR/owl-ref/
24. Web of Knowledge. http://apps.isiknowledge.com

REFERENCES

Allen, R. B. (2011). Category-based models for knowledge representation. In *Information: A fundamental construct*. Manuscript in preparation. Retrieved from http://boballen.info/ISS/

Ananiadou, S., Friedman, C., & Tsujii, J. (2004). Introduction: Named entity recognition in biomedicine. *Biomedical Informatics, 37*, 393–395. doi:10.1016/j.jbi.2004.08.011

Atkins, D., Droegemeier, K., Feldman, S., Garcia-Molina, H., Klein, M., Messerschmitt, D., & Wright, M. H. (2003). *Revolutionizing science and engineering through cyberinfrastructure: Report of the National Science Foundation Blue-Ribbon Advisory Panel on Cyberinfrastructure*. Arlington, VA: National Science Foundation. Retrieved from http://www.nsf.gov/od/oci/reports/atkins.pdf

Bard, J. B. L., & Rhee, S. Y. (2004). Ontologies in biology: Design, applications and future challenges. *Nature Review Genetics, 5*, 213–222. doi:10.1038/nrg1295

Blaschke, C., Hirschman, L., & Valencia, A. (2002). Information extraction in molecular biology. *Briefings in Bioinformatics, 3*, 154–165.

Bodenreider, O. (2004). The Unified Medical Language System (UMLS): Integrating biomedical terminology. *Nucleic Acids Research, 32*, D267–D270. doi:10.1093/nar/gkh061

Clark, T., Martin, S., & Liefeld, T. (2004). Globally distributed object identification for biological knowledgebases. *Briefings in Bioinformatics, 5*, 59–70. doi:10.1093/bib/5.1.59

Cohen, A. M., & Hersh, W. R. (2005). A survey of current work in biomedical text mining. *Briefings in Bioinformatics, 6*, 57–71. doi:10.1093/bib/6.1.57

Crick, F. (1970). Central dogma of molecular biology. *Nature, 227*(5258), 561–563. doi:10.10381227561a0

Dalgleish, R., Flicek, P., Cunningham, F., Astashyn A., Tully, R. E., Proctor, G., ... Maglott, D. R. (2010). Locus Reference Genomic sequences: An improved basis for describing human DNA variants. *Genome Medicine, 2*, 24. doi:10.1186/gm145

de Bruijn, L., & Martin, J. (2002). Literature mining in molecular biology. In R. Baud & P. Ruch (Eds.), *Proceedings of the EFMI Workshop on Natural Language Processing in Biomedical Applications* (pp. 1–5). Ottawa, Canada: National Research Council of Canada.

den Dunnen, J. T., & Antonarakis, S. E. (2000). Mutation nomenclature extensions and suggestions to describe complex mutations: A discussion. *Human Mutation, 15*, 7–12.

Elmasri, R., & Navathe, S. (2000). *Fundamentals of database systems* (3rd ed.). Reading, MA: Addison-Wesley.

Field, D., Garrity, G., Gray, T., Morrison, N., Selengut, J., Sterk, ... P., Wipat, A. (2008). The minimum information about a genome sequence (MIGS) specification. *Nature Biotechnology, 26*, 541–547. doi:10.1038/1360

Fundel, K., & Zimmer, R. (2006). Gene and protein nomenclature in public databases. *BMC Bioinformatics, 7,* 372. doi:10.1186/1471-2105-7-372

Gene Ontology. (2011). *GO ontology relations.* Retrieved from http://www.geneontology.org/GO.ontology.relations.shtml

Gene Ontology Consortium. (2000). Gene Ontology: Tool for the unification of biology. *Nature Genetics, 25,* 25–29. doi:10.1038/75556

Genomic Standards Consortium. (2011). *Minimum Information about a (Meta) Genome Sequence.* Retrieved from http://gensc.org/gc_wiki/index.php/MIGS/MIMS

Go, K., & Carroll, J. (2004a). Scenario-based task analysis. In D. Diaper & N. Stanton (Eds.), *The handbook of task analysis for human-computer interaction* (pp. 117–133). Mahwah, NJ: Lawrence Erlbaum.

Go, K., & Carroll, J. (2004b). The blind men and the elephant: Views of scenario-based system design. *Interactions, 11*(6), 44–53. doi:10.1145/1029036.1029037

Goll, J., Montgomery, R., Brinkac, L. M., Schobel, S., Harkins, D. M., Sebastian, Y., ... Sutton, G. (2010). The Protein Naming Utility: A rules database for protein nomenclature. *Nucleic Acids Research, 38,* D336–D339. doi:10.1093/nar/gkp958

Gorman, M. (2004). Authority control in the context of bibliographic control in the electronic environment. *Cataloging & Classification Quarterly, 38*(3–4), 11–22. doi:10.1300/J104v38n03_03

Greenberg, J. (2009). Theoretical considerations of lifecycle modeling: An analysis of the Dryad Repository demonstrating automatic metadata propagation, inheritance, and value system adoption. *Cataloging & Classification Quarterly, 47,* 380–402. doi:10.1080/01639370902737547

Gulley, M. L., Braziel, R. M., Halling, K. C., His, E. D., Kant, J. A, Nikiforova, M. N., Versalovic, J. (2007). Clinical laboratory reports in molecular pathology. *Archives of Pathology & Laboratory Medicine, 131,* 852–863.

Higgs, P. G., & Attwood, T. K. (2005). *Bioinformatics and molecular evolution.* Malden, MA: Blackwell.

Hodge, G. (2000). *Systems of knowledge organization for digital libraries: Beyond traditional authority files* (CLIR Report 91). Washington, DC: Council on Library and Information Resources. Retrieved from http://www.clir.org/pubs/reports/pub91/pub91.pdf

Institute for Museum and Library Services. (2011). *Specifications for projects that develop digital products.* Retrieved from http://www.imls.gov/assets/1/AssetManager/DigitalProducts.pdf

International Federation of Library Associations and Institutions. (2009). *Functional requirements for bibliographic records: Final report.* Retrieved from http://archive.ifla.org/VII/s13/frbr/frbr_2008.pdf

Joint Steering Committee for Development of RDA (Ed.). (2009). *RDA scope and structure.* Chicago, IL: American Library Association. Retrieved from http://www.rda-jsc.org/docs/5rda-scoperev4.pdf

Juran, J. (1992). *Juran on quality by design.* New York, NY: Free Press.

Khatri, P., Sellamuthu, S., Malhotra, P., Amin, K., Done, A., & Draghici, S. (2005). Recent additions and improvements to the Onto-Tools. *Nucleic Acids Research*, *33*, W762–W765. doi:10.1093/nar/gki472

Krallinger, M., Erhardt, R. A., & Valencia, A. (2005, March). Text-mining approaches in molecular biology and biomedicine. *Drug Discovery Today*, *10*, 439–445. doi:10.1016/S1359-6446(05)03376-3

Krallinger, M., Valencia, A., & Hirschman, L. (2008). Linking genes to literature: Text mining, information extraction, and retrieval applications for biology. *Genome Biology*, *9*(Suppl. 2), S8–S8.14. doi:10.1186/gb-2008-9-S2-S8

Lambe, P. (2007). *Organising knowledge: Taxonomies, knowledge and organisational effectiveness*. Oxford, United Kingdom: Chadons.

Liu, H., Hu, Z., Zhang, J., & Wu, C. (2006). BioThesaurus: A web-based thesaurus of protein and gene names. *Bioinformatics*, *22*, 103–105. doi:10.1093/bioinformatics/bti749

MacMullen, W. J., & Denn, S. O. (2005). Information problems in molecular biology and bioinformatics. *Journal of the American Society for Information Science and Technology*, *56*, 447–456. doi:10.1002/asi.20134

Martin, S., Hohman, M. M., & Liefeld, T. (2005). The impact of life science identifier on informatics data. *Drug Discovery Today*, *10*, 1566–1572. doi:10.1016/S1359-6446(05)03651-2

National Endowment for the Humanities (2011). *Guidance for data management plans for NEH Office of Digital Humanities proposals and awards*. Retrieved from http://www.neh.gov/grants/guidelines/pdf/DataManagementPlans.pdf

National Institutes of Health. (2010). *NIH data sharing policy and implementation guidance* (NIH Publication No. 03–05-2003). Bethesda, MD: Author. Retrieved from http://grants.nih.gov/grants/policy/data_sharing/data_sharing_guidance.htm#goals

National Library of Medicine. (2009). *UMLS reference manual*. Bethesda, MD: Author. Retrieved from http://www.ncbi.nlm.nih.gov/books/NBK9675/

National Science Board. (2005). *Long-lived digital data collections: Enabling research and education in the 21st century* (NSB Report No. 05–40). Arlington, VA: National Science Foundation. Retrieved from http://www.nsf.gov/pubs/2005/nsb0540/nsb0540.pdf

National Science Foundation. (2007). *Cyberinfrastructure vision for 21st century discovery* (NSF Report No. 07–28). Arlington, VA: Author. Retrieved from http://www.nsf.gov/pubs/2007/nsf0728/nsf0728.pdf

National Science Foundation. (2010). *Grant proposal guide* (NSF Publication No. gpg11001). Arlington, VA: Author. Retrieved from http://www.nsf.gov/pubs/policydocs/pappguide/nsf11001/gpgprint.pdf

Open Biological and Biomedical Ontologies. (2011). *Archive of original principles*. Retrieved from http://www.obofoundry.org/crit_2006.shtml

Patton, G. (Ed.). (2009). *Functional requirements for authority data: A conceptual model (FRAD)*. IFLA Working Group on the Functional Requirements and Numbering of Authority Records (FRANAR). IFLA Series on Bibliographic Control (Vol. 34). München: K. G. Saur.

Patterson, D. J., Cooper, J., Kirk, P. M., Pyle, R. L., & Remsen, D. P. (2010). Names are key to the big new biology. *Trends in Ecology and Evolution*, *25*, 686–691. doi:10.1016/j.tree.2010.09.004

Pruitt, K. D., Tatusova, T., Klimke, W., & Maglott, D. R. (2009). NCBI Reference Sequences: Current status, policy and new initiatives. *Nucleic Acid Research*, *37*, D32–D36. doi:10.1093/nar/gkn721

Pruitt, K. D., Tatusova, T., & Maglott, D. R. (2005). NCBI Reference Sequence (RefSeq): A curated non-redundant sequence database of genomes, transcripts and proteins. *Nucleic Acids Research*, *33*, D501–D504. doi:10.1093/nar/gki025

San Gil, I., Hutchison, V., Frame, M., & Palanisamy, G. (2010). Metadata activities in biology. *Journal of Library Metadata*, *10*, 99–118. doi:10.1080/19386389.506389

Seal, R. L., Gordon, S. M., Lush, M. J., Wright M. W., & Bruford, E. A. (2011). Genenames.org: The HGNC resources in 2011. *Nucleic Acids Research*, *39*, D514–D519. doi:10.1093/nar/gkq892

Smalheiser, N., & Torvik, V. (2009). Author name disambiguation. *Annual Review of Information Science and Technology (ARIST)*, *43*, 1–43. doi:10.1002/aris.2009.1440430113

Smith, B., Ashburner, M., Rosse, C., Bard, J., Bug, W., Ceusters, W., ... Lewis, S. (2007). The OBO Foundry: Coordinated evolution of ontologies to support biomedical data integration. *Nature Biotechnology*, *25*, 1251–1255. doi:10.1038/nbt-1346

Stvilia, B., Gasser, L., Twidale M., & Smith, L. C. (2007). A framework for information quality assessment. *Journal of the American Society for Information Science and Technology*, *58*, 1720–1733. doi:10.1002/asi.20652

Svenonius, E. (1986). Unanswered questions in the design of controlled vocabularies. *Journal of the American Society for Information Science*, *37*, 331–340.

Tillett, B. (2004). Authority control: State of the art and new perspectives. *Cataloging & Classification Quarterly*, *38*(3–4), 23–41. doi:10.1300/J104v38n03_04

Turner, P., McLennan, A., Bates, A., & White, M. (2005). *Molecular biology* (3rd ed.). New York, NY: Taylor & Francis.

Unified Medical Language System. (2011). *Metathesaurus release statistics*. Retrieved from http://www.nlm.nih.gov/research/umls/knowledge_sources/metathesaurus/release/statistics.html

UniProt Consortium. (2011). *Protein naming guidelines*. Washington, DC: Author. Retrieved from http://www.uniprot.org/docs/nameprot

Wain, H. M., Bruford, E. A., Lovering, R. C., Lush, M. J., Wright, M. W., & Povey, S. (2002). Guidelines for human gene nomenclature. *Genomics*, *79*, 464–470. doi:10.1006/geno.2002.6748

Wand, Y., & Wang, R. (1996). Anchoring data quality dimensions in ontological foundations. *Communications of the ACM*, *39*(11), 86–92.

Wang, R., & Strong, D. (1996). Beyond accuracy: What data quality means to data consumers. *Journal of Management Information Systems*, *12*(4), 5–35.

Yilmaz, P., Gilbert, J. A., Knight, R., Amaral-Zettler, L., Karsch-Mizrachi, I., Cochrane, G., ... Field, D. (2011). The genomic standards consortium: Bringing standards to life for microbial ecology. *The ISME Journal*, *5*, 1565–1567. doi:10.1038/ismej.2011.39

Yilmaz, P., Kottmann, R., Field, D., Knight, R., Cole, J. R., Amaral-Zettler, L., Glöckner, F. O. (2011). Minimum information about a marker gene sequence (MIMARKS) and minimum information about any (x) sequence (MIxS) specifications. *Nature Biotechnology*, *29*, 415–420. doi:10.1038/nbt.1823

The Intersection of Standards and Professional Knowledge, Skills, and Service: One Road to Ensuring a Functional Future of Bibliographic Control for Serials Acquisition, Management, and Access

NADINE P. ELLERO
Ralph Brown Draughon Library, Auburn University, Auburn, Alabama, USA

DEAN E. CODY
Lovejoy Library, Southern Illinois University Edwardsville, Edwardsville, Illinois, USA

The evolution of libraries to the online format has significant implications for serials acquisitions and work flows. From an acquisitions perspective, the recent development of standards and recommended practices by numerous organizations aims at bibliographic control of the online format including the underlying metadata for accessing full text. This article discusses metadata and standards for their effect on serials bibliographic control. Our literature review reveals the colloquial use of the word standards, *about which we strive for a more precise delineation. We distinguish standards from recommended practices and maintain that a broader librarian participation in developing standards benefits all relevant groups.*

INTRODUCTION

Behind the scenes of library catalogs and discovery tools lie the metadata, systems, and workflows for the bibliographic control of a wide variety of resources. These critical elements of metadata, systems, and workflows are becoming more complex and distributed within libraries (Carpenter, 2011; Hazen, 2011; Ma, 2009; Machovec, 2011, Webster, 2006) and are requiring a multitude of standards (Collins, 2011, 2008) and standards compliance by libraries, publishers, and vendors to ensure seamless and accurate access to resources, especially online ones (Carpenter, 2011). Systems need to be interoperable (Blake, 2010; Chamberlain et al., 2011; Machovec, 2011; Webster, 2006) and the current realities of diminishing staff make this environment for ensuring effective bibliographic control for serials data even more challenging.

This article will highlight existing and emerging standards involving metadata in the acquisition, management, and access of serial resources. Recent developments, such as KBART (Knowledge Bases and Related Tools), SERU (Shared E-Resource Understanding), COUNTER (Counting Online Usage of Networked Electronic Resources), and CORE (Cost of Resource Exchange), to name a few, are helping to offer relief for the needs of serials acquisitions and resources management. As helpful as these guides have been, it is the strong contention of the authors that sustained and deepening participation in standards development needs to increase among library professionals. This work can involve initial draft creation, community review, and continual revision when needed. As technology and systems evolve, these levels of involvement will become more critical and instrumental for building a functional future of bibliographic control serving to foster resource/information discovery in the present time and for generations to come.

The trends and changes in scholarly communication such as open access, open repositories, data set linkages, etc. (Hazen, 2011; Needleman, 2011) will demand many new infrastructures, both human and machine. Almost 64 years ago, Vannevar Bush,[1] a well-known American engineer, made the following observation in *Physics Today*, "It would also be interesting to examine what a pickle this whole movement is getting us into in regard to publication of scientific results, for if we publish fully all that is now being done the libraries would not hold it, and if they could no scientist would have time to examine it all, even in his own rather narrow field" (Bush, 1948, p. 39). This "pickle" today is beyond measure and many disciplines and industries are being challenged with building new complex infrastructures to capture, curate, and connect this information when and wherever needed. Systems need to be "smart" and direct users to the best information because as Bush noted, they would not have the time to examine it all. The National Research Council and the Institute of Medicine are publishing the works of many committees working on these new and emerging infrastructures, such as the National Research Council Committee on an Ocean Infrastructure Strategy for U.S. Ocean Research in 2030 (http://www.nap.edu/catalog.php?record_id=13081) and the Institute of Medicine workshop series on "Digital Infrastructures for the Learning Health System" (http://www.nap.edu/catalog.php?record_id=12912). Our profession is no different and is equally challenged by the very same vastly growing volume of information and quickly emerging new technologies. Furthermore, we may find ourselves embedded in these new information infrastructures if we are to remain relevant and have a vibrant voice in how our future of bibliographic and other knowledge resources, both on the micro and macro levels, will be controlled, managed, indexed, accessed, and supplied. The center of all this, we contend, are standards, as they will become more essential in the effective functioning of these emerging complex infrastructures requiring trust, enabling seamless connectivity, and inspiring organizational and individual discipline for doing things right. No matter the rate of this volume and velocity of change and information, there will most likely be neither funding nor the time to redo or fix inferior work as our world demands excellent research for building knowledge and tools that will, for example, improve medical processes for positive health outcomes and reduced financial burdens.

The authors have firsthand and extensive experience with the review of National Information Standards Organization (NISO) standards from their participation in the Medical Library Association's Technical Services Standards Committee (MLA/TSSC), an effort adding up to well over 20 years. This experience includes leadership at the committee level by both authors and one author having held the official position of voting representative from the Medical Library Association (MLA) to NISO. In April 2010, we conducted an informal survey to query past committee members and voting representatives to glean the professional value of reviewing standards and the acquisition of knowledge and skills gained by these participating librarians.

Additionally, the authors created and maintained a database of ISO/NISO standards reviewed during the years of 2005–2011. A total of 161 standards were reviewed and classified by broad topic (Table 1). Over 50 percent covered some aspect of metadata, impacting bibliographic control and encompassing the coding of data and the development of identifier schemes (Figure 1).

The current literature intersecting standards, serials metadata, and professional participation was reviewed for issues and trends affecting bibliographic control and is summarized in the Literature Review section. Provided in Appendix 1 and Appendix 2 is a guide for reviewing standards that the authors developed as a result of their service on the MLA/TSSC and is discussed in the section "The MLA/TSSC Experience."

KEY DEFINITIONS AND THEIR FACETS

For the purpose of developing our thoughts on the functional future of bibliographic control with respect to the specialty of serials metadata, systems, and workflow, we provide the following definitions of functionality and bibliographic control. While many have defined bibliographic control in

FUNCTIONAL FUTURE FOR BIBLIOGRAPHIC CONTROL

TABLE 1 Topics from Standards Reviewed by MLA (2005–May 2011)

Abbreviations	Accessibility	Archives
Audiovisual	Bibliographic Data	Bibliographic References
Binding	Books	Business Organizations
Calculations	Cataloging	Codes
Collections of Materials	Commands	Computational Linguistics
Country Names	Data Conversion	Data Elements
Data Linking	Data Maintenance	Data Migration
Data Models	Data Protocols	Data Structures
Data Transmission	Digital Evidence	Digital Objects
Digital Rendering	Digitization	Display Requirements
Distribution	Document Management	Electronic Records
File Formats	Filing	Formulas
Identifier Schemes	Indexing	Information Retrieval
Interactive	Language Models	Language Parsing
Libraries, National	Library Holdings	Library Management
Library Materials	Library Names	Library Statistics
Manufacturing	Metadata	Multiple Languages
Music	Names, General	Names, Personal
Natural Language	Paper	Performance Measures
Physical Documents	Preservation	Pricing
Production	Publishing Industry	Quality Measures
Record Requirements	Records Management	Recordkeeping
Registry Services	Searching Text	Security
Serial Number	Storage, Physical Items	Technical Reports
Thesauri	Transliteration	Vocabulary
Vocabulary Mapping	Web	XML

the past several decades,[2] Howarth (2005) provided a succinct background of bibliographic control along with a lengthy discussion describing metadata and bibliographic control. We offer ours, which unites two concepts that are instrumental in our growing digital and networked infrastructures:

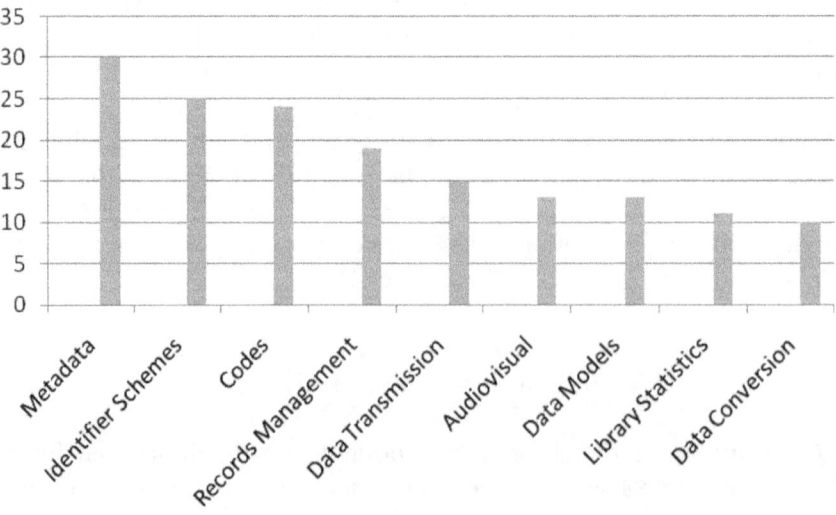

FIGURE 1 Top frequent standards topics September 2005–May 2011.

functionality or utility and bibliographic control that embraces standards and individual and community discipline and compliance.

Functionality

The utility of metadata (Morrissey, 2011), networked systems, and office workflows fosters resource discovery, resource identification, resource accessibility, and resource repurposing/reuse that is fundamentally pragmatic yet invisible to end users. These data and systems must be founded on the core principles/values of accuracy, completeness, consistency, and connectivity/interoperability. Connectivity is twofold, as it operates on both the macro level of systems and networks as well as the micro level of metadata, such as the relationships and user functions of finding, identifying, selecting, and obtaining that is outlined in the Functional Requirements of Bibliographic Records (FRBR) model.[3]

Bibliographic Control

Bibliographic control is a discipline based on philosophical principles and uniform practices utilizing descriptive data/metadata, computational tools, databases (e.g. knowledge bases), web scale networks, and operational workflows that enable multiple levels and layers of resource discovery for end users. Furthermore, we propose that the philosophical foundations of bibliographic control, in order to be effective and enduring, must encompass functionality as defined above and be concentrated on doing the right thing (be disciplined), as opposed to making compromises for short-term gains and expediency. Weinheimer (2010), in his chapter on "Realities of Standards in the Twenty-First Century" states,

> Quality means that some kinds of standards are followed, and that someone using a product that follows those standards, whatever that product happens to be—traveling safely in an airplane, or eating chicken that is free of disease, or drinking water that is clean—can safely rely on it. (p. 203)

We suggest that bibliographic control, boiled down to its essence involves quality and trust and taking the measures to ensure quality in metadata and systems employed for the benefit of resource discovery.

LITERATURE REVIEW

A review of the literature revealed an eclectic assortment of articles, ranging from specific standards for a particular profession, such as the article "Standards for the Academic Veterinary Medical Library" (Murphy, Bedard, Crawley-Low, Fagen, & Jette, 2005), financial accounting standards, various educational standards, and specific library applications such as preservation standards. The literature review, to our surprise, did not reveal any articles addressing the activities of a reviewing body/committee such as ours, nor did they provide any guidelines for reviewing standards.[4] Yet, standards or, more recently, "recommended practices" pervade library operations, with several recent ones involving resource procurement and user access.

The task of reviewing the literature on standards was overwhelming due to the large volume of written material on the general search term *standard*. The word "standard," or "standards," is used in various ways and contexts that it lost meaning in the pursuit of our research. A keyword search of the Library, Information Science & Technology Abstracts (LISTA) database retrieved thousands of hits with everything from ACRL higher education standards to standard operating procedures. Changing the date limit to the range of 2000 to 2011 retrieved well over 9,000 hits. Furthermore, the word "standards" is not a subject heading in LISTA. The word "standard" is a subject heading, but in the context of publisher identifiers and practices, industrial classification numbers, and standardization of subject headings. A keyword search of "ISO Standards" retrieved well over 200 hits. There is significant retrieval of "ANSI Standard" and of "NISO Standard." Clearly the word standard is used in both colloquial and technical contexts. It would seem appropriate and beneficial for EBSCO Publishing to add standard as a thesaurus term to differentiate technical use of the word when referring to a document formally developed or one under development by a standards issuing body. In other word, "standards" in this sense would be a "form of documentation" just as "BIBLIOGRAPHY (Documentation)" is a form of documentation in the LISTA thesaurus.

As evidenced by these growing numbers and needs for information standards, we suggest that there is an important role for professional organizations, such as the MLA, to continue actively encouraging professional involvement with reviewing and developing information standards. This ground is fertile for professional contribution and intellectual growth.

A BRIEF STANDARDS PRIMER

Standards and the organization and access of information, especially in the creation of subject classifications and item arrangements in the form of classification systems, have been integral to libraries and librarianship for several thousand years.[5] However, beginning with the invention of printing in the 15th century and continuing through the current digital environments of the 20th and 21st centuries, there has been an acceleration in the creation of and the need for information related standards to encompass a multitude of library and resource discovery functions. These functions include shared understandings for resource acquisition, knowledge bases for resources accessed via link resolvers, and assessments for resource usage. Along with these evolving library functions are the various types of metadata needed by these functional systems, such as identifier codes (e.g., ISSNs [International Standard Serials Number] and DOIs [Digital Object Identifier]) and descriptive metadata elements such as titles, authors, publishers, and so on.

Library catalogs and cataloging have relied on standards developed or sponsored by the Library of Congress (LC), NISO, Online Computer Library Center, Inc. (OCLC),and so on, for several decades. Coyle (2005) and Webster (2006) provide a concise summary on several of these important standards; MARC21, Z39.50, and the Dublin Core.

To illustrate the complexity and detail of formal standards development, we include the following overview of MLA's relationship with the issuing bodies of NISO up through May 2011. It is unfortunate at this critical time of growth and needs for information standards that MLA withdrew its membership from NISO in May 2011. The MLA was one of many members of NISO, whose membership includes profit, nonprofit, government agencies, and publishers, among others. NISO is a member of the American National Standards Institute (ANSI). A list of members can be found on the websites of NISO and ANSI. Coyle (2005) nicely summed up these relationships between NISO, ANSI, and the ISO (International Standards Organization) stating,

> NISO is a formal standards development organization that is accredited by the American National Standards Institute (ANSI). In addition, NISO is designated by ANSI as the U.S. representative to the International Standards Organization (ISO) Technical Committee 46 on Information and Documentation. (p. 373)

When MLA was fully a member of NISO, the MLA/TSSC members submitted their reviews of each draft standard or standard up for review to MLA's appointed NISO voting representative, who in turn submitted the reviews along with a final vote to NISO.

Due to MLA's past association with NISO, and the latter's relationship with ISO's Technical Committee (TC) 46, almost all of the draft standards we reviewed were from ISO's TC 46. The title of that Committee is "Information and Documentation." Currently, TC 46 is made up of four active subcommittees (SC). Table 2 outlines these subcommittees with their scope of coverage.

RECENT TRENDS IN STANDARDS DEVELOPMENT

One of the ways we elicited trends in standards development and the review process was to analyze the activity of SC 4 and 9. During the period of August 2007 to May 2011, the SC's involvement with metadata was evidenced by 35 drafts submitted for review; SC10 whose title is Physical Keeping of Documents submitted 3; SC 2 on Conversion of Written Languages submitted 4 drafts for review; and SC 8 on Quality, Statistics, and Performance

TABLE 2 ISO Subcommittees

Subcommittees in TC 46	Scope
SC4 Technical Interoperability	Standardization of protocols, schemas, etc., and related models and metadata for processes used by information organizations and content providers, including libraries, archives, museums, publishers, and other content producers
SC8 Quality-Statistics and Performance Evaluation	Standardization of quantitative and qualitative data for the management of information organizations and content providers, e.g., libraries, archives, museums and publishers
SC 9 Identification and Description	Standardization of information identifiers, description and associated metadata and models for use in information organizations (including libraries, museums, and archives) and the content industries (including publishing and other content producers and providers
SC 11 Archives/Records Management	Standardization of principles for the creation and management of documents, records, and archives as evidence of transactions and covering all media including digital multimedia and paper

Evaluation submitted 5 drafts for review. Furthermore, SC 10 is not listed as an active committee. While this is clearly not an exhaustive review of submitted drafts, the trend is obvious. The ISO is concerned with online applications to libraries.

Standards development is a reaction to online developments in libraries. Standards development in the ISO consists of stages. The initial stage is a new work proposal in which the author explains the need for a new standard or for a change to an existing standard. Assuming that the reviewing bodies vote to approve the proposal, each draft standard then undergoes a series of reviews and edits prior to final approval as a published standard. In addition, existing standards undergo a periodic review every few years. Our Committee participated at each stage of this process. It is our observation that the vast majority of standards we reviewed in recent years reflect the shift to the online and networked library. In fact, in the period from July 2008 to June 2009 only one of 29 standards we reviewed had an obvious application to the print library. That one had to do with binding materials. Others in that period dealt with such wide-ranging topics as

- Dublin Core metadata
- The reliability of preserving online information
- Electronic archiving
- RFIDs
- Archiving the web

The period from July 2009 to June 2010 also reflected this trend. Only 2 standards out of more than 30 had obvious application to the past primarily print library and they involved aspects of archival paper. Other standards covered statistics and standardizing number systems (i.e. various identifier codes). From a business perspective, the modern academic library's records are now primarily online. Instead of multisheet carbon paper purchase orders, this information is now captured digitally in a spreadsheet, database, or electronic resource management (ERM) system. The accepted form of business communication is predominantly email, not a typed and printed letter. Accordingly, there are standards for preserving records in an electronic office workflow. During this period we reviewed high profile standards such as the DOI system and others detailing the interoperability of thesauri with other systems.

This online preponderance for business records is evidenced by the work proposals, which appeared in 2005 and are listed in Table 3. The continuing rise of digitization and electronic workflows clearly is seen in the library world and is equally being felt in the academic research world. A need for well developed and implemented standards continues to swell. Schreier, Wilson, and Resnick (2006) note, "Given the importance of good research records, it is somewhat surprising that formal standards for such records are the exception, rather than the rule in academic research laboratories ... Academic researchers prefer informal guidelines rather than formal standards for record-keeping" (p. 42). They go on to state that the trends

TABLE 3 Business Records Reviewed by MLA

Proposal/Draft	Date	Date Reviewed by MLA
Requirements for Long-Term Preservation of Electronic Records (ISO/TC 46 SC 11 N617). Proposal.	2005-09-13	December 8, 2005
Document Management-Information Stored Electronically—Recommendations for Trustworthiness and Reliability (ISO/TC 171/SC3). Proposal	2008-07-3	August 22, 2009
Digital Records Conversion and Migration Process (ISO/TC 46 SC 11 N865). Proposal.	2008-07-29	October 14, 2008
Implementation Guidelines for Digitization of Records (ISO/TC 46 SC 11 N13028). Proposal.	2009-02-19	May 4, 2009
Principles and Functional Requirements for Records in Electronic Office Environments (ISO/DIS 16175-1). Draft–Fast Track Process.	Began as a publication of the International Council on Archives, © 2008	May 19, 2010

they see in challenging academic research are "(1) the rise of large research groups; (2) the introduction of research instruments and methods that self-recorded data either on paper printouts or photographically (e.g., X-ray films, slides, and photographs); and (3) the rise of computers in the laboratory" (p. 43).

The length of standards has changed. It is our observation that the length of standards dealing with the past primarily print library range from 7 to 10 pages, whereas the length of standards dealing with the online library are much longer. Many are 30 to 40 pages long. The longest draft that came before the MLA/TSSC was 858 pages, for Document Management Applications (ISO/WD32000-2). Since that was too long to distribute via email, the Committee abstained from voting. The online library has changed the way the MLA/TSSC conducts its business. Previously, the Committee chair would make copies for each committee member then distribute draft standards via the postal system. When the MLA/TSSC was a voting member of NISO, PDF (Portable Document File format) versions were made available that the chair distributed as email attachments.

Besides the obvious growth in the number and topical scope of information standards, we have noticed a significant change in terminology and possibly the "strength" and viability of these documents issued under the auspices of NISO. Many of the emerging "standards" for library functions mentioned previously are actually *recommended practices*. Even Pesch's (2011a) article "E-Resource Standards You Should Know About" calls these "standards" the title attributes, yet they are clearly qualified as *recommended practices*. We challenge this philosophically, as *recommended practices* implies they are not or can't ever be qualified as full-fledged standards. From what we have gathered, NISO has its own technical use of the word standard. It distinguishes standards from recommended practices. This is a conceptual as well as a procedural distinction. For NISO standards, development involves rigorous peer review and votes by member organizations. Thus, NISO-developed standards have the potential to include a wide representation from the library community—a democratic approach. Further, NISO-developed standards undergo a review every five years. Cunningham (2001) states, "The existence of commonly agreed standards defined and adopted by a professional community of experts saves people the time and effort of having to 'reinvent the wheel'" (p. 275). On the other hand, recommended practices are intended to provide guidance to the user. Such documents are intended to be leading edge. Accordingly, they are discretionary and may be adjusted or revised as needed by the user thereby providing creative flexibility as well as a potential risk for creating problems via inconsistent metadata (Pesch, 2011a). Webster (2006) observed, "Divergent implementations of the standard [i.e. the Bath profile[6]] limited its usefulness" (p. 384). These loose notions of "standards" cause us concern as we see our developing digital world in a critical time of complex infrastructure challenges that need to be built on strong foundations of standards to ensure functionality, quality, and trust in order to be useful and enduring.

STANDARDS AFFECTING SERIALS: AN ACQUISITIONS PERSPECTIVE[7]

We discussed previously the colloquial use of the word standard, which leads to ambiguity of its use in the literature. Standard as used in a technical sense in library literature refers to any formally developed document(s) affecting functionality among libraries, publishers, agents, and societies.

The evolution of libraries to an online environment continues to require a new set of documents to address resulting problems and challenges. Recent years have seen the development of the following NISO-recommended practices, each affecting serials bibliographic control: SERU (Shared Electronic Resource Understanding), a project that involves an agreement between publishers and libraries replacing the time-consuming–license-approval process; PIE-J (Presentation and Identification of E-Journals), another project encouraging publishers and aggregators to display accurate and complete title information for journals, which includes ISSN and citation displays on the journal/aggregator website; CORE (Cost of Resource Exchange) aims to facilitate the transfer of cost and related financial information among any two business applications (e.g. a library's ILS to its ERMS). COUNTER (Counting Online Usage of Networked Electronic Resources) is not a NISO project though it has worked with NISO vis-à-vis SUSHI (Standardized Usage Harvesting Initiative) protocol. COUNTER is an organization requiring paid membership. Its list of members is organized around industry organizations, library consortia, libraries (corporate and academic, from the United States and Europe), smaller publishers, and vendors.

The documents mentioned above address activities in the lifecycle of electronic resource management and analysis of their return on investment (ROI). For example, with an online serial there is initially the pursuit of an agreement to purchase or license its access and use. Added to this scenario is the nature of serials, which frequently undergo title changes involving a whole new set of problems and workflows for the business operations of library technical services departments. In addition to serials changing titles, they frequently change publisher platforms and undergo a transfer process. The *TRANSFER Code of Practice* (Version 2.0) details recommended practices for timely action with respect to both the transferring publisher and the receiving publisher. An effective transfer process requires accurate and complete bibliographic metadata, technical access metadata (such as registering the DOI), and license/administrative metadata for current and perpetual access holdings by local institutions (Hutchens, 2011). Due to recent technological capabilities, journal articles may now include supplemental materials in a variety of formats (e.g. data sets and multimedia files), potentially located disparately from the "core journal article" but whose contents is "owned, published, and hosted by the journal publisher (or the journal's contracted publisher or online platform host)" as described by NISO/NFAIS (2012) in *Recommended Practices for Online Supplemental Journal Article Materials* (p. 2). At the present time distinction is made between integral and additional supplemental content with the hope that eventually integral content will be embedded within the core journal article as it is vital to the article's content and not provided for additional information to the reader. Part B of this document, not publically available at the time of this writing, will detail "the information and metadata required to ensure that the context, linking, and preservation recommendations" addressed in this recommended practice are implemented (p. 4).

Many serials-related metadata problems are listed in section 4.2 of KBART's "Illustration of Specific Data Accuracy Problems" (2010) recommended practices document. During the lifecycle of these serial subscriptions there is the vigilant tracking of its use, which aids the ROI decisions to keep or cancel a subscription; low use, no use, and/or exorbitant prices usually lead to cancelations. This is all to highlight the critical need for accurate and complete metadata, both static and changing, as they are vital for libraries to effectively manage online resources, from acquisitions to access. Connaway and Dickey (2011) highlight this in their article on publisher names in bibliographic data. Publisher names, like journal titles, can change and merge frequently and are essential in workflows for identification and record keeping in ERM systems as well as user discovery and access systems. They further develop their work on creating publisher profiles to include "advanced collection analysis" by looking at languages, formats, and subjects that characterize publisher output. Yasser (2011) analyzed and categorized several types of problems in metadata records and applications. He concluded that "the importance of creating reliable metadata cannot be overstated. With the unprecedented growth of digital resources, it can be anticipated that metadata will become increasingly more important for supporting discovery and management of resources" (p. 61).

In the midst of writing this paper and studying the latest versions of the KBART-, SERU-, and COUNTER-recommended practices, Pesch's (2011b) article outlining these was published. While it is encouraging to see articles discussing standards appearing more frequently in library literature, we still have yet to see an article encouraging deeper participation on a standards committee or offering guidance on how to review a standard, especially for anyone coming to this as a new pursuit or job responsibility. Lynch (1999) has long been a proponent of standards development and noted that

> We need new economic models that continue to insure financial underwriting of the legitimately costly standards process, but not at the

expense of access or broad participation, particularly at a time when the new networked information environment offers so much opportunity to expand and leverage the value of standards work. (p. 10)

One purpose of this article is to focus on the future of bibliographic control with an acquisitions twist. Namely, we point out that core bibliographic data are necessary not only for general resource discovery but for effective acquisitions business operations, such as the procurement and electronic resource management lifecycle previously discussed. Just as catalogers cannot afford to reinvent the same MARC record multiple times over, acquisitions librarians, and those involved in electronic resource management, cannot afford to reinvent knowledge base core data feeding Electronic Resource Management Systems (ERMSs) and link resolver tools such as those provided by Serials Solutions or SFX. Acquisitions and electronic resource librarians need to devote their time to the volatile/changing data such as those encompassing specific institutional holdings for purchased or licensed resources. These specific and unique holdings are used by link resolvers, analyzed for use, and carefully represented by license terms for legal agreements on access and use by all parties concerned.

The KBART recommended practice is a guideline aimed at encouraging content providers, developers and librarians to follow best practices, such as providing complete and accurate metadata, in a timely manner, for managing lists of titles when creating and providing seamless access to online resources. (Zhu, Pollack, Wells, & Llewellin, 2011) These systems and practices are dependent upon standardized metadata such as journal title and variant title, ISSN, publisher/aggregator name, and holdings information (e.g. standardized embargo terminology) for ensuring accurate data management (Farb & Riggio, 2004). While section 5 of the KBART recommendations states,

> Our recommendations also exclude information that is more appropriately classed as bibliographic data than holdings metadata, for example, language, alternate titles, content type, or relationship to other titles. Since this data is more static than holdings data and does not need to be exchanged on such a regular basis, it is outside of the scope of the KBART recommendations. (NISO/UKSG Working Group, 2010, p. 12)

This is in conflict with section 4.2 "Illustration of Specific Data Accuracy Problems." Section 4.2 lists identifier inconsistency (i.e. ISSN's), title inconsistencies, and incorrect date coverage. So while the focus of KBART is on volatile metadata, such as holdings, this volatile data must have a strong connection with the static data. In a digital world of complex data, interconnections and systems interoperability will continue to increase and our standards and recommended guidelines must be accurately synchronized to ensure a functional future (Chamberlain et al., 2011). An example of this is seen in the efforts that OCLC is providing with their WorldCat knowledge base,[8] which is aiming to foster interoperability of several discovery and access functions such as the online catalog, an OpenURL link resolver, and interlibrary loan services. We point out that these services are "cloud-based" and accommodating both public and private environments. While there is contention surrounding OCLC and its business practices and goals, the WorldCat bibliographic database is global and has been a trusted source for bibliographic and ILL metadata for 40 years. Whatever systems prevail they must allow multiple levels of cooperation (local, national, consortial, and global) for the creation and maintenance of many types of metadata and associated services (Webster, 2006). Standards will stand at the center to facilitate multiple levels of functionality. Gorman wrote of this centrality with authority control (2005) and international cooperation for systems and databases with agreed-upon standards (2003).

THE MLA/TSSC EXPERIENCE

Writing Standards Reviews

It is something of a misnomer to say that MLA/TSSC members write reviews of standard drafts issued by ISO/NISO. From our experiences of soliciting membership for MLA/TSSC and attempts at increasing the professional-activity points earned for credentialing in the Academy of Health Information Professionals (AHIP), we observed that few people fully understand the work involved in the process of reading and writing reviews of ISO/NISO standards.

Accordingly, we feel the need to address the reviewing process in which MLA/TSSC has been engaged so as to illustrate its rigor and impact as a needed and important activity and professional contribution. Whereas book reviews in the arts and sciences are published documents, our reviews are not published. Book reviews serve as one form of scholarly communication, although their importance in that communication has been debated. The impact of book reviews on book sales has been decreasing as there is lag time in the publication of the review. Additionally, the book-selection process in academic libraries no longer relies heavily on book reviews and many purchases or licenses are made on a package level rather than title by title, especially for electronic versions. However, the intellectual significance of reviews by MLA/TSSC members is that the review contributes to the creative process of developing and updating standards affecting all aspects of librarianship, as well as nonlibrary-related issues. Our digital information ecosystem is built upon and dependent upon standards. Yet it is ironic to see such a low prestige and recognition of the reviewing process, whether the review is of a book or of a draft library standard having great potential impact upon libraries and their services. The need for standards plays a vital and pivotal role in many disciplines (as seen in the distribution of topics in Table 1) as well as contributing to the growth and maintenance of digital information infrastructures. Furthermore, our observations are paralleled by scholarly reflections on the processes of writing general book reviews. Hartley (2006) noted that "not a lot is known about how people read and write book reviews" (p. 1194) and also that "book reviews still do not figure highly in the promotion stakes for academics" (p. 1194). Eisenman (2002) likewise mentioned the low value of book reviewing in academia.

We consider these observations of reviews and reviewing as unrecognized and undervalued to be alarming. The work of reading and writing reviews, be they books or ISO/NISO standards, is one essential way to facilitate professional growth and contribution. Many of us do not have the luxury of time to conduct full-scale research and write complete books, book chapters, or articles. Attending conferences and presenting papers and posters is also becoming a challenge in these economically difficult times. We strongly suggest that greater credit and recognition be given in our professional organizations for the unique and arduous work of reading and writing reviews of ISO/NISO standards. As suggested by our survey, discussed in a later section, engaging in this work allows professionals to grow in knowledge, acquire analytical reading skills, and contribute to the development and maintenance of international standards affecting many aspects of library and information structures and services. Two years ago when we first began our research and writing on the service of reviewing standards, 21st-century mechanisms were not employed to offer open and easy participation as it is today. Very recently, NISO has greatly opened up this process and advertises, via its website and newsletter, "calls for public comment" on draft standards. The website provides a downloadable PDF and ballot form. As of this writing, a call was placed for public comment on "NISO RP-14–201X, NISO SUSHI Protocol: COUNTER-SUSHI Implementation Profile," open from December 1, 2011, to January 20, 2012, as well as for the previously mentioned *Recommended Practices for Online Supplemental Journal Article Materials* (January 30, 2012, to February 29, 2012).

In 2005 when we gathered a new body of standard reviewers for the MLA/TSSC, we quickly realized that we had no document by which to train them or provide guidance. Thus began our brainstorming of how best to train and carry on these skills that we have developed over the years. While the author's strengths and styles are different, a complementary tandem developed, blending philosophical insights with practical rigors of critical reading and writing concise reviews, which has resulted in this article. In recognizing this gap, we developed a framework for reviewing standards (Appendix 1: Reviewer Guidelines) and a guideline for writing standards reviews (Appendix 2: Guidelines for Writing Reviews) that we hope will foster continued and deepening engagement, contribution, and intellectual growth in the library profession. The infusion of technology will continue to create more sophistication in the ways information is created, linked, and utilized, which in turn will necessitate an imperative for standardization in the details of information creation, linking, and utilization across disparate systems, disciplines, and cultures. Standards will help lead the way in fostering deeper connections with data and enliven the "Semantic Web" as envisioned by Tim Berners-Lee.[9]

Another aspect of our research explored what had been the long-term participation of the MLA in the international effort to create and publish standards affecting all aspects of librarianship. One of our motivations to write this article was to highlight the value of this work in light of the continuing growth, trends, and needs for information standards and to encourage professional contribution on all levels of engagement from initial draft writing to implementation of tools and services by our profession. We surveyed past and present members of the MLA/TSSC to determine their commitment and personal satisfaction with regard to this work. The MLA/TSSC has participated for more than 20 years in the reviewing of NISO/ISO standards and had the opportunity to draft one standard from start to finish. We, the authors, have both served on this committee and as voting representatives from MLA to NISO for the past 10 years, with one author serving close to 20 years.

The MLA/TSSC Survey and Findings

In seeking a level of objectivity for our observations, we designed and administered a voluntary and anonymous survey to mitigate our obvious bias with long-held personal passions for reviewing standards (See Appendix 3). We also obtained Institutional Review Board (IRB) clearance from both of our institutions to ensure no harm would be incurred by any survey participants.[10] An Access database was developed to track and index by topic each of the standards that were reviewed by the MLA/TSSC from 2005 through 2011. These topics were the same ones used in the survey instrument for question No. 8 eliciting specific topics about which the respondents felt they had learned most through being a reviewer. The most selected topics were Identifier Schemes (80%); Metadata and Records Management (60%); and Coding of Data, Data Elements, Library Statistics, and Vocabularies (50%). Figure 1 shows the most-frequently-occurring topics from highest to lowest as they appeared in the titles of the standards drafts. "Metadata" was in the lead position and this is no surprise as metadata underlies much of the work of our information profession. The MLA/TSSC participants widely represented the usual technical services departments with several respondents having collection development responsibilities, which is often not included in technical services.

One way to view professional growth is via one's curriculum vitae (CV). A CV tracks professional accomplishments for submission to reviewing bodies responsible for decisions regarding tenure, promotion, and merit-based raises, or to potential employers. In response to the question querying participation on the MLA/TSSC as a means to enhance one's CV, nine of ten either strongly agreed (4) or agreed (5). One respondent strongly disagreed.

Overall, respondents indicated a positive experience of professional growth as a result of their work. Professional growth can be measured in terms of what we learn. Draft standards address many aspects of librarianship, so there is the opportunity to learn about a topic with thoughtful reading. Six respondents were affirmative, four agreed, and two strongly agreed that their librarianship skills improved as a result of their committee involvement. Three respondents disagreed that their committee work enhanced their scholarship, and three had no opinion. So while only four respondents indicated belief that their scholarship abilities improved, it was our experience as committee chairs that draft standards were consistently reviewed by the same small number of MLA/TSSC members. Due to the anonymous nature of the survey we can't make any direct correlations.

Another aspect of professional growth can come via personal relationships developed with colleagues. Professional relations can foster learning as we communicate, discuss problems, share successes, or develop a sense of mission and obligation to each other as we fulfill the charge of a committee. In answer to the question whether the respondent believed their committee work to have developed meaningful relationships with colleagues, eight out of ten either strongly agreed (5) or agreed (3), while only two disagreed. No one strongly disagreed.

Yet another way to consider professional growth is whether we believe we are making a contribution to the library profession or to the MLA in particular. There can be personal satisfaction in serving a large organization as this level of involvement can add fulfillment to one's career. All ten respondents strongly agreed that as a result of their committee work they are serving the profession in a meaningful way. Narrowing our focus to the MLA, in answer to the question investigating committee work as a way to serve the MLA, nine of ten either strongly agreed (8) or agreed (1), while only one strongly disagreed.

Survey and Study Limitations

The survey size was not as large as we would have liked. Relying on our collective memory over a 20-year period, we could only identify and contact 16 past and present members of the MLA/TSSC. Of the 16, we had a response rate of about 50 percent. Another way of thinking about this is that the small number of committee members over 20 years speaks to their level of commitment to this mission and to the MLA.

There are numerous other library organizations participating in the editorial process of reviewing draft standards. We did not consult with representatives from those organizations, which could have shed light on their workflow and the extent of their reviewing process.

We are unable to develop a complete review of all drafts for the 20 years of involvement, as the archival records are located in the MLA archives in Chicago. At the very least our work will serve to document 10 years of MLA/TSSC standards review work.

THE INTERSECTION OF STANDARDS AND PROFESSIONAL WORK

Professional growth can come in many forms. The most obvious is the growth the MLA/TSSC members experienced as each studied, researched, and reviewed the draft standards. Additionally there are the more mundane gains such as working under pressure due to tight deadlines and lots of writing practice.

The workflow involved in reviewing standards has changed drastically over the years. Just as the standards currently under development reflect changes in libraries, committee workflow reflects those changes. Previously, everything had to be physically mailed. Committee chairs would have to photocopy each draft standard, and then mail it through the postal system. Because some standards can be as long as one hundred pages or more, the time and expense of copying and mailing was considerable. The Chair received the standard in physical form in the mail, read it, reviewed it, and wrote a review. The reviews were either mailed or written into the message of an email correspondence. Now, this process is much more seamless and user friendly due to the technology of the Internet and document attaching in email systems. Since then, the Committee Chair learned the importance of tracking workflow. The following is a list of items tracked:

- the ISO committee authoring the draft
- the draft title
- the due date for MLA's NISO representative to cast the ballot
- the due date assigned for reviews (these are important since the NISO representative reads and considers each review in the ballot-casting process)
- the date email was sent issuing the review, as there is often a high frequency of drafts to review

A spreadsheet using Microsoft Excel was devised to track this workflow. Arranging this information in a spreadsheet is important due to the heavy workload, especially when reviews of several drafts are due on the same date. Further, we believe it is important to track the amount of participation contributed by each committee member. Conceivably a member may ask for a letter of recommendation. This serves as an official record of what has been done and can aid in writing letters of recommendation.

We have been reviewing standards spanning two decades in our roles as NISO voting representative and Chair of the MLA/TSSC. Each of us has learned by trial and error and sheer trench work. We boldly embraced this work with little guidance but with lots of enthusiasm and satisfaction in knowing that we would be adding to a needed and valued service. Armed with ideals, determination, and the desire to contribute to our profession we have carried on this challenging mission. Indeed this work is not for the faint of heart or those who fear anything beginning with a Z and ending with a number!

We were compelled to write this article for several reasons: to provide a useful guide for new reviewers, to let others know of this valuable professional pursuit, to acknowledge the history of the MLA/TSSC work, and, last but not least, to make a call for more participation by librarians. With standards in a vital and pivotal role, there is a need for many more of us to be involved in this work of standards development and to champion the cause for a high caliber, functional future of bibliographic control.

Entering the world of standards is always interesting and nothing short of mind expanding, as our world becomes more and more technologically sophisticated and computing languages and machine interoperability are a backdrop for most information standards.

We have pointed out that many of the emerging standards address the issue of metadata. Robu, Robu, and Thirion (2006) state, "Librarians and library activities can contribute in many ways to the SW [semantic web] on a practical level ... get well acquainted with metadata standards such as DC [Dublin Core] and the various ways in which they may be expressed (HTML, XML, RDF)" (p. 204). Not only are Committee members getting acquainted with metadata standards, each is assisting in the writing, revision, and review process of each standard.

CONCLUSION

A significant aspect of our functional future is systems interoperability and the effective and timely exchange of many types of functional/actionable metadata elements utilized by technical, administrative, and financial systems that are invisible to information seekers but vital behind the scenes for libraries, vendors, and publishers. This tripod of library operations supports services from acquisitions to access and is built upon standards and recommended practices aiming to encourage quality metadata flowing in and out of local systems and workflows as well as metadata capturing serial life cycles and publisher/vendor supply chains (Chamberlain et al., 2011). A January 2012 NISO white paper, *Making Good on the Promise of ERM: A Standards and Best Practices Discussion Paper* addresses the complexities and need for systems interoperability enabled by accurate, complete, and timely metadata and fostered by the dedication of libraries, publishers, and vendors to reconcile differences, build consensus, and encourage practice compliance with recommended practices (NISO ERM Data Standards and Best Practices Review Steering Committee, 2012). These measures of discipline and desire for doing the best and right thing will significantly aid in a functional future of bibliographic control and metadata so integral to our core systems of information provision, acquisition, discovery, and access.

The authors strongly contend that continued and deepening participation in the review and creation of standards by librarians will significantly add to building a functional future of bibliographic control that is vibrant and flexible enough to handle the volume and velocity of daily changes associated, in particular, with the nature of online serials and the lifecycle management of acquiring, evaluating, and ensuring seamless access for information seekers. Many minds applied to these challenges will hopefully produce a healthy yield of functional products and workflows. Participating in standards reviewing and development is an excellent avenue for gaining knowledge and skills while serving the profession and helping to foster a functional future of bibliographic control. The ultimate end goal of all these efforts is to enable users to discover the information and resources they need for study, scholarship, and invention.

ACKNOWLEDGMENTS

The authors express acknowledgment and gratitude for the aid of Katie Corcoran in the structure and hosting of the survey on the MLA website and for Leopoldo M. Montoya who was one of the original authors of the *Reviewer Guidelines* and *Guidelines for Writing Reviews*.

NOTES

1. See additional background information on Vannevar Bush at http://www.ibiblio.org/pioneers/bush.html

2. See Taylor, A. G. (Miller, D. P.). (2004). *Wynar's introduction to cataloging and classification* by Arlene G. Taylor, with the assistance of David P. Miller (Rev. 9th ed., pp. 3–6). Westport, CT: Libraries Unlimited.

3. See "What is FRBR?: A conceptual model for the bibliographic universe" at http://www.loc.gov/cds/downloads/FRBR.PDF

4. See Needleman, M. H. (2011); Coyle, K. (2005a, 2005b).

5. Weihs, J., A Brief History of Classification, Part 1, Technicalities. 2010 Jan/Feb; 30(1): 14–16. Ibid., A Brief History of Classification, Part 2. Technicalities. 2010 Mar/Apr; 30(2): 16–19. Ibid., A Brief History of Classification, Part 3. Technicalities. 2010 May/June; 30(3): 15–18.

6. For information on and applications of the Bath Profile, see OCLC's Bath Profile Compliance Checklist: http://www.oclc.org/support/documentation/firstsearch/z3950/bath/; SRU (Search/Retrieval via URL and the Bath Profile: http://www.loc.gov/standards/sru/resources/bath-profile.html; and an archived document of the 2004 standard at http://www.collectionscanada.gc.ca/bath/ap-bath-e.htm. Email received 12/14/2011 from the Library and Archives Canada Standards Office, written by Laura M. May, confirmed that this standard is no longer being updated.

7. Listed here are the links to the standards/recommended practices discussed in this section: SERU (http://www.niso.org/workrooms/seru), PIE-J (http://www.niso.org/workrooms/piej), CORE (http://www.niso.org/workrooms/core/), COUNTER (http://www.projectcounter.org/about.html), SUSHI (http://www.niso.org/workrooms/sushi), and KBART (http://www.niso.org/workrooms/kbart).

8. See full WorldCat® knowledge base description at http://www.oclc.org/knowledgebase/default.htm.

9. See the Scientific American article, "The Semantic Web: A new form of Web content that is meaningful to computers will unleash a revolution of new possibilities," May 17, 2001 available at http://www.scientificamerican.com/article.cfm?id=the-semantic-web

10. Nadine P. Ellero was employed by the Claude Moore Health Sciences Library, University of Virginia, Charlottesville, Virginia, when the survey was developed and distributed.

REFERENCES

Blake, K. (2010). Controlling chaos: Management of electronic journal holdings in an academic library environment. *Serials Review, 36*, 242–250.

Bush, V. (1948). Trends in American science. *Physics Today, 1*, 5–7, 39.

Carpenter, T. (2011). The value of standards in electronic content distribution: Reflections on the adoption of NISO standards. *Journal of Electronic Publishing, 14*(1), 51–58.

Chamberlain, C., McDonald, R., Blackburn, J., McQuillan, B., & Carlson, A. (2011). Serials management in the next-generation library environment. *The Serials Librarian, 60*(1–4), 37–52.

Collins, M. (2008). Electronic resource management systems (ERMS) review. *Serials Review, 34*, 267–299.

Collins, M. (2011). Serials literature review 2008–9: Embracing a culture of openness. *Library Resources & Technical Services, 55*(2), 60–80.

Connaway, L. S., & Dickey, T. J. (2011). Publisher names in bibliographic data: An experimental authority file and a prototype application. *Library Resources & Technical Services, 55*(4), 182–194.

Coyle, K. (2005a). Libraries and standards. *Journal of Academic Librarianship, 31*(4), 373–376.

Coyle, K. (2005b). Standards in a time of constant change. *Journal of Academic Librarianship, 31*(3), 280–283.

Cunningham, A. (2001). Six degrees of separation: Australian metadata initiatives and their relationships with international standards. *Archival Science, 1*, 271–283.

Eisenman, R. (2002). Some realities of book reviewing. *Journal of Information Ethics, 11*(1), 22–25.

Farb, S. E., Riggio, A. (2004). Medium or message? A new look at standards, structures, and schemata for managing electronic resources. *Library Hi Tech, 22*(2), 144–152.

Gorman, M. (2003). Cataloging in the twenty-first century. In Michael Gorman (Author), *The enduring library: Technology, tradition, and the quest for balance* (pp. 82–93). Chicago, IL: American Library Association.

Gorman, M. (2005). Authority control in the context of bibliographic control in the electronic environment. In Arlene G. Taylor and Barbara B. Tillett (Eds.), *Authority control in organizing and accessing information: Definition and international experience* (pp. 11–21). Binghamton, NY: Haworth Information Press.

Hartley, J. (2006). Reading and writing book reviews across the disciplines. *Journal of the American Society for Information Science and Technology, 57*(9), 1194–1207.

Hazen, D. (2011). Lost in the cloud: Research library collections and community in the digital age. *Library Resources & Technical Services, 55*(4), 195–204.

Howarth, L. (2005). Metadata and bibliographic control: Soul-mates or two solitudes? *Cataloging & Classification Quarterly, 40*(3/4), 37–56.

Hutchens, C. (2011). Journal title transfers: The process, the complexities, the problems, and what the Transfer and KBART Working Groups are doing to address them. *The Serials Librarian, 61*(3/4), 389–395.

Lynch, C. (1999). The case for new economic models to support standardization efforts. *Information Standards Quarterly, 11*(2), 5–10. Retrieved from http://www.niso.org/publications/white_papers/wp-lynch/

Ma, J. (2009). Metadata in ARL libraries: A survey of metadata practices. *Journal of Library Metadata, 9*, 1–14.

Machovec, G. (2011). An interview with Ted Koppel, Auto-Graphics, regarding standards. *The Charleston Advisor*, January, 61–64.

Morrissey, S. M. (2011). "More what you'd call 'guidelines' than actual rules": Variation in the use of standards. *Journal of Electronic Publishing, 14*(1), 79–92.

Murphy, S. A., Bedard, M. A., Crawley-Low, J., Fagen, D., Jette, J.-P. (2005). Standards for the academic veterinary medical library. *Journal of the Medical Library Association, 93*(1), 130–132.

Needleman, M. H. (2011). Linked data: What is it and what can it do? *Serials Review, 37*, 234. This is a one page "Standards Update" in Serials Review.

NISO ERM Data Standards and Best Practices Review Steering Committee. (2012). Making good on the promise of ERM: A standards and best practices discussion paper. Retrieved from http://www.niso.org/apps/group_public/download.php/7946/Making_Good_on_the_Promise_of_ERM.pdf

NISO/NFAIS. (2012). Recommended practices for online supplemental journal article materials. Retrieved from http://www.niso.org/apps/group_public/document.php?document_id=7964&wg_abbrev=suppbusiness

NISO/UKSG KBART Working Group. (2010). KBART knowledge bases and related tools: A recommended practice of the National Information Standards Group (NISO) and UKSG. Retrieved from http://www.uksg.org/sites/uksg.org/files/KBART_Phase_I_Recommended_Practice.pdf

Pesch, O. (2011a). E-Resource standards you should know about. *The Serials Librarian, 61*(2), 215–230.

Pesch, O. (2011b). Perfecting COUNTER and SUSHI to achieve reliable usage analysis. *The Serials Librarian, 61*(3/4), 353–365.

Robu, I., Robu, V., Thirion, B. (2006). An introduction to the semantic web for health science librarians. *Journal of the Medical Library Association, 94*(2), 198–205.

Schreier, A. A., Wilson, K., & Resnick, D. (2006). Academic research record-keeping: Best practices for individuals, group leaders, and institutions. *Academic Medicine, 81*(1), 42–47.

TRANSFER Code of Practice: Version 2.0. (2008). Retrieved from http://www.uksg.org/sites/uksg.org/FILES/TRANSFER_Code_of_%20Practice_2_0.pdf

Weinheimer, J. (2010). Realities of standards in the twenty-first century. In Conversations with catalogers in the 21st century. Libraries Unlimited. 188–205.

Webster, P. (2006). Interconnected and innovative libraries: Factors tying libraries more closely together. *Library Trends, 54*(3), 382–393.

Yasser, C. M. (2011). An analysis of problems in metadata records. *Journal of Library Metadata, 11*(2), 51–62.

Zhu, J., Pollack, G., Wells, R., & Llewellin, M. (2011). KBART-providing standardized, accurate and timely metadata: Methods and challenges. *Against the Grain, 23*(1), 24.

APPENDIX 1

Reviewer Guidelines (by Nadine P. Ellero and Dean E. Cody)

The aim of these revised guidelines is to serve as an instructional guide or framework for reviewing ISO/NISO standards by new and continuing members of the Technical Services Standards Committee of the Medical Library Association (TSSC/MLA) or as an individual reviewer, which is encouraged by NISO (see: http://www.niso.org/participate/). A preliminary version, from which these guidelines emerged, was authored by Nadine P. Ellero and Leopoldo M. Montoya in August 2005. As of this writing, no like guide has been developed by ISO/NISO or any other professional organization, to our knowledge.

Reviewing standards can be a very rewarding experience, incorporating both intellectual challenge and the acquisition of knowledge as one reads a standard and becomes enlightened with particular topics of the standards read and studied.

The following six steps are a suggested framework for the engagement and discipline of reviewing standards and can be used as a checklist for organizing one's work.

1. Plan your review and note due dates
2. Be prepared to learn
3. Acknowledge your limitations and/or biases
4. Consider the context
5. Evaluate the need for the standard
6. Evaluate the general structure and style

Plan Your Review: This step, while mundane, is essential. Work days are consumed with job responsibilities and the due dates for standard reviews come quickly. Many standards are well over a hundred pages and very technical, requiring a long time to read and study. We suggest that you mark your calendars upon notification and make a copy of the standard with the due date marked on the first page. To effectively pace yourself, consider studying smaller sections at a time to avoid becoming overwhelmed and/or rushed in your reading. Make notes in the margins of a copy of the standard to trigger later pondering, checking of information, noting errors, etc.

Be Prepared to Learn: Try not to allow the length or technicality of the standard to intimidate you in the task of reading and review. One of the benefits of being a reviewer is that you also are a learner. When you come across a concept that you do not know or understand, take the time to conduct research, or call a colleague who is an expert or may know of an expert. Conducting research via an Internet search is often successful for finding additional background reading. As you read, try to not make assumptions or fill in gaps. Instead, notice the gaps, as they provide valuable clues to the standard's weakness and where it needs further development. This may seem obvious, but it is easy to unconsciously make assumptions and fill in gaps. Making unwanted assumptions especially happens when reading too quickly.

Acknowledge Your Limitations and/or Biases: It is not expected that you be an expert in all standards topics, and stating your limitations will provide a context for the standards developers as they read your review. Stating that you are not an XML expert or are unable to comment on the actual code or schema is helpful for them. However, you are encouraged to discuss certain functions or aspects to make sure that those elements are adequately addressed in the technical code. Be careful not to assume that a particular aspect is or might be addressed when you are unable to decipher technical codes or languages. Be confident in what you read and understand and communicate your concern or question.

Consider the Context: The answers to what, where, when, and who, serve as the context in which the standard is to apply. Reading the preface or introduction to the standard often supplies this background information. However, the preface or introduction is often considered to not be part of the actual standard. A formal review of the introduction is not expected and it serves only as background information. However, there have been instances in which the introduction contained information that should have been in the body of the standard or was in conflict with what was actually contained in the standard. These potential discrepancies should be noted and made part of the formal overall review, ideally in the opening of your review (see Guidelines for Writing Reviews). Many of the standards complement or are related to other standards and this should be acknowledged in the introduction, a related standards list, or other appropriate section.

Evaluate the Need for the Standard: Consider if there still is a current need for the standard or if it will soon be obsolete. Discern the parts that are still valid and/or those that may require further development or revision to address emerging technologies or significant changes in the topic or discipline to which the standard applies.

Evaluate the general structure and style: A standard is a formally written document and should follow rules of proper grammar, syntax, and semantics. There should be no ambiguity in expression and the writing should be logical and easily followed. Diagrams should enhance or summarize the text or be used for quick reference. Take note of the absence of tables or diagrams that would aid complicated or detailed specifications. Glossaries are especially needed for standards containing lots of technical terms or acronyms. Make sure that there is consistency between definitions of terms within the text and the glossary.

APPENDIX 2

Guidelines for Writing Reviews (by Nadine P. Ellero and Dean E. Cody)

We propose the following guidelines for writing a standard review that is submitted to the ISO/NISO working committee as part of a representative organization or as an individual where online submission is encouraged (see http://www.niso.org/participate/). During MLA's NISO membership tenure, members of the Technical Services Standards Committee Association (MLA/TSSC) submit individual reviews via email to the Chair of the MLA/TSSC. The MLA/TSSC Chair compiles the reviews into one document and sends the compiled document to the NISO/MLA voting representative. The NISO/MLA voting representative submits all the written reviews and, if appropriate at the time, submits a final vote on behalf of MLA.

We encourage individual reviews to reflect the creativity and expertise of the reviewer. The ultimate goal is to provide an orderly, well thought out, succinct and useful communication that will ultimately be seen by the standards authors, committees, NISO Board, etc. The following format, comprising an opening, an analysis, and a closing, is suggested.

Opening: Compose a full paragraph or a sentence or two depending on the standard. Express any limitations that you have in reviewing the standard, either in full or in part. Address in general terms, how well the standard appears to function for its intended purpose, audience, and context.

Analysis: List in detail, the areas of strength and weakness. Always reference specific sections, using the outline numbering in the standard itself or referencing a specific page and paragraph/sentence location. Make suggestions for sections that need to be revised or embellished whenever possible.

Likewise, provide actual examples of what is in error regarding grammar, syntax, semantics, etc.

Closing: Summarize how you would vote on this standard if you were asked or what recommendations you would make for its next developmental step. Some examples are

- *"This standard is in overall excellent shape and should be forwarded to the next step in the development process."*
- *"This standard has a good beginning but lacks specificity and purpose to make it useful; please rewrite to accommodate the insufficiencies described in the analysis."*
- *"This standard has been well developed and is needed to further XYZ in the world of information access and deserves a yes vote."*
- *"This standard is now obsolete because of ABC and should not be updated."*

APPENDIX 3

The MLA/TSSC Survey (2010)

The Medical Library Association has participated for many years, on a national and an international level, in the review and development of standards, issued by ANSI/NISO and ISO, affecting all aspects of libraries and librarianship. The authors of this study are interested in determining the impact and value that this work has had on the careers of past and present members of the Medical Library Association's Technical Services Standards Committee and MLA-Board-appointed NISO Representatives, MLA, and the profession.

We request 10 to 15 minutes of your time to reflect on your past or present service as you answer the following survey questions. The results of this survey will be anonymous and tabulated for observations in a paper that we are writing entitled "Professional Development, Standards, and the Medical Library Association: Reflections on Ten Years Experiences and Their Value" to be presented at a future MLA Annual Meeting and/or published in a library journal.

1. Please select your identifying category/MLA role (select all that apply)
    - Past Standards Committee member
    - Past NISO voting representative
    - Current Standards Committee member
    - Past NISO voting representative
2. How long was your tenure in this role?
    - Less than one year
    - More than one but less than two years
    - Three to five years
    - More than five years

3. In what range of years did you serve or are you serving? (please select all that apply)
   - 1990–1995
   - 1996–2000
   - 2001–2005
   - 2006–2010
4. Which of the following areas best describes your technical services work for your institution? (please select all that apply)
   - Administration
   - Acquisitions
   - Cataloging
   - Collection development
   - Electronic resources management
   - Other, please specify
5. Please provide your opinion on the following statements about your committee work or role as an appointed representative:

	Strongly Agree	Agree	Disagree	Strongly Disagree	No Opinion
My committee role or work as an appointed representative has improved my librarianship skills.					
My committee role or work as an appointed representative has improved my scholarship abilities.					
I consider my committee work or work as an appointed representative as a way to enhance my CV.					
As a result of my committee work or work as an appointed representative, I have developed meaningful relationships with my colleagues.					
I consider my committee work or work as an appointed representative as a way to serve the Medical Library Association.					
I learned a lot about the processes standards undergo in International and National Organizations (ISO/NISO) during my tenure as a committee member or appointed representative.					

6. Additional comments about any of the above statements:
7. The amount of work expected of me during my tenure on the committee or as an appointed representative was
   - Just right
   - Too much
   - Not enough

8. The following is a list of topics covered by the Standards Committee or by appointed representatives to NISO. Identify the topics about which you learned the most from reading and writing reviews of standards that were in development or under review. Please select all that apply:
   - Abbreviations
   - Archives
   - Bibliographic Data
   - Binding
   - Cataloging
   - Coding of Data
   - Data Conversion
   - Data Elements
   - Data Linking
   - Data Models
   - Data Protocols
   - Data Retrieval
   - Data Structures
   - Data Transmission
   - Display Requirements
   - File Formats
   - Identifier Schemes
   - Information Retrieval
   - General Statistics
   - Library Holdings
   - Library Statistics
   - Metadata
   - Name Authority/Person Names
   - National Libraries
   - Performance Measures
   - Preservation
   - Records Management
   - Storage of Physical Materials
   - Text Searching
   - Transliteration
   - Vocabularies
   - XML
   - Other. Please identify.
9. Please provide any additional comments regarding your experience in reading and writing reviews for various developing standards or standards that were being revised:

Thank you for your time. We believe your comments will be an important part of our research.

Could the Functional Future of Bibliographic Control Change Cataloging Work? An Exploration Using Abbott

GRETCHEN L. HOFFMAN

School of Library and Information Studies, Texas Woman's University, Denton, Texas, USA

Abbott's (1988) The System of Professions *theory is used to understand how technology has changed cataloging work in academic libraries, and if the functional future of bibliographic control could change cataloging work. Abbott says technology can destroy and create professional work. Technology has somewhat destroyed professional cataloging work by enabling more efficient cataloging processes. Professional cataloging work has been passed to nonprofessional staff and vendors. The Web has created new forms of metadata work, but catalogers and metadata librarians may be competing for it. Cataloging must claim new work to survive.*

INTRODUCTION

Cataloging is the process of describing and providing access to library resources using various standards for descriptive cataloging and subject analysis. The current code for descriptive cataloging, *Anglo-American Cataloguing Rules, Second Edition, Revised* (2002)—AACR2—was developed in the 20th century when academic libraries collected physical materials and users accessed library collections through a card catalog. Technological changes facilitated by computers and the Web, however, have changed what libraries collect and how library collections are accessed. Instead of collecting physical materials only, academic libraries are collecting electronic and digital resources. Instead of a card catalog, users access library resources through sophisticated online catalogs and databases available on the Web. Users are accessing library collections in a networked environment, and their needs are evolving. At the same time, cataloging units are under pressure from administrators to catalog more efficiently and at lower costs.

In response to these needs, the International Federation of Library Associations and Institutions (IFLA) "initiated a fundamental re-examination of cataloguing theory and practice on an international level" (IFLA Study Group, 1998, p. 1). This reexamination resulted in three models: the *Functional Requirements for Bibliographic Records* (FRBR), a model of the bibliographic universe that maps bibliographic entities, attributes, and relationships in bibliographic records and defines user tasks (IFLA, 1998); the *Functional Requirements for Authority Data* (FRAD), an extension of the FRBR model that maps entities, attributes, and relationships in authority records (IFLA Working Group, 2009); and the *Functional Requirements for Subject Authority Data* (FRSAD), a further extension of the FRBR model that maps entities, attributes, and relationships in subject authority records (IFLA Working Group, 2010). Together, these models give a rich and detailed understanding of bibliographic and authority data, and they define the functional future of bibliographic control. These models are important because they have influenced cataloging principles and standards, and are facilitating the move from a paper-based environment to a networked information environment. For example, the models are incorporated in the *Statement of International Cataloguing Principles* (IFLA Cataloguing Section, 2009), which are "principles ... intended to guide the development of cataloguing codes" (p. 2). In addition, the FRBR and FRAD models form the structure of the new descriptive cataloging code, *Resource Description and Access* (RDA). Because RDA is partially based on these models, RDA is meant to help users find and access library resources in a networked environment. RDA is intended to describe and provide access to all resources (digital and physical) and to show the relationships among them in a better way than AACR2.

Lastly, the Library of Congress (LC) recognizes that even with its planned implementation of RDA in March 2013, the MARC 21 encoding standard is struggling to meet the demands of the new networked information environment. In October 2011 the Library of Congress announced it was moving forward to develop "in collaboration with librarians, standards experts, and technologists a new bibliographic framework that will serve the associated communities well into the future" (Library of Congress, 2011a, para. 4). The interesting possibilities that will emerge with this new functional future will most certainly change cataloging work in academic libraries, and with that comes uncertainty in how catalogers can adapt their work habits in response. One theory that can inform an understanding of these possible changes is Andrew Abbott's *The System of Professions* (1988), which focuses on how professions define their jurisdictions and compete for new tasks. In this paper, Abbott's theory is used as a framework to explore how the functional future of bibliographic control could change cataloging work in academic libraries. It will discuss two technological changes that have changed cataloging work, and how the functional future could change cataloging work. For the purposes of this paper, the broad, general trends in cataloging work in academic libraries are presented with the caveat that the paper may not describe changes in cataloging work in all academic libraries.

ABBOTT'S SYSTEM OF THE PROFESSIONS

In his *The System of Professions* (1988), Andrew Abbott presents a theory of professions. Law, medicine, engineering, and library and information Science (LIS) are examples of professions that claim an area of expertise separate from other professions. Professions control professional work through "abstract, formal knowledge systems" (p. 53) that set them apart from other professions. This knowledge is disseminated by formal education, which gives professions legitimacy both to the outside world and to its members. Professions have the power to define their work jurisdiction and to determine the legitimate work of the profession; they control and define the tasks of the profession. In the system of professions, professions are interrelated and operate in a system tied to tasks. Professions compete for new tasks in a struggle to claim jurisdiction. New tasks are created primarily "through changes in technologies and organizations" (p. 92), but it is change through technology that is of interest in this paper. Abbott says that technology can both create and destroy professional work. On one hand, technology opens up new areas of work for professions to claim; professions can claim work that falls within their work jurisdiction. However, new work is not always easily claimed by one profession. Competing professions may fight for jurisdiction and the right to perform new work. On the other hand, technology can destroy professional work and prompt professions to redefine their work jurisdictions. Professional work can be given away, taken away, or simply abandoned. Professional workers can pass routine and undesirable work to lower-level or nonprofessional workers in favor of work that is deemed more appropriate to their professional status.

Professions are not homogeneous groups. Abbott (1988) says professions include areas of specialization that have different work methods and separate definitions of legitimate work. Cataloging is one such specialization in LIS. The primary job of catalogers is to create bibliographic records that describe and provide access to library resources. Catalogers are directed in their work by many complicated standards developed and endorsed by the library profession, and catalogers are expected to accurately and consistently apply these standards in their work (Taylor, 2006). This makes cataloging work complex because standards do not cover all exceptions. Often, catalogers must use judgment and apply standards in nonstandard ways. Because cataloging standards are complex and cataloging work requires judgment, it cannot be performed by all workers in a library. It takes years of ongoing specialized education and training to become a proficient cataloger. Because this work is specialized, many academic libraries have dedicated cataloging units responsible for this work.

Abbott's theory has been applied previously in LIS. For example, O'Connor (2009) used it to understand how information literacy legitimized school and academic librarianship. Burnett and Bonnici (2006) used the theory to understand jurisdictional disputes surrounding information technology education. Trosow (2001) applied Abbott's theory to the fields of law and law librarianship. In this paper, Abbott's theory is used as a framework to show how technological change has both destroyed and created cataloging work in academic libraries, and if the functional future of bibliographic control could create new kinds of cataloging work.

HOW TECHNOLOGY HAS CHANGED CATALOGING WORK

According to Abbott, technology can both create and destroy professional work. Technology, especially the computer and the Web, changed how cataloging work is performed in academic libraries. To understand if the functional future of bibliographic control could affect cataloging work in academic libraries, it is important to explore how these two technological developments have both destroyed cataloging work and created metadata work in academic libraries.

The Computer: Online Catalogs, Bibliographic Utilities, and Shared Cataloging

Historically, cataloging was performed by professional catalogers who transcribed bibliographic information on paper cards that were filed in a card catalog. The development of the computer led to several significant changes to cataloging work starting in the late 1960s and 1970s. The MARC format was developed that enables computers to read bibliographic information. Online public access catalogs (OPACs) were developed to give users computerized access to library collections. Academic libraries began moving their bibliographic information from cards available in the card catalog to electronic bibliographic records available in the online catalog (Millsap, 1996). Bibliographic utilities, such as the Online Computer Library Center (OCLC), were developed that allow catalogers to create and share electronic bibliographic records. Together, these technological developments changed the cataloging process. Cataloging is no longer a time- and labor-intensive process of typing bibliographic information on multiple cards and filing them in a card catalog. Electronic bibliographic records created by catalogers around the world can be found on a bibliographic utility and downloaded quickly into libraries' online catalogs. These developments led to a more efficient and quicker cataloging process.

As a result of this efficiency, routine cataloging work in academic libraries has been passed from professional catalogers down to nonprofessional staff, called paraprofessional catalogers or copy catalogers, who quickly and cheaply copy catalog bibliographic records from bibliographic utilities. Today, much of the cataloging work in academic libraries is performed by these paraprofessional catalogers. Braden reports that in 1977, 50% to 65% of academic libraries used paraprofessionals to perform copy cataloging (which was then called "adaptive cataloging") and only 12% to 15% to perform original cataloging (as cited in Eskoz, 1990). Compare this to the 2011–2012 *The Survey of Academic Library Cataloging Practices* (2011), which reports that 81.43% of academic libraries use paraprofessionals to perform copy cataloging and 31.43% use paraprofessionals to perform original cataloging. Some academic cataloging units even have passed copy cataloging work down to student assistants (Gatti, 2005).

In addition to passing professional cataloging work down to paraprofessional catalogers and student assistants, this work is also increasingly outsourced to contract catalogers (Baker, 1998; Scheschy, 1999) and library vendors who sell bibliographic records along with library materials (*The Survey of Academic Library Cataloging Practices*, 2011). Outsourcing cataloging is cost efficient and gives users faster access to materials, but it also makes academic libraries dependent on library vendors to provide bibliographic information. Furthermore, using outsourcers and library vendors limits the ability of catalogers to customize bibliographic records (e.g., adding local subject headings, additional access points, etc.) to meet local users' needs, because it is more cost efficient to accept these records "as is" without customizing them (Jansen, 2003; Simpson, 2007). As a consequence, less customization is done on bibliographic records today than in the past.

While cataloging work has been passed to paraprofessional catalogers and library vendors, the work of professional catalogers has changed. They still catalog, but they are no longer needed to perform the routine cataloging work in cataloging units. Professional catalogers perform original cataloging and difficult copy cataloging, and they manage the paraprofessional catalogers (Buttlar & Garcha, 1998; El-Sherbini & Klim, 1997). As a consequence, their numbers are decreasing. Since the 1980s, academic cataloging units (and technical services departments) have lost many professional cataloger positions. Wells (2004) reports that due to budget cuts, 72.7% of technical services units in academic libraries have lost professional librarian positions, while only 50% of these units have lost paraprofessional positions. Most positions were lost in cataloging. Wilder (2002) reports a 35% drop in staff and a 46% drop in hiring new employees from 1985 to 2000 in technical services/cataloging departments in academic libraries belonging to the Association of Research Libraries (ARL). Passing professional cataloging work to paraprofessional catalogers coupled with a loss of professional cataloger positions have led some to suggest that cataloging has been deprofessionalized (e.g., Harris, 1992; Jeng, 1997).

Technology enabled catalogers in academic libraries to share bibliographic records and develop more efficient cataloging processes. Following Abbott, technology has changed the professional status of cataloging work. Technology also has destroyed professional cataloging work, in a certain sense, because the work has been passed to paraprofessional catalogers and library vendors. Abbott explains how technology has done this, "[Technology] required, as the price for the services, near total standardization in descriptive cataloging and indexing, which deeply invaded the area of judgment that made librarians professionals" (p. 220). Yet, as stated above cataloging work has not been completely destroyed. It still occurs in academic libraries, but as academic libraries seek ever more efficient cataloging processes, the work may be eroded further. As more cataloging work is given away, catalogers must find new areas of work to claim.

The World Wide Web: Electronic Resources, Institutional Repositories, and Digital Collections

The World Wide Web is a technological change that has created three areas of work in academic libraries. Electronic resources, institutional repositories, and digital collections are becoming a part of the regular workflow in many academic libraries (Ayers, et al., 2009; Boock & Vondracek, 2006; Lopatin, 2010). The Web has enabled electronic publishing and the creation of new electronic formats. Academic libraries are collecting more electronic resources, including electronic books and electronic journals. To provide access to them, bibliographic records in the MARC format are purchased from vendors and downloaded into a library's catalog. Many academic libraries also are building institutional repositories to capture an institution's intellectual output (see e.g., Giesecke, 2011; Lynch, 2003). Finally, many academic libraries are digitizing special collections and/or archival materials and making them available through content management software such as CONTENTdm or DSpace. For example, Boock and Vondracek (2006), in a survey of 40 academic libraries, found that 97% of them were involved in digitization projects. Non-MARC metadata schemes like Dublin Core, Encoded Archival Description (EAD), VRA (Visual Resources Association) Core, etc., are used to describe and provide access to these resources.

However, this work is not necessarily being performed by catalogers in cataloging units. To handle this new work, some academic libraries have created professional librarian positions devoted to electronic resources and metadata. The positions are given various titles such as Metadata Librarian, Electronic Resources Librarian, Digital Collections Librarian, etc. (Han &

Hswe, 2010). These professionals manage the electronic journals and databases, manage/create the metadata for institutional repositories, and/or manage/create the metadata for digital collections. For example, in Boock and Vondracek's (2006) survey, 76% of academic libraries created new positions devoted to digitization projects. This work can include tasks such as digitization, metadata creation, project management, web page design, and digital preservation (p. 200). The work of an "Electronic Resources Librarian" involves managing electronic journals and databases; the tasks can include "acquisitions, renewals, and cancellations of [electronic resources]; license and pricing negotiations; and troubleshooting technical problems" (Albitz & Shelburne, 2007, p. 21). These areas are a new source of professional work. For example, Ayers, et al. (2009) surveyed libraries, archives, and museums in the Research Library Group (RLG) and found that 77% of the libraries use professional librarians (with an MLIS degree) and 67% use professional staff (without an MLIS degree) to do this work.

Furthermore, these new positions are not necessarily housed in cataloging units or even technical services units. For example, Albitz and Shelburne (2007) surveyed ARL libraries and found that only 52% of electronic resources librarians performed electronic resources work in technical services units. For institutional repository and digital collections work, it may be done by a dedicated metadata or digital collections unit, or performed collaboratively by different units across a library. For example, Han and Hswe (2010) report that beginning in 2004, metadata positions began to be housed in library units with names like Digital Library Unit, Scholarly Resources Integration Department, Metadata and Systems Development, etc. (p. 132). This is supported by Boock and Vondracek (2006) who report that 50% of the academic libraries in their survey "created new units to handle aspects of digitization," but only 20% of these new units reported to technical services units (pp. 200–201). Ma (2006) also states that digital projects often are performed collaboratively by units across a library, not just in cataloging units.

Competing for the New Work

Professional librarian positions have been created in academic libraries. The work may be seen as a new source of work for professional catalogers and cataloging units. However, they are struggling to claim it. For electronic resources work, library vendors may have claimed the cataloging work, because bibliographic records in the MARC format are purchased from library vendors and are uploaded into library catalogs. There is no work for catalogers to perform. For institutional repositories and digital collections that work with non-MARC metadata, catalogers may be struggling to claim the work here, too. This can be seen in Hoffman's (2010) multiple case study of three academic cataloging units. Hoffman found that the cataloging units were giving away routine and less desirable work (book cataloging) to vendors and were trying to claim new areas of work in special cataloging projects, electronic resources, and digital collections. The units were able to claim special cataloging projects only because the work fell within the jurisdiction of cataloging units. It was difficult to claim electronic resources work because it had been claimed by vendors. Lastly, digital collections could not be claimed, because digital initiatives units and information technology units were competing with cataloging units for the work.

Following Abbott, metadata librarians and catalogers may be competing to claim metadata work. This is an interesting competition, because metadata work is very similar to cataloging: Both types of work describe and provide access to library resources. Yet, each group believes it should perform the work. On one side, some metadata librarians believe that metadata work is different from cataloging and requires separate skills. For example, Clair (2010) argues that metadata librarians are different from catalogers. He writes:

> The skills of traditional cataloging will always be useful for metadata librarians as they process digital resources and make them available ... These skills are being applied in new and sometimes unexpected ways in response to the demands, promise, and challenges associated with the networked environment. Some of the tasks that have arisen before metadata librarians as a result of this process are indeed brand new and require skills that set metadata librarians apart from their colleagues in library technical services units. (p. 280)

The idea that metadata librarians need special skills is supported by Han and Hswe (2010), who analyzed metadata librarian job descriptions between 2000 and 2008. They found that "knowledge of emerging technologies" is the difference between metadata librarian and cataloging librarian positions (p. 137). They report that qualifications for metadata librarian positions require more knowledge in digital library development and technology, digital management software, metadata standards outside of MARC, and markup languages.

On the other side, some catalogers believe they could learn these skills and perform this work. For example, Veve and Feltner-Reichert (2010) report that 90% of catalogers working with non-MARC metadata feel that metadata work is "a natural extension of catalogers' responsibilities" (p. 205). There also have been many calls for catalogers to claim metadata work (see e.g., Banush, 2008; Boydston & Leysen, 2006; DeZelar-Tiedman, 2004; Gorman, 2003; Schottlaender, 2003). There is even some evidence that professional catalogers are willing to give up cataloging work to perform metadata work. For example, Riemer (2009) argues that professional catalogers should pass their work, such as editing master records on OCLC and subject analysis, to paraprofessional catalogers, so professional catalogers can perform metadata work. In addition, professional cataloger positions are starting to require an understanding of non-MARC metadata and digital resources (Chapman, 2007; Park & Lu, 2009; Park, Lu, & Marion, 2009; Zhu, 2008).

Some cataloging units are starting to reorganize in order to perform metadata work. For example, the Cataloging Department at the University of Oklahoma has gotten involved in metadata work for digital libraries "through the use of redesigned workflows, agreed on metadata standards, customized training for cataloging department staff, and improved communication between the Cataloging Department and those tasked with implementing digital libraries" (Valentino, 2010, p. 549). In some academic libraries, the same staff members are starting to create both MARC and non-MARC metadata (Ayers et al., 2009). Han and Hswe (2010) report that some cataloging units have changed names to reflect metadata work, such as "Cataloging and Metadata Unit" (p. 132). In fact, changing names may be necessary for cataloging units to claim metadata work. The word *cataloging* is often associated with print and "old" ways of organizing information using MARC, while *metadata* is often associated with digital resources and "new" ways of organizing information using non-MARC metadata schemas. Including both types of work in a name may show library administrators that cataloging units want to do the work.

COULD THE FUNCTIONAL FUTURE CHANGE CATALOGING WORK?

Professions are tied to tasks (Abbott, 1988). If tasks are given away or abandoned, then professions need to claim new tasks to survive. This puts cataloging in a tenuous position. Technology has destroyed professional cataloging work in a sense by allowing cataloging work to be passed to paraprofessional catalogers and library vendors. It logically follows that if more cataloging work is given away, catalogers will need to claim new work to survive. One new area of work is in metadata, but as stated previously catalogers are competing with metadata librarians over it and may not be able to claim it fully.

Given this situation, could the functional future of bibliographic control change cataloging work? The Web has enabled academic libraries to provide access to electronic and digital resources. Many people even predict that library collections may be primarily electronic in the future (e.g., Vogh, 2011). Managing and providing access to electronic resources and digital collections may increase in importance as cataloging and providing access to physical collections may decrease in importance. The functional future's models (FRBR, FRAD, and FRSAD) and RDA were developed to respond to the changes facilitated by the Web and to account for how users search for information in a networked information environment. The functional future of bibliographic control may expand current cataloging work and create new areas of work, but given the situation in academic libraries, could catalogers claim it?

RDA: Showing Relationships and Expanding Authority Control Work

RDA is based in part on the FRBR and FRAD models and it could expand cataloging work in academic libraries. Using RDA, catalogers could show more relationships between resources to users. Oliver (2007) explains, "[RDA] encourages the description of relationships between related resources and between resources and persons or bodies that contributed to the creation of that resource" (p. 251). Relationships would be shown on bibliographic records through relationship designators that explain the responsibility, like "artist," "author," or "composer." This is different from current cataloging practice where designators are added only for certain relationships, such as illustrators for children's books, and for certain formats, such as sound recordings. In addition, there could be more work to show bibliographic relationships among the FRBR group 1 entities: Work, Expression, Manifestation, and Item.

RDA also could expand authorities work. Authority control is essential to library catalogs because it helps users find and access library resources by providing unique and consistent names, titles, and subjects in bibliographic records. Authority records contain authorized forms of names, titles, and subjects, as well as variant forms. RDA expands authority work by allowing catalogers to describe much more detailed information about persons, families, corporate bodies, and works than is possible with AACR2. This could mean more authority control work for catalogers in terms of linking materials and showing relationships.

Authority Control Beyond the Library Catalog

Another possible area of work is performing authority control for library resources available/indexed outside of a library's catalog. Currently, authority control is performed on bibliographic records in a library's catalog. This gives users access to library materials. In the functional future, however, catalogers could perform authority control for all library resources available/indexed in the library catalog, databases, and digital collections. This would help users, because they would need to use one interface only, instead of having to search each system separately. This is problematic for users, however, because there is no authority control across these systems. Each system uses its own form of names, titles, and subjects. Without authority control, users may not receive all names, titles, and subjects in a search.

The need for authority control across systems has increased, because many library catalogs can search multiple systems at once. For example, ExLibris's *Primo* product allows users to search a library's catalog, digital collections, and databases at the same time. Searching all systems at once would be useful to users, but lack of authority control means that search results are not collocated. When performing a search for an article using *Primo*, for example, a user receives multiple entries for the article, one entry for each database that indexes the article. Authority control and the FRBR model could help this situation. Catalogers could create a single "work" record for the article and attach an item for each individual database. This would be a more efficient way to collocate articles and organize search results for users. The same problem exists for names. Databases and library catalogs use different forms of names. When a user performs a search for a name, there is no authority control to bring together variant forms of a person's name or to differentiate people who have the same name. In addition, authority files in academic libraries only contain names of people who are responsible for books and other items in library collections. Library catalogs do not provide access to individual articles in serial publications; databases provide this access. Authority files used in libraries do not necessarily include names of people who have written journal articles only. If authority control is performed across a library's catalog and databases, a user could retrieve all of the works by a particular author available in the library (books, articles, reviews, etc.). The same problem exists for subjects. Library catalogs and databases use different controlled vocabularies and subject descriptors. Bringing together all forms of a subject would help users find library resources on the same subject.

Could Cataloging Perform the Work of the Functional Future?

According to Abbott, professions compete for new work. The functional future has the potential to expand and create new cataloging work in academic libraries, but could catalogers claim this work? One reason catalogers could claim the work is that cataloging rules may change, but many of the cataloging processes may essentially stay the same. As stated in the previous section, catalogers could certainly lay claim to work to provide authority control across a library's catalog, digital collections, and databases. They already know and perform the detailed processes of authority control work.

However, there are several reasons why they may not be able to claim it. One reason is that to perform this work, cataloging units may need more catalogers. As this paper has shown, library units are lacking catalogers because the professional cataloging work has been passed down to paraprofessional catalogers or outsourced to library vendors. As a consequence, there are fewer professional catalogers performing cataloging today, and many cataloging units have even lost some paraprofessional cataloger positions as well. In truth, there are fewer catalogers working in academic libraries today than when AACR2 was implemented in the late 1970s. If there are no catalogers, then there is no one to claim the new forms of cataloging work. In addition, catalogers would need training, but due to current economic considerations, academic libraries may not have the money or resources for more catalogers and training. Those catalogers who are currently working may not have been trained properly in the process of authority work.

Another reason catalogers may not claim this work is because it has already been claimed by vendors. Many academic libraries already purchase bibliographic records from library vendors and/or hire them to perform authority control. It may be more cost efficient to hire vendors to do this work than to hire additional catalogers to perform this work. In addition, database vendors could claim authority control work, too. In essence, there may not be enough cataloging work to go around.

Finally, catalogers may find it difficult to claim this work because academic libraries may soon no longer use MARC-based bibliographic and authority records. Non-MARC metadata work is increasing in academic libraries and using multiple encoding standards may not serve a library's needs. It is incumbent upon current and new catalogers to learn new methods of description and encoding of library catalog data. Fortunately, LC's initiative into "a new bibliographic framework" to replace the MARC format (Library of Congress, 2011a) could create conditions favorable for this new learning and new work for catalogers. This initiative is in response to reports from the national RDA test, as well as the Library of Congress's (2008) report *On the Record,* and the feeling that the potential of RDA and other future developments may be limited by the MARC format. The initiative states:

> Although the format is deeply embedded in the infrastructure, changing technologies and changing resource description practices mandate a transition to a more current and forward looking data creation and interchange environment. The semantic web and related linked data model hold interesting possibilities for libraries and cultural heritage institutions. (2011b, para. 1)

It details the requirements for the new environment and the approaches LC will take to create the new framework. Specifically, there should be broad accommodation of content rules and data models; provision for types of data that logically accompany or support bibliographic description; accommodation of textual data, linked data with URIs [Uniform Resource Identifiers] instead of text, and both; consideration of the relationships between and recommendations for communications format tagging, record input conventions, and system storage/manipulation; consideration of the needs of all sizes and types of libraries; continuation of maintenance of MARC until no longer necessary; compatibility with MARC-based records; and provision of transformation from MARC 21 to a new bibliographic environment (LC, 2011b). One of the main focuses of this initiative will involve employing Linked Data and the Resource Description Framework (RDF) (LC, 2011b, para. 11). In particular, LC feels that:

> Embracing common exchange techniques (the Web and Linked Data) and broadly adopted data models (RDF) will move the current library-technological environment away from being a niche market unto itself to one more readily understandable by present and future data creators, data modelers, and software developers. (para. 13)

A non-MARC-based functional future may help cataloging claim the work of the functional future. The knowledge of past and present practices is vital to the creation of the new practices and to the transition of the cataloging profession.

CONCLUSION

In this article, Abbott's (1988) *The System of Professions* theory was used as a framework to understand how technology has changed cataloging work in academic libraries and if the functional future of bibliographic control could change cataloging work. Technology has changed cataloging work in two ways. The development of computers, the MARC format, online catalogs, and bibliographic databases led to shared cataloging and a more efficient cataloging process. As a consequence of this efficiency, cataloging work lost its professional status and has been passed down to paraprofessional catalogers and out to library vendors. Professional catalogers now perform original cataloging, difficult copy cataloging, and manage the paraprofessionals, and there are fewer professional cataloger positions in academic libraries. The development of the Web facilitated developments in electronic publishing and digitization, and academic libraries are collecting electronic publications and providing access to digital resources. This has created new areas of metadata work in electronic resources, institutional repositories, and digital collections. Many academic libraries have created professional "metadata librarian" positions to perform this work, and catalogers and metadata librarians seem to be competing for this work.

If cataloging wants to survive as a specialization in LIS, it will need to claim new work. The functional future of bibliographic control has the potential to expand and create new areas of work, such as showing relationships and performing more authority control work using RDA, and performing authority control for library resources available/indexed in a library's catalog, databases, and digital collections. Cataloging, however, may not be able to claim this work because there are fewer catalogers in cataloging units, competition from vendors, and academic libraries may not want more MARC-based bibliographic and authority data. If LC develops a non-MARC bibliographic framework, catalogers and cataloging units may be able to claim the work of the functional future and possibly non-MARC metadata work as well. Cataloging has the power to secure a place in the functional future; catalogers just need to claim the work.

REFERENCES

Abbott, A. (1988). *The system of professions: An essay on the division of expert labor.* Chicago, IL: University of Chicago Press.

Albitz, R. S., & Shelburne, W. A. (2007). Marian through the looking glass: The unique evolution of the electronic resources (ER) librarian position. *Collection Management, 32,* 15–30.

Anglo-American Cataloguing Rules, Second Edition, Revised. (2002). Chicago, IL: American Library Association.

Ayers, L., Camden, B. P., German, L., Johnson, P., Miller, C., Smith-Yoshimura, K. (2009). *What we've learned from the RLG partners metadata creation workflows survey.* Dublin, Ohio: OCLC Research. Retrieved from http://www.oclc.org/research/publications/library/2009/2009-04.pdf

Baker, B. B. (1998). Resource sharing: Outsourcing and technical services. *Technical Services Quarterly, 16,* 35–45.

Banush, D. (2008). Stepping out: The expanding role of catalogers in academic libraries and academic institutions. *Cataloging & Classification Quarterly, 45,* 81–90.

Boock, M., & Vondracek, R. (2006). Organizing for digitization: A survey. *Portal: Libraries and the Academy, 6,* 197–217.

Boydston, J. M. K., & Leysen, J. M. (2006). Observation on the catalogers' role in descriptive metadata creation in academic libraries. *Cataloging & Classification Quarterly, 43,* 3–17.

Burnett, K. M., & Bonnici, L. J. (2006). Contested terrain: Accreditation and the future of the profession of librarianship. *Library Quarterly, 76,* 193–219.

Buttlar, L., & Garcha, R. (1998). Catalogers in academic libraries: Their evolving and expanding roles. *College & Research Libraries, 59,* 311–321.

Chapman, J. W. (2007). The roles of the metadata librarian in a research library. *Library Resources & Technical Services, 51,* 279–285.

Clair, K. (2010). Creative disorder: The work of metadata librarians in the 21st century. In S. Walter & K. Williams (Eds.), *The expert library: Staffing, sustaining, and advancing the academic library in the 21st century* (pp. 270–291). Chicago, IL: Association of College and Research Libraries.

DeZelar-Tiedman, C. (2004). Crashing the party: Catalogers as digital librarians. *OCLC Systems & Services: International Digital Libraries Perspectives, 20,* 145–147.

El-Sherbini, M., & Klim, G. (1997). Changes in technical services and their effect on the role of catalogers and staff education: An overview. *Cataloging & Classification Quarterly, 24,* 23–33.

Eskoz, P. A. (1990). The catalog librarian: Change or status quo? Results of a survey of academic libraries. *Library Resources & Technical Services, 34,* 380–392.

Gatti, T. H. (2005). Utilization of students as cataloging assistants at Carnegie category I institution libraries. *Library Resources and Technical Services, 49,* 27–31.

Giesecke, J. (2011). Institutional repositories: Keys to success. *Journal of Library Administration, 51,* 529–542.

Gorman, M. (2003). Cataloging in an electronic age. *Cataloging & Classification Quarterly, 36,* 5–17.

Han, M., & Hswe, P. (2010). The evolving role of the metadata librarian: Competencies found in job descriptions. *Library Resources & Technical Services, 53,* 129–141.

Harris, R. (1992). *Librarianship: The erosion of a woman's profession.* Norwood, NJ: Ablex.

Hoffman, G. L. (2010). Negotiating normative institutional pressures and maintaining legitimacy in a complex work environment: A multiple case study of three academic cataloging units. *Advances in Library Administration and Organization, 29,* 243–292.

IFLA Cataloguing Section and IFLA Meetings of Experts on an International Cataloguing Code (2009). *Statement of international cataloguing principles.* Retrieved from http://www.ifla.org/files/cataloguing/icp/icp_2009-en.pdf

IFLA Study Group on the Functional Requirements for Bibliographic Records (1998). *Functional requirements for bibliographic records: Final report.* Munich, Germany: K. G. Saur. Retrieved from http://www.ifla.org/files/cataloguing/frbr/frbr.pdf

IFLA Working Group on Functional Requirements and Numbering of Authority Records (FRANAR) (2009). *Functional requirements for authority data: A conceptual model.* Munich, Germany: K. G. Saur.

IFLA Working Group on the Functional Requirements for Subject Authority Records (FRSAR) (2010). *Functional requirements for subject authority data (FRSAD): A conceptual model.* Retrieved from http://www.ifla.org/files/classification-and-indexing/functional-requirements-for-subject-authority-data/frsad-final-report.pdf

Jansen, L. (2003, spring). The craft of local practice: How catalogers are gaining efficiency but losing control. *OLA Quarterly, 9*(1), 5–8.

Jeng, L. H. (1997). Knowledge, technology, and research in cataloging. *Cataloging & Classification Quarterly, 24,* 113–140.

Library of Congress. (2011a, Oct. 31). *A bibliographic framework for the digital age.* Retrieved from http://www.loc.gov/marc/transition/pdf/bibframework-10312011.pdf

Library of Congress. (2011b, Oct. 31). *A bibliographic framework initiative general plan.* Retrieved from http://www.loc.gov/marc/transition/news/framework-103111.html

Library of Congress Working Group on the Future of Bibliographic Control. (2008). *On the record.* Retrieved from http://www.loc.gov/bibliographic-future/news/lcwg-ontherecord-jan08-final.pdf

Lopatin, L. (2010). Metadata practices in academic and non-academic libraries for digital projects: A survey. *Cataloging & Classification Quarterly, 48,* 716–742.

Lynch, C. A. (2003). Institutional repositories: Essential infrastructure for scholarship in the digital age. *ARL: A Bimonthly Report*, 226. Retrieved from http://www.arl.org/resources/pubs/br/br226/br226ir.shtml

Ma, J. (2006). Managing metadata for digital projects. *Library Collections, Acquisitions, & Technical Services, 30*, 3–17.

Millsap, L. (1996). A history of the online catalog in North America. In L. C. Smith & R. C. Carter (Eds.), *Technical services management, 1965–1990: A quarter century of change and a look to the future* (pp. 79–91). New York, NY: Haworth Press.

O'Connor, L. (2009). Information literacy as a professional legitimation: The quest for professional jurisdiction. *Library Review, 58*, 272–289.

Oliver, C. (2007/5). Changing to RDA. *Feliciter*, 250–253.

Park, J., & Lu, C. (2009). Metadata professionals: Roles and competencies as reflected in job announcements, 2003–2006. *Cataloging & Classification Quarterly, 47*, 145–160.

Park, J., Lu, C., & Marion, L. (2009). Cataloging professionals in the digital environment: A content analysis of job descriptions. *Journal of the American Society for Information Science and Technology, 60*, 844–857.

Riemer, J. J. (July/Aug. 2009). Copy cataloging as a catalyst for new metadata roles in cataloging units. *Technicalities, 29*(4), 1, 9–11.

Scheschy, V. M. (1999). Outsourcing: A strategic partnership. *Technical Services Quarterly, 16*, 31–41.

Schottlaender, B. E. C. (2003). Why metadata? Why me? Why now? *Cataloging & Classification Quarterly, 36*, 19–29.

Simpson, B. (2007). Collections define cataloging's future. *The Journal of Academic Librarianship, 33*, 507–511.

The survey of academic library cataloging practices, 2011–12 edition (2011). New York, NY: Primary Research Group.

Taylor, A. G. (2006). *Introduction to cataloging and classification* (10th ed.). Westport, CT: Libraries Unlimited.

Trosow, S. E. (2001). Jurisdictional disputes and the unauthorized practice of law: New challenges for law librarianship. *Legal Reference Services Quarterly, 20*, 1–18.

Valentino, M. L. (2010). Integrating metadata creation into catalog workflow. *Cataloging & Classification Quarterly, 48*, 541–550.

Veve, M., & Feltner-Reichert, M. (2010). Integrating non-MARC metadata duties into the workflow of traditional catalogers: A survey of trends in perceptions among catalogers in four discussion lists. *Technical Services Quarterly, 27*, 194–213.

Vogh, B. S. (2011). Opportunities and challenges for libraries: An open letter. *College & Undergraduate Libraries, 18*, 97–103.

Wells, K. L. (2004). Hard times in technical services: How do academic libraries manage? A survey. *Technical Services Quarterly, 21*, 17–30.

Wilder, S. J. (2002). Demographic trends affecting professional technical services staffing in ARL libraries. *Cataloging & Classification Quarterly, 34*, 51–55.

Zhu, L. (2008). Head of cataloging positions in academic libraries: An analysis of job advertisements. *Technical Services Quarterly, 25*, 49–70.

The Ship Has Sailed and We Aren't On It: How Catalogers Could Support User Tasks and Why We Won't

MARY Z. ROSE

Technical Services Department, Southern Illinois University Edwardsville, Edwardsville, Illinois, USA

The article begins by describing the possible characteristics of a catalog interface built to leverage a future FRBR bibliographic framework and discussing the viability of a FRBR-ized catalog interface. The author then examines current trends in interface design, which leverage conventional cataloging data structures. This survey of the literature is followed by recommendations for adapting cataloging practices to enhance the efficacy of current interface designs. The author concludes by proposing that catalogers have a choice to make about the direction of functional cataloging initiatives.

INTRODUCTION

Functional cataloging supports the generic user tasks of finding, identifying, selecting, and obtaining relevant library resources. How a person approaches these tasks is controlled by the interface available for conducting a search of a library's catalog. Cataloging that helps the seeker achieve success with that interface is functional.

Catalogers have long been discussing how we can reorder the bibliographic universe to inspire better catalog interface designs. In the meantime, interface designers have developed new ways to manipulate the bibliographic descriptions currently available. These innovations would be even more effective if as catalogers we revised some of our cataloging ideals to support the emerging interface functionality. However, doing so would undermine the FRBR (Functional Requirements for Bibliographic Records) ideal that has been central to the cataloging discussion for well over a decade.

In this article, I begin by describing the FRBR cataloging philosophy and the possible characteristics of a catalog interface built to leverage a future FRBR bibliographic framework. I also discuss the viability of a "FRBR-ized" catalog interface. Next is an examination of current trends in interface design, which leverage conventional cataloging data structures, followed by recommendations for adapting cataloging practices to enhance the efficacy of current interface designs. Finally I propose that catalogers have a choice to make about the direction of functional cataloging initiatives.

I have adopted the generic user tasks of finding, identifying, selecting, and obtaining relevant resources as the basis for functional cataloging. These tasks are described by the International Federation of Library Associations (IFLA) Study Group in the September 1998 *Functional Requirements for Bibliographic Records: Final Report* (IFLA Study Group, p. 8) as follows:

- using the data to *find* materials that correspond to the user's stated search criteria (e.g., in the context of a search for all documents on a given subject, or a search for a recording issued under a particular title);
- using the data retrieved to *identify* an entity (e.g., to confirm that the document described in a record corresponds to the document sought by the user, or to distinguish between two texts or recordings that have the same title);
- using the data to *select* an entity that is appropriate to the user's needs (e.g., to select a text in a language the user understands, or to choose a version of a computer program that is compatible with the hardware and operating system available to the user);
- using the data in order to acquire or *obtain* access to the entity described (e.g., to place a purchase order for a publication, to submit a request for the loan of a copy of a book in a library's collection, or to access online an electronic document stored on a remote computer).

For the rest of this article, I will concentrate my discussion on the first three tasks of finding, identifying, and selecting, since these are the tasks most affected by cataloging practices.

THE FRBR IDEA

The FRBR Philosophy

FRBR is a structural framework for cataloging developed by IFLA and described in the 1998 *Functional Requirements for Bibliographic Records: Final Report* (IFLA Study Group). The intent is to support the user tasks of finding, identifying, selecting, and obtaining resources.

FRBR uses a relational database approach to organize data into attributes about entities and relate the entities to each other. IFLA defines three groups of entities. Group 1 entities are *work*, *expression*, *manifestation*, and *item*. These entities recognize that an intellectual creation may be realized or perceived in different ways, which in turn may be embodied and transmitted using different modes and technologies. Group 2 entities are *person* and *corporate body*. These represent the creators of and contributors to a resource or, possibly, the subject of a resource. The Group 3 entities further organize subject data into *concept*, *object*, *event*, and *place*. The Group 1 entities, known colloquially as WEMI (the acronym formed by their initials), are the focus of the following exposition.

Separating attributes of a bibliographic description into four separate WEMI components represents a dramatic change in how catalogers think. Catalogers are accustomed to dealing with an individual resource—an *item*. For illustrative purposes, suppose the item I'm holding is a book called *Undersea Pottery* by Dilbert Cousteau, published by Hillsboro Press in 2000. I recognize that the bibliographic description of this item represents multitudes of essentially identical items other people in other libraries are holding in their hands just as accurately as it describes the particular item I happen to be holding. The entity "the book *Undersea Pottery* by Dilbert Cousteau published by Hillsboro Press in 2000 that is held at several libraries" is a *manifestation*. In essence, the bibliographic records created by catalogers usually describe manifestations.

The book *Undersea Pottery* by Dilbert Cousteau published by Hopscotch Press in 1973 is a different manifestation of the same *work*. A work is defined by the creator(s) and the content. The electronic version of Cousteau's book published by Vincent Online Press in 2012 is another manifestation, just employing a different mode of transmission. But if I digitally record myself reading the book cover-to-cover and then post it on YouTube, the result constitutes a different *expression* of the same work. The quality of expression can be thought of as the medium of perception, in this case sound versus text. The content and creator are the same, so it is the same work. Language is another perceptual element that constitutes a different expression.

One problem with the WEMI reduction is that it isn't always clear what constitutes a new work. For example, if someone translates Cousteau's book to French but in the process changes some of the cultural references to better resonate with French readers, is the content really still the same? Or has the translator become an additional creator, making the result a new work instead of simply a new expression of the original work? If in my YouTube recording I summarize the boring chapters instead of reading them completely through, is this abridged version just a different expression of the original work, or is it a different work? If the Hillsboro Press edition has some annotations by Cousteau's grandson, is it a manifestation of the original work or a new work?

It's important to make these distinctions between work, expression, and manifestation in order for FRBR to be an effective cataloging framework. Some attributes of a catalog description belong to the work, some to the expression, others to the manifestation, and others to the item. For a given library acquisition, the cataloger records the manifestation attributes: title, publisher, date of publication, edition, etc. In conventional cataloging, the cataloger also records the work-level and expression-level attributes in the same bibliographic record. But in a FRBR-based catalog, the work-level attributes would probably be imported from a separately created work record. This record could include the author, uniform title, classification, subjects, and the original creation date. The same work attributes thus would be connected automatically and consistently to all of the manifestations of a work. From a cataloging perspective, a cataloger would no longer describe an item top-to-bottom, back-to-front. Instead he would first determine whether it is a manifestation of a previously identified work or expression. Also, if it is a new work in some derivative way (e.g., an abridgement), the cataloger would note that this new work is closely related to the original work and would make the nature of that relationship explicit in his cataloging.

Characteristics of a FRBR-ized Catalog Interface

The hypothetical FRBR-ized interface organizes this information in a hierarchical display for the user. Fritz and Fields (2011) provide an illustration of what this display looks like. In their depiction, the creator is at the top of the hierarchy; individual works are listed below. Each work can be expanded to show expressions in normalized groupings: "Text, English," "Text, German," "Audio." Each of these groups can be expanded to reveal the manifestations. Two different publications of the English text version of *Madeline* by Ludwig Bemelmans, one published in 1939 by Simon and Schuster and one in 1993 by Puffin Books, are represented in their example. At the bottom of the list of works, the user can expand an option labeled "Related works" to see descriptions of movies and television programs based on the book *Madeline*.

The advantages of a FRBR-ized interface are obvious. Instead of today's bewildering list of disparate manifestations of various expressions ordered only by some obscure "relevancy" algorithm, the catalog searcher would receive a results list in which manifestations are collocated by work. This approach supports the user's ability to identify and distinguish between similar manifestations (e.g., print books with different publishers and dates of publication). It also helps the user to select a manifestation by mode of transmission (e.g., electronic versus print) or an expression by medium of perception (e.g., sound versus text).

The disadvantages are also obvious. The hypothetical FRBR-ized display requires several clicks to view a bibliographic description. But what if the user is searching for a known item? Should she have to drill down through works and expressions to find it? Also, many works—some estimates are as high as 80 percent—only have one manifestation (Tillett, 2003). If that estimate is accurate, then is creating a WEMI structure worth the tremendous effort required to reorder the bibliographic universe?

Viability of a FRBR-ized Catalog Interface

I believe this is a moot question, because I am convinced that the time has passed in which holding out for a FRBR-based catalog was a viable option. If the new Resource Description and Access (RDA) cataloging guidelines, developed to replace the conventional AACR2 (Anglo-American Cataloging Rules, 2nd edition), had proven to be a robust framework for implementing FRBR, there might have been a way to steer interface design in a FRBR direction. But as released in 2010, twelve years after the IFLA Study Group's report, RDA is viewed by many as a disappointment. Although it uses FRBR vocabulary and a WEMI organization to discuss bibliographic data, RDA perpetuates the conventional cataloging tradition of providing work/expression attributes in work/expression identifiers only as needed to identify a work as unique, not to fully describe the creator(s) and content of the work (Joint Steering Committee, 2010). As previously discussed, attaching descriptive attributes at the appropriate levels is vital to any FRBR-based catalog and its presentation via a FRBR-ized interface.

In addition, RDA has usability issues, prompting the Library of Congress (LC) and the other national libraries to delay its implementation until it is extensively revised (U.S. RDA Test Coordinating Committee, 2011). At this writing, LC has identified a target implementation date of March 31, 2013 (Library of Congress, 2012). LC has also given a vote of no-confidence to MARC as an encoding format for RDA/FRBR (Library of Congress, 2011). This means that even after RDA is improved, catalogers will need to wait for a MARC replacement before FRBR-based cataloging can be implemented in a way that enables a FRBR-ized catalog interface. The reality is that the philosophical and logical frameworks for realizing a FRBR-ized interface are many years away.

In the meantime, catalog interface developers have been designing new interface functionality that leverages the conventional cataloging AACR2 and MARC data structures. These designs are very different from the hypothetical interface based on the FRBR data structure model. The next section identifies some of the current trends in catalog interface design.

CURRENT INTERFACE DESIGN TRENDS: A REVIEW OF THE RECENT LITERATURE

Wynne and Hanscom (2011) list several trends in the design of public interfaces for library catalogs, often described in the literature as "next generation catalogs." Developments such as automatic spell-checking and word variant searching, relevance ranking of search results, and "more like this" suggestions help users find useful information. Thomas (2000) states that relevance ranking is particularly helpful for users with lower logical reasoning skills. The ability to narrow results by subject facets, and enhancements like book-cover images and reviews, helps users differentiate between similar resources and identify which resources are most interesting to them. Naun (2010) observes that newer interfaces often allow users to restrict search results to items that are available, which is among the user-identified characteristics of helpful interface features summarized by Thomas and Buck (2010). Along with a display of delivery options, this component helps users obtain items of interest. Displays that incorporate format icons to represent books, sound recordings, video recordings, electronic resources, and other forms help users select the resource format that is best suited to their needs. Clickable facets for narrowing results to a particular format further support the user task of selection.

Interfaces are also trending toward a brief default display rather than a full display of catalog data, although there is no consensus on which fields to display and which to omit. Does this facilitate or impede user tasks? Thomas (2000) asserts that fuller displays help users identify which resources are not relevant to their information need. However, Thomas also found that users typically perceive only a couple of data fields as being important to them. One conclusion from his study was that more subject data in a brief display helped users make decisions about relevancy without having to view the fuller display. Yee (2006a) asserts that users need the full record display for the user task of identifying and distinguishing between similar resources.

In interface design, the post-search ability to narrow a retrieved recordset by subject or topic is generally achieved by parsing precoordinated Library of Congress subject heading (LCSH) strings into a list of clickable facets reflecting topic, region, and era. The list is often ordered according to the number of items retrieved in the initial search that corresponds to the facet. Naun (2010) observes that this combines the power of keyword searching with controlled vocabulary: Users are led to the controlled vocabulary through their keyword search. However, it must be remembered that the act of narrowing a search by clicking on a facet in the list executes a second search *within* the retrieved set; it doesn't repeat the original search with the preferred authorized term. In other words, records omitted from the initial set because they lack the keyword search term remain outside the results set, even if they contain the subsequently clicked controlled vocabulary synonym facet. Naun also notes that subject or topic faceting based on classification is offered in some current interfaces. He observes that classification-based subject access helpfully offers the user a smaller set of subject area variables to review compared to the typically lengthy set of LCSH facets. This works well in a search like "stonehenge" that crosses disparate subject areas (e.g., technology, world history, fine arts, etc.), for users intending to approach the topic from a particular perspective. In some interfaces this is the only manner in which the system leverages classification data, beyond merely displaying it.

Interfaces seem to be trending away from utilizing authority records. This dramatically disables the user looking for resources by a creator who is known by more than one name. In the past, users searching for names were forced to access the name authority file first and then click on a choice within it to retrieve bibliographic records. Yee (2005) envisions a system that searches authority record cross-references for a user's author search term and then displays the bibliographic records containing the corresponding authorized forms. This would result in retrieval sets that aren't transparent to the user, since the user's search term would not necessarily appear in the retrieved bibliographic records. To borrow Yee's example, a user searching for "Samuel Clemens" would retrieve everything in the library written by Mark Twain, but she wouldn't know why. In another article, Yee (2006b) imagines an interface in which the user's author keyword search activates a search of name authority records instead of bibliographic records. This is a return to an earlier catalog interface model–a forced intervening assessment of name authorities instead of immediate access to bibliographic descriptions–with the twist that it is a keyword search rather than a browse search and the user is liberated from a left-anchored last-name-first mode. It seems unlikely that modern interface design will retreat from a Google-driven tempo between search and final result to incorporate this type of intermediary step. Yee proposes the same model for subject keyword searches. Naun (2010) observes that the latter would be overwhelming for novice users and ineffective in a case where the search word is a ubiquitous term like "history."

Implicit to interfaces designed to rigorously manipulate MARC coding in order to create faceted displays is the need to create bibliographic records that are consistent and include all of the relevant metadata. Wynne and Hanscom (2011) note that inaccurate, inconsistent, and missing data are exposed to a greater extent in these interfaces than they were in previous interfaces. The authors report that data cleanup projects and their automation become higher cataloging priorities in this environment.

PROPOSED CATALOGING ADAPTATIONS IN RESPONSE TO SELECTED TRENDS

As previously noted, current interfaces are based upon conventional cataloging structures rather than a FRBR framework for cataloging data, which is several years away from feasible implementation. I submit that conventional cataloging can and should advance to maximize the performance of new interface features while retaining the AACR2 and MARC structures. The first step is to identify and implement simple changes in cataloging practice that will make current interface functionality more effective.

Keyword Searching

Keyword searching across fields or within a field has replaced browse searching entirely in many current interfaces; where it is still offered, browse searching is de-emphasized and has to be intentionally selected by the user as a search mode. Interfaces that mimic Google functionality employ a default Boolean "AND" between search terms. To maximize the helpfulness of this trend for users, I recommend focusing cataloging efforts on enhancing keyword access in effective and nonredundant ways.

My first recommendation is to provide formatted contents notes (i.e., contents notes coded to identify data as title or contributor data) whenever this information is meaningful. Specific instances include: individual songs included in musical sound recordings, with composers and performers (except in the case of "classical music" recordings, which I will address subsequently); individual essays or chapters in anthologies, including authors when the anthology includes multiple contributors; and individual works of short fiction in anthologies whether by a single contributor or multiple contributors, including contributor names in the latter case. In current cataloging practice, contents notes are required for musical sound recordings but are left to the cataloger's judgment in the remaining scenarios. In all of the cases, the title and contributor formatting is currently optional.

I do not recommend supplying analytical uniform title or name-title added entries (i.e., added entries for each included song or story in normalized, LC-authorized forms) when formatted contents notes are provided, except when the resulting keywords vary materially from the contents note. This means that the bibliographic description of a book of 20 short stories might contain name-title added entries for only 3 of the included stories. Also, at some libraries it is local practice to include uncontrolled title added entries (740 fields) when the corresponding formatted contents note element begins with an article: This practice, which is done to support browse searching, should be discontinued.

My next recommendation, for scores and sound recordings that are compilations of individual "classical music" works, takes the opposite approach. For these resources, I recommend supplying uniform name-title added entries in lieu of detailed contents notes. Many current interfaces offer the ability to narrow retrieval by title facet, which could be configured to display uniform titles. This would greatly enhance the common music user task of selecting multiple recordings of the same work or versions of the same score. In cases where keyword access would be meaningfully enhanced by including variant titles found on the item or known from another source, these should be supplied in a note.

For example, the bibliographic description of a sound recording including Beethoven's piano sonatas numbers 5 through 8 would include corresponding uniform name-title entries in the form of "Beethoven, Ludwig van, 1770–1827. Sonatas, piano, no. 5, op. 10, no. 1, C minor." It would also contain a note to the effect of: "Includes the Pathétique sonata and three other piano sonatas." Doing this would represent a change in current cataloging practice, which requires all added access points to be explicitly justified elsewhere in the catalog record. Similarly, I recommend eliminating the credits notes (508 and 511 fields) from video-recording records in favor of providing normalized personal name added entries with relater terms (for example: 700 1_ Eastwood, Clint, $d 1930- $e director).

Refinement of Retrieval Set Using Subject/Topic Facets

Subject facets are generated in current interfaces in two ways: through subject headings and through classification. In the former case, post-coordinated LC subject headings composed of a main heading modified by a subdivision or multiple subdivisions are broken apart into specific geographic, topic, period, and/or form facets. An example of a post-coordinated LC subject heading exhibiting all of these types of subdivisions in the order listed is Women—China—History—20th century—Maps. Perhaps this would describe a resource depicting demographic information about Chinese women on separate maps for each decade of the 20th century. In current catalog interfaces that offer the user the ability to narrow a search by subject facet, each of these terms ("Women," "China," etc.) would be presented to the user as a separate clickable facet if this resource were among those retrieved by the user's search. Similarly parsed headings and subdivisions represented in other retrieved resources would also appear as facet options for narrowing the search. For most searches, this results in a lengthy list of subject facet options.

My first recommendation regarding facets focuses on topical subdivisions. Topical subdivision modifiers separated from the main heading are virtually meaningless. To use the above example, consider the user who performs a keyword search for "china" and is presented with the facet option "history." Clicking on it would generate a results set that includes the resource described above, and a book with the subject heading "China—History—221 B.C.-960 A.D.," and every other resource with a subject heading containing both the keyword "china" and the topical subdivision "history." It could include a novel about an American pioneer named "Samuel China." I therefore recommend discontinuing the use of topical subdivisions in bibliographic records.

However, I do not recommend omitting form subdivisions. Although some current interfaces don't display form subdivisions (650 $v subfields) as facet choices, they could easily be configured to conflate them with genre/form headings (655 fields), displaying them together as genre/form facets. I know this because interfaces currently conflate geographic subdivisions (650 $z subfields) with geographic subject headings (651 fields). Therefore, my second recommendation is to retain the use of form subdivisions in bibliographic descriptions and configure interfaces to display them.

In the case of geographic subdivisions, the issue for catalogers is to ensure that the geographic heading appears one way or another in the bibliographic record when it is appropriate. Problems arise when a heading is inherently geographic. An example is the subject heading "Jazz," which is the Library of Congress authorized heading used instead of "Jazz—United States." By clicking on the "United States" facet, users will eliminate records with the heading "Jazz" from their retrieval set (unless the record also includes a different subject heading containing "United States"). Therefore, my third recommendation is to add an explicit geographic heading (651 field) to records with subject headings in which the geographic term is implied. In the environment of facet-based interfaces that either don't offer or de-emphasize browse subject searches, it doesn't matter whether the phrase "United States" appears as a main subject or a geographic subdivision.

My final recommendation regarding topic facets deals with facets based on the LC class number assigned to a resource. Classification-based topic facets are generated by mapping class numbers to top-level topics in the classification outline. The topics are then displayed as subject area facets represented by the retrieved resources. This subject breakdown results in a shorter list of more general topic groups compared to the list based on subject headings. However, if a library doesn't classify certain types of resources such as sound recordings, video recordings, or electronic resources, these resources will not be represented in the classification-based facet display. I recommend providing a top-level classification for these resources. For instance, bibliographic records for musical sound recordings that lack an LC call number (090 or 050 field) should be supplied with an 090 field that looks like this: 090 __ $a M.

Absence of Authority Control

The fact that many current interfaces fail to leverage authority control in interpreting searches is a disservice to users. As previously discussed, Yee (2005; 2006b) in particular has offered thorough delineations of how authority control could be integrated into interface design. I am convinced that Yee's suggestions could be realized with current interface technology, but to my knowledge this has not happened. The implication is that interface designers believe users simply will not tolerate a return to a mode that involves any delay between search input and a "hit list." This is a grim reality that makes transparent authority control impossible. I do not advocate authority control without transparency.

What can catalogers do to maximize the searcher's ability to find, identify, and select resources without the benefit of authority control? Although on the surface it sounds counter-intuitive, one way to mitigate the damage is to make authority work a cataloging priority. The regular cleanup of names used in bibliographic records to match authorized forms will enable users to utilize name facet displays effectively, since works by authors will be collocated by the facet. This obviously doesn't solve the main problem with variant name forms, exemplified by Yee's (2005) scenario of the person seeking works by Samuel Clemens coming up empty-handed. We can only hope the unfortunate user will ask a librarian why the library has nothing by this author. But diligent maintenance of access points will ensure that she won't find a stray resource with a bibliographic record containing a personal name access point for Clemens and walk away with a potentially dangerous false sense of accomplishment. Subject heading cleanup is another priority for the same reason (i.e., the collocation of subject-related resources in a facet option).

THE CATALOGING JOURNEY

The cataloging journey I propose is more than reforming some cataloging rules: It is a radical paradigm shift. As this paper demonstrates, it isn't possible for catalogers to catalog for a future FRBR-based catalog and simultaneously modify cataloging practices to promote the effectiveness of current interface design. The differences between the FRBR ideal and the current catalog interfaces are too fundamental. The FRBR-ized interface concept is that the catalog's response to a search would be an array of resource categories based on normalized relationships. The user would access bibliographic descriptions only after selecting the category that matches his need. In contrast, current interfaces are committed to immediately delivering bibliographic descriptions in response to a keyword search. The descriptions are loosely organized; the interface relies on post-search refinement to transform the retrieval into a relevant subset. The imagined FRBR-ized catalog interface would rely extensively on manipulating "work records" that would essentially be enhanced author-title authority records. On the opposite end of the spectrum, current interfaces don't employ any means of leveraging existing authority control. The cataloging recommendations I have offered in this paper contradict the FRBR philosophy by opposing the use of normalized access points that are redundant or meaningless in the current interface design environment. My recommendations instead concentrate on supplying keywords and access points that are useful, meaningful, and reliable in this environment.

The ship of current interface design is continuing to gain speed. The wind is in its sails. The designers and users aboard will be just that much further along their current course ten years or so from now, when everything is in place to design a FRBR-ized interface. At the moment the ship isn't too far away. With some determined effort we could jump into john boats and paddle out to join it. How can we redirect the ship's course in a FRBR direction without a vigorous RDA product and an alternative to MARC? I submit that we cannot. But we can roll up our sleeves and pitch in to make the boat sail faster and smarter in its current direction, by changing cataloging practices to optimize the effectiveness of the catalog interfaces being developed. We can collaborate with interface designers to identify new ways of leveraging the current cataloging data structures. But in many ways catalogers are idealists, so we are not likely to do this as a group. We will likely remain on the shore building our FRBR sand castle, expecting the ship to come back for us when we're finished.

REFERENCES

Fritz, D. A., & Fields, L. (2011). Cataloging correctly (someday) using RDA. In S. S. Intner, J. F. Fountain, & J. Weihs (eds.), *Cataloging correctly for kids: An introduction to the tools* (5th ed., pp. 73–103). Chicago, IL: American Library Association.

International Federation of Library Associations, IFLA Study Group on the Functional Requirements for Bibliographic Records (FRBR). (1998). *Functional requirements for bibliographic records: Final report* (As amended and corrected through February 2009.) Retrieved from http://archive.ifla.org/VII/s13/frbr/frbr_2008.pdf

Joint Steering Committee for Development of RDA. (2010). *RDA toolkit*. Retrieved from http://access.rdatoolkit.org/

Library of Congress. (2011, October 31). *A bibliographic framework for the digital age*. Retrieved from http://www.loc.gov/marc/transition/news/framework-103111.html

Library of Congress. (2012, March 2). *Library of Congress announces its long-range RDA training plan*. Retrieved from http://www.loc.gov/catdir/cpso/news_rda_implementation_date.html

Naun, C. C. (2010). Next generation OPACs: A cataloging viewpoint. *Cataloging and Classification Quarterly*, *48*(4) 330–342.

Thomas, D. H. (2000). The effect of interface design on item selection in an online catalog. *Library Resources and Technical Services*, *45*(1), 20–46.

Thomas, T., & Buck, S. (2010). OCLC's WorldCat Local versus III's WebPAC. *Library Hi Tech*, *28*(4), 648–671.

Tillett, B. B. (2003). FRBR (functional requirements for bibliographic records). *Technicalities*, *23*(5), *1*, 11–13.

U.S. RDA Test Coordinating Committee. (2011, June 13). *Report and recommendations of the U.S. RDA Test Coordinating Committee: Executive summary*. Retrieved from http://www.loc.gov/bibliographic-future/rda/source/rda-execsummary-public-13june11.pdf

Wynne, S. C., & Hanscom, M. J. (2011). The effect of next-generation catalogs on catalogers and cataloging functions in academic libraries. *Cataloging & Classification Quarterly, 49*, 179–201.

Yee, M. M. (2006a, September). Applying FRBR to library catalogues: A review of existing FRBRization projects. Draft of paper presented at the National Library of Australia Australian Committee on Cataloging Beyond the OPAC: Future directions for web-based catalogues conference, Perth, Western Australia. Retrieved from http://www.nla.gov.au/lis/stndrds/grps/acoc/papers2006.html

Yee, M. M. (2006b, September). Beyond the OPAC: future directions for web-based catalogues. Draft of keynote address presented at the National Library of Australia Australian Committee on Cataloging conference of the same name in Perth, Western Australia. Retrieved from http://www.nla.gov.au/lis/stndrds/grps/acoc/papers2006.html

Yee, M. M. (2005). FRBRization: A method for turning online public finding lists into online public catalogs. *Information technology and libraries, 24*(3), 77–95.

Subject Access: Conceptual Models, Functional Requirements, and Empirical Data

OKSANA L. ZAVALINA

Department of Library and Information Sciences, University of North Texas, Denton, Texas, USA

One of the central functions of bibliographic control is providing subject access. However, numerous studies conducted over decades have shown that users routinely experience problems with subject access in library catalogs and databases. These problems are often due to inadequate quality of subject metadata, which is greatly influenced by complexity of subject representation. The fact that major cataloging standards (e.g., AACR2 and its predecessors) have been overlooking the importance of subject access and have not addressed subject cataloging is arguably one of the reasons behind problems in organization of subject access. The new cataloging code—Resource Description and Access (RDA)—attempts to fill this gap. Upon examination of how subject access is addressed in RDA and its underlying conceptual models that specify functional requirements for bibliographic control—FRBR, FRAD, and FRSAD—this article presents results of a study that used FRBR model as an analytical framework in examination of user search queries in a large-scale digital library. The findings of this study provide empirical data to inform the development of RDA sections that cover subject access, particularly subject entities and relationships.

INTRODUCTION

Subject access has been one of the central topics of research in library and information science for decades, particularly in regard to information seeking and information retrieval (IR) theory (Hjørland, 1997). The importance of organizing information by subject is continuing to increase (Svenonius, 2000). As defined by Cochrane (1985), subject access means systematic (e.g., classification system), topical (e.g., subject headings), and natural (e.g., title, abstract words) approaches to the subject matter of information resources and encompasses both processes of subject cataloging by information professionals and information seeking and retrieval by the users. Subject access in information retrieval systems is provided through metadata—"structured data about an object that supports functions associated with the designated object" (Greenberg, 2003, p. 1876). Supporting the user tasks defined by the Functional Requirements for Bibliographic Records model (IFLA, 1998; 2008)—find, identify, select, and obtain information objects—is the major function of metadata in information systems.

Creators of information objects, especially textual, play a certain role in subject access by assigning titles to their works (in cases when such titles are not abstract but semantically meaningful). However, the two major players in subject access are

- users who seek information by subject through search queries and browsing, and
- information professionals who perform subject analysis and create subject metadata—metadata that describes subject matter or aboutness of information objects.

There are a number of problems that each of these two players face in the process of subject access. These are summarized below.

Users of Information Systems Engaged in Subject Access

Searching and browsing are two major types of interactions between the users and information systems (Wilson, 2000). As defined by Lipetz (1970), subject searching is a type of search in which "the user is interested in both identifying and locating one or more documents pertaining to some known topic" (p. 43). Historically, subject searching has been recognized as one of the two major approaches employed by users in catalog searching, along with known-item searching (Krikelas, 1972). According to Lee (2003), subject exploration (including subject search and subject browse)—"purposive exploration on chosen subjects"—is one of the three general types of scholarly information seeking, along with locating specific information and/or documents and general scanning for nonspecific information (p. 424).

User subject access to information systems (specifically catalogs and bibliographic databases) has long been investigated (e.g., Jackson, 1958; Larson, 1991b; Lipetz, 1970; Matthews, Lawrence, & Ferguson, 1983; Tagliacozzo & Kochen, 1970). Researchers have identified subject access problems such as search failure and information overload (cf., Larson, 1991a) and named a range of reasons behind these problems, including users' subject domain and conceptual knowledge (e.g., Allen, 1991; Borgman, 1996; Markey, 2007), their understanding of how the information retrieval system functions (Borgman, 1996), their knowledge of sources to search and ordering of their searches (Markey, 2007), and mismatches between multiple vocabularies involved in subject access—those of authors, documents, searchers, indexers, syndetic structures, and queries (Buckland, 1999). One of the prominent reasons behind the problems with subject access is quality and application of subject metadata: controlled vocabularies applied in information systems (e.g., Cochrane, 1986, 2000), the structure of subject headings (e.g., Farradine, 1970; Taube, 1953; Weinberg, 1995), etc.

Information Professionals Creating Subject Metadata

Achieving adequate subject representation in metadata for effective subject access and information retrieval is a task of increasing complexity. Subject representation is based on subject analysis, which consists of three major steps: (1) determining the subject of an information resource, (2) translating, and (3) assigning subject terms/notations. Each of these steps is complicated.

According to Taylor (2006), determining subject, or "aboutness," of a document depends on at least two factors: (1) indexer's knowledge and/or opinion about the world and (2) judgment. These subjective factors lead to definitional problems regarding subjects of works in the library and information science literature. As Bates stated, "It is practically impossible to instruct indexers or catalogers how to find subjects when they examine documents" (1986, p. 360).

Although there is no one right way to determine aboutness, several models have been influential (e.g., Broughton, 2004; International Organization for Standardization, 1985; Langridge, 1989; Šauperl, 2002). Langridge (1989), for example, argues that there are two types of subject: knowledge forms/fundamental categories (e.g., philosophy) and topics/perceived phenomena (e.g., morals). She suggests examining document characteristics such as viewpoint or bias, intellectual level, audience, bibliographic forms, and textual characteristics. Various accepted subject analysis models share the recommendations to examine the item's title, subtitle, author, table of contents, chapter headings, introduction, dust jacket, and if necessary, sample text. Analyzing author's intention and possible uses of information—two other important parts of determining aboutness, captured by several models (e.g., Beghtol, 1986; Hjørland, 1998; Šauperl, 2002; Wilson, 1968)—seem to be an especially challenging part of subject analysis, as each indexer might have a different interpretation of author intention and prediction of possible uses; moreover, these interpretations and predictions can change over time. Šauperl emphasizes relating the topic to existing collection(s), including an institution's own collection, Library of Congress, WorldCat, and collections similar to the institution's collection; the nonlinearity of Šauperl's model captures the nature of the iterative process of subject analysis.

Alternative models of determining aboutness that, in particular, have been employed in automatic indexing, are *objective-quantitative method* (Wilson, 1968), according to which concepts with most references in text of an information package are treated as its subjects, and *grammatical model* (described by Svenonius, 2000), which assumes that a subject of a document can be inferred from the grammatical subjects of its sentences. The objective-quantitative approach has been criticized (Hjørland, 1997) for not acknowledging context-dependence and for the lack of pragmatic aspects such as potential uses. The grammatical model's major limitation is the ambiguity of natural language. Although language is sometimes used in a propositional mode (e.g., in sciences), much more often it is used in expressive/emotive mode (in humanities, in general, but especially in movies, poetry, and fiction) (Svenonius, 2000). Hjørland (1997) proposed viewing a document's subjects as its "intellectual potential," which can differ for the same document at different periods of time and stages of society development, across different domains, etc.

It is at the second stage of subject analysis that translation problems begin. One of which is that "there is no such thing as unambiguous, uniform classification system ... no classification system can reflect either the social or the natural world fully accurately" (Bowker & Star, 1999, pp. 322–323). Of course, this is true not only for classification systems but for any subject heading or indexing system in general. Another important translation problem, as identified by Bates (1998), is an expertise gap between the user and the indexer: even PhDs are naïve searchers and usually do not realize that there are any ambiguities or problems with a term, having in mind just one sense of the term that interests them. Expertise gap is one of the reasons user and indexer terms very often do not match.

In the final step of subject analysis, the indexer represents the subject matter of an information object, expressed in natural language, with the terms from one or more "subject languages" (Svenonius, 2000, p. 127): subject terms from "alphabetic subject languages" (i.e., controlled-vocabulary lists of subject terms or thesauri), and/or "classificatory subject languages" (i.e., classification notations built according to certain a classification scheme). This step is complicated because the subject representation process is affected by limitations of available subject languages. An additional level of complexity is added by the fact that subject representation should be guided by the desired balance between specificity and exhaustivity. Hjørland (1998, p. 95) claims that since virtually any document has an infinite number of subjects, the subject analysis is "a process of giving priority to those subjects which best serve the needs of the user of the information system in question"; assigning subject headings that correspond to the "most probable long-term utility" of the information resource.

The various complexities of determining subjects of an information resource and subject representation in metadata that were described above obviously influence subject access. Moreover, the fact that major cataloging standards (e.g., Anglo-American Cataloging Rules, International Standard Bibliographic Description) have been overlooking importance of subject access and have not been addressing subject cataloging is arguably one of the reasons behind the problems in organization of subject access. Although Charles Ammi Cutter's library catalog objectives recognized subject access as an important function of an information system as early as 1876 (Cutter, 1904), the developers of the 20th-century cataloging standards did not pay adequate attention to subject access. Neither the revision of Cutter principles by Lubetzky (1960) nor the Paris Principles (1961)—a set of cataloging principles adopted by the International Federation of Library Associations (IFLA) and taken as the basis for the cataloging codes developed worldwide since 1960s—included subject access issues. Instead, these two influential documents focused solely on descriptive cataloging issues. As a result, neither the first (1967) edition of the Anglo-American Cataloguing Rules, nor the subsequent revisions dealt with subject access. Although the recent IFLA Statement of International Cataloguing Principles (2009) has significantly updated and broadened the scope of the Paris Principles, the issues of subject access and subject cataloging are still nearly absent from its text (Guerrini, 2009). In 1998, IFLA's working group on Functional Requirements for Bibliographic Records (IFLA, 1998) included subject access into its model of the bibliographic universe, but the cataloging standard in use at that time—second edition of Anglo-American-Cataloguing Rules or AACR2—did not reflect this important change. The Resource Description and Access commonly known under the acronym RDA (Joint Steering Committee on the Development of RDA, 2010)—the new unified cataloging code that is scheduled to start replacing AACR2 in 2013 (some 137 years after the first publication of the Cutter principles)—attempts to finally fill this gap.

MODELING SUBJECT ACCESS IN FRBR FAMILY OF MODELS AND RDA

The future of bibliographic control is often associated with RDA, whose structure is largely based on the Functional Requirements for Bibliographic Records (commonly known under the acronym FRBR) entity-relationship model of the bibliographic universe. The FRBR model was first developed in 1990s. Based in part on Cutter's principles of library catalog, FRBR model (Functional Requirements for Bibliographic Records, 1998) defined user tasks as: find, identify, select, and obtain. In regard to subject access, these user tasks can be specified as (1) find the works on a given subject, (2) find the works in which a concept is significantly treated, (3) select a work by its main subject only, (4) search for works on related subjects, and (5) search for works in which related or connected subjects are handled (Buizza & Guerrini, 2002). Additional user tasks, such as navigation (Svenonius, 2000), use (e.g., Morgan, 2006), and others have been discussed at different points of time but are not included in the FRBR model. The FRBR model was revised in 2008, and two related models have been released since then: Functional Requirements for Authority Data (commonly known under the acronym FRAD) and Functional Requirements for Subject Authority Data (commonly known under the acronym FRSAD). One more user task of "explore" was added by the FRSAD model (IFLA, 2010). Collectively, FRBR, FRAD, and FRSAD are now called the FRBR family and are considered parts of a larger general model. Arguably, all three models in the FRBR family of models demonstrate weakness in their coverage of subject access—a weakness that is inherited by RDA. The discussion of the treatment of subject entities, attributes, and relationships in FRBR, FRAD, and FRSAD models, as well as in RDA, follows.

Subject Entities

The FRBR model (IFLA, 2008, pp. 16–29) defines a set of ten entities that can serve as a subject of a work (Figure 1) that belong to three groups:

- Group 1
  - *work*
  - *expression*
  - *manifestation*
  - *item*
- Group 2
  - *person*
  - *corporate body*
- Group 3
  - *concept*
  - *object*
  - *event*
  - *place*

Of these ten FRBR entities, four Group 3 entities—*concept, object, event*, and *place*—are considered the major types of subjects.

The FRAD model (IFLA, 2009) added a *family* entity to the initial set of ten FRBR entities that can be a subject of a work and modified the definition of the *person* entity by including groups of people working under the same pseudonym (e.g., Ellery Queen) or trademark (e.g., Betty Crocker).

The new *thema* entity introduced by FRSAD model (IFLA, 2010) is a superclass of all entities that can be subjects of a *work*. FRSAD model developers state that *thema* can encompass any of the ten FRBR entities, or any other application-specific or domain-specific subject entities (p. 17). FRSAD also defined *nomen*—"any sign or sequence of signs (alphanumeric characters, symbols, sound, etc.) that a *thema* is known by, referred to, or addressed as" (p. 15)—as a separate entity instead of an attribute, as in FRAD model. However, FRSAD model does not explicitly predefine any subject entities in Group 3; it is limited to three entities: *work*, *thema*, and *nomen*.

The set of bibliographic entities included in the FRBR family of models is not comprehensive, and other candidate entities have been discussed. For example, the FRBR model has been criticized for a lack of granularity relating to groups of individuals other than *corporate body* (e.g., *communities*, *societies*, etc.), as they are lumped together without differentiation under the *object* or *concept* entities (Delsey, 2005). Researchers (e.g., Delsey, 2005; Zeng & Salaba, 2005) have also suggested revisiting Group 3 by adding *time* and *process*, differentiating between a dynamic *event* and a static *situation*, between *concrete* and *abstract concepts*. Maxwell (2008) has pointed out that *genre/form* could be considered a subclass of the *concept* entity. Recently, however, some researchers have suggested replacing Group 3 by *has a subject* property and freeing Group 3 entities from a Group 3 box "to make them usable anywhere" (Coyle, 2010, p. 272) or even completely removing the Group 3 of entities from the FRBR model as only "useful to some" (Gemberling, 2010, p. 449).

Alternative approaches to bibliographic entities, and to their subject matter, have also been discussed. For example, Svenonius (2000) used a set-theoretic approach rather than entity-relationship approach taken by FRBR model developers. She took a document—a material embodiment of information content—as the most basic entity and maintained that documents can be grouped in sets with respect to attributes they have in common. Svenonious defined and discussed the five most important sets—*work*, *superwork*, *edition*, *author*, and *subject*—and mentioned other potential sets such as *text*, *impression*, *imprint*, *archive*, and *collection*. Although Svenonious maintained that the subject set is one of the five most important sets of bibliographic entities, unlike the developers of the FRBR model, she did not attempt to define and discuss specific kinds of subjects.

Unlike its predecessors AACR and AACR2, Resource Description and Access (RDA) cataloging code aims to address subject access. The RDA code reserves Chapter 23 for general guidelines on recording the subject of a work. However, the work on this chapter started only in 2011, after the publication of FRSAD model (Tillett, 2011). Since the FRBR family of models supplies underlying structure for the development of RDA, the new cataloging code also devotes a number of its chapters to discussion of specific FRBR entities. Nine of these chapters are placeholder chapters reserved for the Group 3 subject entities *concept*, *object*, *event*, and *place*. RDA currently does not introduce any new entities but works with the ones suggested by FRBR family of models. However, a proposal has been recently made (Tillett, 2011) to the Joint Steering Committee for the Development of RDA to extend the definition of *event* to include conferences, exhibitions, expeditions, meetings, etc. (p. 6), and to introduce a *time* entity previously omitted by FRBR family of models.

Table 1 below shows subject entities in FRBR, FRAD, and FRSAD models, and in RDA.

Subject Attributes

While Group 1 (*work, expression, manifestation*, and *item*) and Group 2 (*person* and *corporate body*) entities in the FRBR model are well defined and have a number of attributes and characteristics, Group 3 entities (*concept, object, event*, and *place*) have limited definitions and lack elaborated characteristics. Both the first edition and the second revised version of FRBR model list only one attribute for each of the Group 3 entities—the term for the entity—with two characteristics under it: a subject heading and a classification number.

In the FRAD model, a number of attributes were added. The *concept* entity received a new *type of concept* attribute; the *object* entity received 5 new attributes: *type of object, date of production, place of production, producer/fabricator*, and *physical medium*. The list of *event* attributes was expanded to include *date associated with the event* and *place associated with the event*, while two new attributes—*coordinates* and *other geographical information*—were added for the *place* entity.

The FRSAD model introduced a variety of attributes for its new entities—*thema* and *nomen*. In the FRSAD model, *thema* has two major attributes: *type of thema* (FRSAD specifies that FRBR and FRAD entities are valid types of *thema* but that there can be other types as well) and *scope note*. The *nomen* entity in the FRSAD model has eleven attributes: *type, scheme, reference source, representation, language, script, script conversion, form, time of validity, audience*, and *status*. In RDA, chapters 12 through 16 are meant to deal with recording the attributes *concepts, objects, events*, and *places*. However, out of these five chapters, only one has been written—Chapter 16 "Identifying Places"—while others still remain "to be developed after the initial release of RDA." The only four RDA elements that represent attributes for *concept, object, event*, and *place* entities are *identifier, source consulted, status of identification*, and *term* or *name* (the latter with two sub-elements: *preferred term/name* and *variant term/name*). However, a proposal has been recently made (Tillett, 2011) to the Joint Steering Committee for the Development of RDA to introduce *"date and location/place"* attribute for *object* and *event* entities and *date* attribute for *place* entity.

Table 1 below shows subject attributes in FRBR, FRAD, and FRSAD models and RDA.

TABLE 1 Subject entities, attributes, and relationships in the FRBR family of models and RDA

	FRBR	FRAD	FRSAD	RDA

Entities	• Work
	• Expression
	• Manifestation
	• Item
	• Person
	• Corporate body
	• Concept
	• Object
	• Event
	• Place
		• Work
		• Expression
		• Manifestation
		• Item
		• Person
		• Family
		• Corporate body
		• Concept
		• Object
		• Event
		• Place
			• Thema
			  ○ Work
			  ○ Expression
			  ○ Manifestation
			  ○ Item
			  ○ Person
			  ○ Family
			  ○ Corporate body
			  ○ Concept
			  ○ Object
			  ○ Event
			  ○ Place
				• Work
				• Expression
				• Manifestation
				• Item
				• Person
				• Family
				• Corporate body
				• Concept
				• Object
				• Event
				• Place

Attributes	• Concept
	  ○ term for the concept (subject heading; classification number)
	• Object
	  ○ term for the object (subject heading; classification number)
	• Event
	  ○ term for the event (subject heading; classification number)
	• Place
	  ○ term for the place (subject heading; classification number)
		• Concept
		  ○ term for the concept (subject heading; classification number)
		  ○ type of the concept
		• Object
		  ○ term for the object (subject heading; classification number)
		  ○ date of production
		  ○ place of production
		  ○ type of object
		  ○ representation
		  ○ producer/fabricator
		  ○ physical medium
		• Event
		  ○ term for the event (subject heading; classification number)
		  ○ date associated
		  ○ place associated
			• Thema
			  ○ type of a *thema*
			  ○ scope note
			• Nomen
			  ○ type
			  ○ reference source
			  ○ language
			  ○ script
			  ○ script conversion
			  ○ form
			  ○ time of validity
			  ○ audience
			  ○ status
				• Concept
				  ○ identifier
				  ○ source consulted
				  ○ status of identification
				  ○ term (preferred; variant)
				• Object
				  ○ identifier
				  ○ source consulted
				  ○ status of identification
				  ○ name (preferred; variant)
				• Event
				  ○ identifier
				  ○ source consulted
				  ○ status of identification
				  ○ name (preferred; variant)

(Continued on next page)

TABLE 1 Subject entities, attributes, and relationships in the FRBR family of models and RDA. *(continued)*

	FRBR	FRAD	FRSAD	RDA

		• Place
		  ○ term for the place (subject heading; classification number)
		  ○ coordinates
		  ○ other geographical information
				• Place
				  ○ identifier
				  ○ source consulted
				  ○ status of identification
				  ○ name (preferred; variant) *to be developed after the initial release of RDA*

Relationships	• has a subject	• name/corresponding subject term or classification number relationship	• Work ↔ Thema
			  ○ has a subject
			  ○ is a subject
			• Thema ↔ Nomen
			  ○ has an appellation
			  ○ is an appellation
			• Thema ↔ Thema
			  ○ hierarchical
			  ○ generic
			  ○ whole-part
			  ○ instance
			  ○ perspective hierarchical
			  ○ polyhierarchical
			  ○ associative
			  ○ other semantic
			• Nomen ↔ Nomen
			  ○ equivalence
			  ○ whole-part	

Subject Relationships

Clarifying the relationships between the bibliographic entities plays a crucial role in assisting users of information systems to "complete the tasks of finding, identifying, selecting and obtaining and are the key to navigating through the bibliographic universe" (Oliver, 2009, p. 34). Table 1 shows subject relationships in FRBR, FRAD, and FRSAD models and RDA.

Among many other relationships, the FRBR model considers a subject relationship (Figure 1). According to FRBR model, a *work* entity can have a one-way[1] *has a subject* relationship to any of the FRBR entities: another *work, expression, manifestation, item, person, corporate body, concept, object, event,* or *place*. However, as in the case with the attributes discussed above, relationships between entities other than *work*, which can be very useful in representing subjects, are not specified in the FRBR model. For example, as pointed out by Maxwell (2008), relationships between Group 2 entities (*person*-to-*person, person*-to-*corporate-body*), and between a *person* entity and Group 3 entities (e.g., "Edith Piaf" and "Singers," "Actresses," "Authors, French") have been overlooked by the FRBR model.

The FRAD model focuses mainly on three kinds of nonsubject relationships: (1) relationships between different *works*, (2) relationships between various *persons, families,* and *corporate bodies* associated with the

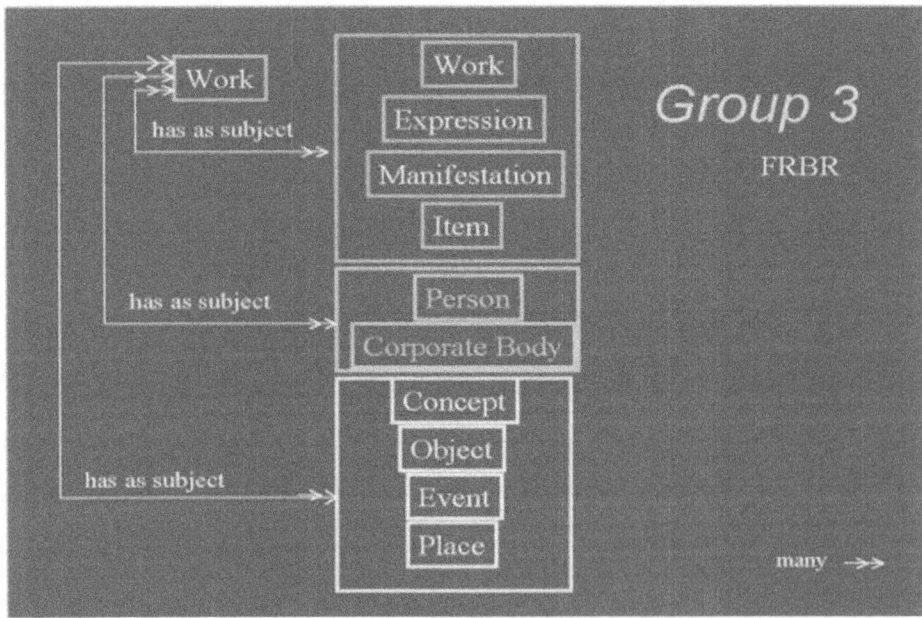

FIGURE 1 Subject entities and relationships in the FRBR model. From Tillett, B. (2004). What is FRBR? (p. 3). http://www.loc.gov/cds/downloads/FRBR.PDF. (Color figure available online.)

works, and (3) relationships between *works, persons, families,* and *corporate bodies* on one side and the *names* that denote them on the other side. In the FRAD model, the only type of relationship in which *concept, object, event,* and *place* entities participate is the *name/corresponding subject term or classification number relationship*. This includes the *known by* relationship to the *name* entity and the *assigned* relationship to *identifier* entity. Interestingly, no true subject relationships such as FRBR's *has a subject* relationship are considered in the FRAD model.

The FRSAD model considers two major sets of relationships: relationships between different types of entities and relationships between the entities of the same type. *Work* to *thema* and *thema* to *nomen* are FRSAD relationships of the first kind. Unlike in FRBR model, these relationships are two-way: a *work* has as subject *thema* while a *thema* is a subject of a *work*, and a *thema* has an appellation of a *nomen* while a *nomen* is an appellation of a *thema*. The FRSAD model also considers relationships between the same types of entities: *thema-thema* relationships (e.g., hierarchical, generic, whole-part, instance, perspective hierarchical, polyhierarchical, associative, and other semantical) and *nomen-nomen* relationships (e.g., equivalence and partitive).

Because *thema* is a much broader entity than any of the FRBR entities, it is unclear from the FRSAD model which specific relationships are envisioned for *concepts*, *objects*, *events*, and *places*. However, one can see that some of the FRSAD *thema-thema* relationships apply to subject entities. For example, whole-part relationships may exist between *places* (e.g., the United States is a whole while Texas is a part) or *objects* (e.g., a train is a whole while a coach is a part). In her recent memorandum to the Joint Steering Committee for Development of RDA, Tillett (2011, p. 13) clarifies that three major types of *thema-thema* relationships in FRSAD are hierarchical, associative, and other semantic relationships. The memorandum also specifies the subtypes of these relationships. For hierarchical type, the generic, whole-part, instance, polyhierarchical, and "other hierarchical" subtypes are listed. For the associative type the much more detailed Cause/Effect, Process/Agent, Action/Product of the Action, Action/Patient or Target, Concept or Thing/Properties, Thing or Action/Counter-agent, Thing/Its part, Raw Material/Product, Action/Property, and Field of study/Objects of phenomena studied subtypes are listed.

Section 0.6. *Core Elements* of RDA includes a subsection 0.6.7. *Recording Subject Relationships* with the following guidelines:

> When recording relationships between a work and an entity that is the subject of that work, include as a minimum at least one subject relationship element.
>
> When using an access point to represent the subject entity, the access point may be formulated using either the preferred name, title, or term for the entity, or a classification number representing the entity. Formulate

the access point representing the subject entity following the standards for subject access points and classification numbers used by the agency creating the data.

Unlike the conceptual models in the FRBR group of models, the RDA acknowledges the existence of relationships within Group 3. For each of the RDA subject elements—*concept, object, event,* and *place*—RDA provides *related concept, related object, related event,* and *related place* elements. However, these and other relationships of Group 3 entities are not detailed by RDA. Although chapters 34 through 37 of RDA are reserved for guidelines on recording relationships to *concepts, objects, events,* and *places* associated with information resources, at the time this paper is written (December 2011) these four chapters remain placeholders "to be developed after the initial release of RDA." However, a proposal has been recently made to the Joint Steering Committee for the Development of RDA to include broader/narrower and related relationships between *concepts* (Tillett, 2011, p. 5); "all the relationships to other entities (including relationships to owners—provenance) and other *objects* that we have in RDA for items" (p. 6) for *objects*; to add relationships to "persons, corporate bodies, families, places, etc." (p. 7) for *events*; relationships with "other entities (Group 1, Group 2, and Group 3) and other places—hierarchical, whole-part relationships with broader areas or contained places" (p. 8) for *places*. Tillett (2011) also suggests to consider inclusion of relationships to the *place* where the *object* or *event* "was found, where it has resided, where it currently resides" (pp. 6–7).

The above analysis of Resource Description and Access (RDA) unified cataloging code and its underlying conceptual models—FRBR, FRAD, and FRSAD—demonstrates that subject access is not currently sufficiently addressed by any of these documents. Arguably, the lack of empirical data to support/develop the handling of subject entities, attributes, and relationships plays its role in this underrepresentation. In fact, the "need to verify and validate the FRBR model [or family of models] against real data and in different communities to make sure the model is valid and applicable" is named (Zhang & Salaba, 2009, p. 240) as one of the top 10 critical issues and challenges within the FRBR research and development community. Meeting this challenge is impossible without research into how subject searching is done in practice, and this need has been emphasized by the members of the IFLA FRBR review working group (Riesthuis & Žumer, 2004).

The aim of the empirical study presented below has been to start bridging this research gap. Transaction logs recorded by the servers of information systems provide a wealth of data for analysis of various patterns of user information-seeking expressed through queries—sets of one or more symbols (e.g., words, phrases, etc.) combined with other syntax and used as a command for an information retrieval system to locate potentially relevant content indexed by that system. Transaction log analysis—"the study of electronically recorded interactions between online information retrieval systems and the persons who search for the information found in those systems" (Peters, 1993, p. 37)—is a widely used research method. Transaction log data are most often analyzed quantitatively, for example, to compare search query length in different information systems (e.g., Jansen, Spink, and Pedersen, 2004). However, there are also a variety of uses for transaction log data in qualitative research, in particular, for conceptual analysis of search queries. For instance, the Getty study of humanities scholars online searching (Bates, 1996) observed that names of individuals, geographical names, chronological terms, and discipline terms are the key types of search queries. Studies by Spink, Jansen, Wolfram, and Saracevic (2002); Koshman, Spink, and Jansen (2006); Beitzel, Jensen, Chowdhury, Frieder, and Grossman (2007); Jansen, Spink, and Koshman (2007) also categorized Web search queries into the categories such as people, places, and things. The study described below used FRBR family of models entities to categorize user search queries in a large-scale digital library and investigate relationships between the search categories.

FINDINGS OF THE EMPIRICAL STUDY INTO SUBJECT ENTITIES AND RELATIONSHIPS IN USER SEARCH QUERIES

The study's purpose was to analyze user searching in a large-scale cultural heritage digital library and compare the results with the subject entities and relationships of the FRBR family of models. The IMLS-funded Opening History—currently the largest cultural heritage digital library in the United States, with more than 1,500 participating digital collections and more than a million harvested digital items—was a target of this study. This study used transaction log analysis as its research method, with a focus on individual search queries rather than on complete sessions. One year of search log data—January 1 through December 31, 2010—was analyzed. The data set was derived from the Opening History transaction log data collected by the Google Analytics application. The data set contained 4,470 search queries, many of which occurred more than once. Grouping of identical search queries together resulted in 2,551 unique search queries, which were then categorized into 10 search categories. Despite all of the benefits of search log analysis as an unobtrusive method of observation, one of its limitations is its inability to detect from the user's search query what exactly the user is expecting to find: any expression of a specific abstract *work*, its particular *expression* (e.g., translation into Italian), *manifestation* (e.g., 3rd edition), or a specific digital *item/copy* embodying the work. Moreover, although the library cataloging of print materials has traditionally focused on the *manifestation* level, metadata records describing digital objects seldom adhere to Dublin Core "one-to-one" principle and often combine descriptions of various *manifestations* with descriptions of *items* (e.g., Urban, 2010).

For these reasons, only *work,* the broadest FRBR Group 1 entity, was adopted as a search category for this analysis. The other eight categories included six FRBR Group 2 and Group 3 entities (*person, corporate body, concept, object, event,* and *place*), one FRAD Group 2 entity (*family*), and two additional categories derived from the earlier study (Zavalina, 2007): *class of persons* and *ethnic group.*

Polysemic user search queries were assigned to multiple categories. For example, a "network" search query was categorized as *concept* and *object* while a "cologne" search category was categorized as *object* and *place*. Most phrase queries also belonged to multiple categories. For example a "two eagles cherokee" query was categorized as *object, person,* and *ethnic group,* while an "Atlanta 1864 map" query was categorized as *place, event,* and *object*. As a result of this approach, search queries were on average assigned to 1.54 categories.

Whenever possible, foreign-language search queries were translated into English and categorized into appropriate search categories (e.g., German-language query "Anti faschisten," which translates as "anti-fascists," was placed into the *class of persons* category). Due to these efforts, only 4.27% of all search queries (e.g., "meau," "4042A," "msg000027") remained uncategorized. To maximize validity and generalizability of the findings, the following measures were taken: the detailed coding manual was developed and used by the two coders in assigning the search queries to search categories, and the intercoder reliability was measured on a subset of 5% of the search queries. Overall intercoder reliability constituted 93.36%: The highest agreement between the coders was observed in assigning the search queries to the *class of persons* category (99.22%), while the lowest agreement was observed in assigning the search queries to the *work* category (88.28%). The results presented below are based on 2,442 unique search queries that researchers were able to assign to one or more search categories.

As shown in Figure 2, the top two categories observed in search queries were *place* (e.g., "Chile") with 34.34% of searches, and *object* (e.g., "drinking vessel"), with 31.06% of searches. It is worth noting that these categories belong to FRBR Group 3 of entities, or subject entities. Another Group 3 search category—*concept* (e.g., "civil right")—was the fourth most often occurring search category, with 17.44% of search queries. However, the fourth FRBR Group 3 subject entity—*event* (e.g., "1935 meat strike")—was observed less often in the search queries than the other three (10.39%) and was the sixth most frequently occurring search category among ten. The FRBR Group 2 search categories—*person* (e.g., "Alfred R. Glancy Jr.") and *corporate body* (e.g., "Dana College," "Kappa Alpha Psi")—were observed in 25.52% and 14.11%, respectively, of the search queries. The *work* (e.g., "Find It Illinois," "how a colored woman aided John Brown") search category was observed in 7% of the search queries, while the *class of persons* (e.g., "fashion designers") and *ethnic group* (e.g., "Cheyenne") search categories were observed in

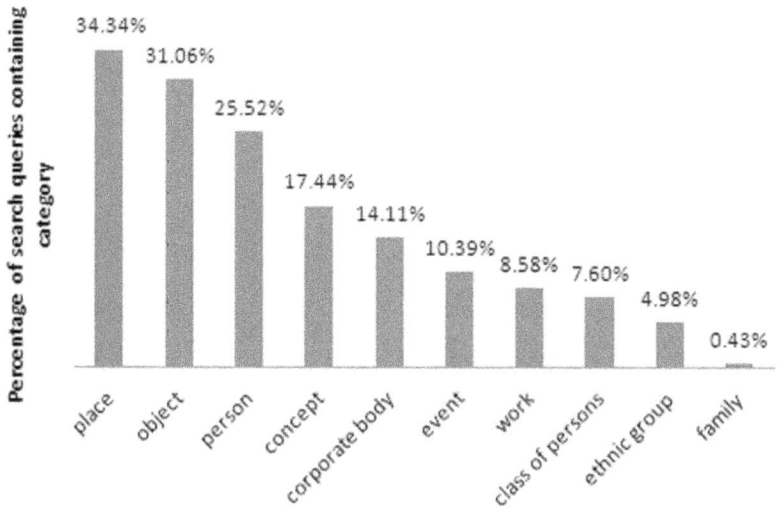

FIGURE 2 Distribution of search categories in unique search queries. (Color figure available online.)

7.60% and 4.98% of user searches, respectively. Finally, *family* (e.g., "Wright brothers") search category was observed in only 0.43% of unique search queries.

Of course, not all of the search queries belonged to a single search category. Although the median number of search categories per search query was one, a search query covered 1.54 search categories on average. Almost 45% of all unique search queries in the data set were multicategory search queries that combined between two and seven search categories. Figure 3 below demonstrates that two-category searches constituted almost one-third of all search queries, while three-category searches accounted for almost 10% of all search queries. From this author's understanding, a high proportion of multicategory search queries indicates that users reflect perceived relationships between the entities of interest to them in the search queries they construct.

The top five highest rates of co-occurrence were observed mostly between the subject search categories—Group 3 FRBR subject entities (see Table 2). *Place* and *object* categories co-occurred the most often, in 256 unique search queries (23.5% of all multicategory unique search queries). *Concept* and *object* search categories co-occurred in 146 unique search queries (13.4% of multicategory unique search queries), followed by *place* and *corporate body* (130 cases of co-occurrence, or 11.9% of multicategory unique search queries), *object* and *corporate body* (109 cases of co-occurrence, or 10.0% of multicategory unique search queries), and *event* and *place* (103 cases of co-occurrence, 9.5% of multicategory unique search queries). Some of the co-occurrence can be explained by search

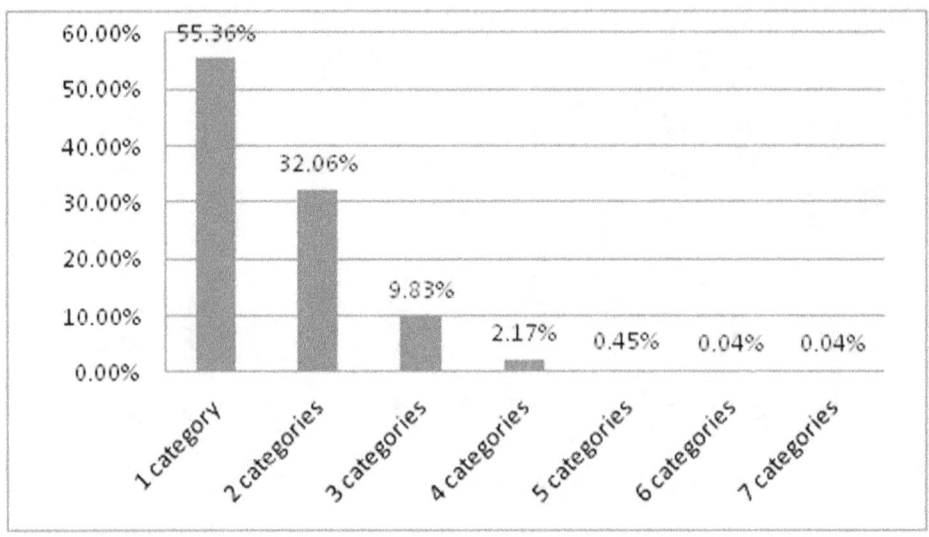

FIGURE 3 Distribution of search queries by the number of search categories in a query. (Color figure available online.)

ambiguity (e.g., with the search query "football" the user may be searching for information about the game, i.e., *concept*, or about the ball that is used in the game, i.e., *object*). However, the high level of co-occurrence between some search categories, especially within FRBR Group 3 of entities, indicates that search queries express strong relationships between these highly co-occurring search categories. For example, an *event* is associated with the *place* where this *event* happened, and a *corporate body* such as a manufacturing company is associated with the kinds of *objects* it manufactures and with the names of the *person*(s) who founded it.

A total of 134 different combinations of search categories were observed in user search queries, but only 25 of them were found in 1% or more of

TABLE 2 Co-occurrence of search categories in unique search queries ($n = 2442$)

	Concept	Object	Event	Place	Person	Family	Class of persons	Ethnic group	Corp. Body	Work
Concept		**146**	53	95	23	0	43	22	37	37
Object	146		81	**256**	89	3	40	35	**109**	71
Event	53	81		**103**	22	0	22	9	19	23
Place	95	256	103		47	0	52	40	**130**	71
Person	23	89	22	47		9	38	9	47	55
Family	0	3	0	0	9		3	3	4	6
Class of persons	43	40	22	52	38	3		14	24	29
Ethnic group	22	35	9	40	9	3	14		10	12
Corp. Body	37	109	19	130	47	4	24	10		26
Work	37	71	23	71	55	6	29	12	26	

TABLE 3 Distribution of multicategory search queries by combinations of categories

Combination of search categories	Combination of FRBR Groups	Percentage of multi-category unique search queries ($n = 1089$) containing this combination
concept + object	Group 3 + Group 3	7.62%
place + corporate body	Group 3 + Group 2	5.51%
event + place	Group 3 + Group 3	4.59%
object + corporate body	Group 3 + Group 2	4.13%
object + person	Group 3 + Group 2	3.12%
concept + place	Group 3 + Group 3	2.85%
concept + event	Group 3 + Group 3	2.57%
place + work	Group 3 + Group 1	2.57%
object + place + corporate body	Group 3 + Group 3 + Group 2	2.48%
object + event + place	Group 3 + Group 3 + Group 3	2.30%
object + event	Group 3 + Group 3	2.20%
person + corporate body	Group 2 + Group 2	2.20%
person + work	Group 2 + Group 1	2.02%
concept + class of persons	Group 3 + Group 2?	1.93%
place + person	Group 3 + Group 2	1.93%
person + class of persons	Group 2 + Group 2?	1.93%
concept + object + place	Group 3 + Group 3 + Group 3	1.65%
place + ethnic group	Group 3 + Group 2?	1.56%
object + ethnic group	Group 3 + Group 2?	1.38%
concept + corporate body	Group 3 + Group 2	1.29%
object + work	Group 3 + Group 1	1.29%
place + class of persons	Group 3 + Group 2?	1.29%
object + person + work	Group 3 + Group 2 + Group 1	1.19%
concept + place + corporate body	Group 3 + Group 3 + Group 2	1.01%

multicategory unique search queries (Table 3). These 25 combinations included 22 two-category combinations and 3 three-category combinations. Importantly, the vast majority of these most frequently occurring combinations (22 out of 25) included one or more of FRBR Group 3 subject entities: *concept, object, event*, or *place. Concept* occurred in the five most frequent combinations, *object* in 10, *place* in 11, and *event* in 4. While in most cases the combinations occurred between two or more FRBR Group 3 subject entities, four more additional search categories were found in the most frequent combinations of search categories: FRBR Group 2 *corporate body* (in six of the 25 most frequent combinations) and *person* (also in six of the 25 most frequent combinations), a FRBR Group 1 *work* (in four of the 25 most frequent combinations), and a *class of persons* (in 3 of the 25 most frequent combinations) category that is not an entity in the FRBR family of models but as a superset of individual *persons* fits Group 2. The most frequently occurring two-category combination was *concept* and *object*, with almost 8%

TABLE 4 Participation of search categories in multicategory search queries

Search category	Number of multi-category combinations containing this search category	Percentage of multi-category queries in all search queries containing this category
Family	4	90.9%
Work	47	83.56%
Class Of Persons	44	81.96%
Event	43	81.13%
Corporate Body	42	76.89%
Concept	41	73.47%
Object	63	71.48%
Ethnic Group	34	69.29%
Place	59	62.78%
Person	42	33.64%

of multicategory search queries. Among the three-category search queries, a combination of *object*, *place*, and *corporate body* in a search query was the most frequently occurring (2.48% of multicategory search queries).

Most entities that can serve as subjects of a work, according to the FRBR family of models, exhibited a high level of participation in multicategory user search queries. With exception of *person* category, FRBR entities were found to be part of multicategory queries much more frequently than in a single-category query (Table 4). Between 62.78% (*place*) and 81.13% (*event*) of search queries containing FRBR Group 3 search categories were multicategory search queries. An even higher percentage of search queries containing *family*, *work*, or *class of persons* search categories were multicategory search queries: between 81.96% for *class of persons* and 90.90% for *family*. The *person* category was found to combine with other categories in the search queries the least frequently (33.64% of all search queries contained *person* category), albeit in a variety of different combinations (42).

As demonstrated by the data in Table 4, the number of multicategory combinations in which search categories participated ranged from 4 to 63, with 90% of search categories participating in at least 34 multicategory combinations. The FRBR Group 3 *object* search category was found in the highest number of multicategory combinations (63), followed by *place* (59) and *work* (47).

CONCLUSION AND FUTURE RESEARCH

This empirical study found that both FRBR Group 3 (*concept*, *object*, *event*, and *place*) and Group 2 entities (*person* and *corporate body*), as well as *work*, one of the Group 1 entities, are widely represented among the user searches in the Opening History digital library. Additional entities emerged that are important for the understanding of subject access in large-scale cultural heritage digital libraries: *class of persons* and *ethnic group*.

Overall, the FRBR-based search query categorization analysis revealed the prevalence of subject searching (including *concept, object, event, place, class of persons*, and *ethnic group* search categories). This finding provides insight into the kinds of information that should be present in metadata records to facilitate subject access to digital collections. The findings of this study provide empirical evidence for the importance of relationships between the subject entities. Thus, they suggest that paying more attention to detailing these relationships in RDA and underlying conceptual models would be beneficial. The priority in this work should be given to relationships occurring most often in user search queries: relationships of *objects* to other entities, in particular to other FRBR Group 3 entities of *event, concept*, and *place*.

While contributing to testing FRBR model against the subject searching data, this empirical study produced results of somewhat limited generalizability, primarily due to its exploratory nature. Further research will address these limitations. The more generalizable results will be produced by a comparative analysis of search queries in multiple large-scale digital libraries of different subject scope. Session-level analysis of user interactions with large-scale digital libraries can provide important contextual information for individual search queries: query reformulation, etc. While transaction log analysis accurately and unobtrusively captures objective data on the actions of information system users, this research method's obvious limitation is that it is unable to provide data on users' motivations and reasoning behind these actions. Triangulation of transaction log analysis results with results obtained through other methods (e.g., through think-aloud protocol observations of users) would help improve the understanding of subject relationships inherent in user search queries and provide valuable data for further development of RDA. These efforts will provide important building blocks for the functional future of bibliographic access.

ACKNOWLEDGMENTS

The empirical study reported in this paper was partially supported by the University of North Texas Junior Faculty Summer Research Grant and Research Initiation Grant. The author wishes to thank members of research and implementation team of the IMLS-funded Digital Collections and Content project at the University of Illinois at Urbana-Champaign for making the Opening History digital library transaction log data available for this research.

NOTE

1. Interestingly, there is no reciprocal relationship *is a subject of* in FRBR model.

REFERENCES

Allen, B. (1991). Cognitive research in information science: Implications for design. *Annual Review of Information Science and Technology, 26*, 3–37.

Bates, M. (1996). The Getty end-user online searching project in the humanities: Report no. 6—Overview and conclusions. *College & Research Libraries, 57*, 514–523.

Bates, M. (1998). Indexing and access for digital libraries and the Internet: Human, database, and domain factors. *Journal of the American Society for Information Science, 49*(13), 1185–1205.

Bates, M. (1986). Subject access in online catalogs: A design model. *Journal of the American Society for Information Science, 37*(6), 357–376.

Beghtol, C. (1986). Bibliographic classification theory and text linguistics: Aboutness analysis, intertextuality and the cognitive act of classifying documents. *Journal of Documentation, 42*(2), 84–113.

Beitzel, S., Jensen, E., Chowdhury, A., Frieder, O., & Grossman, D. (2007). Temporal analysis of a very large topically categorized Web query log. *Journal of the American Society for Information Science and Technology, 58*(2), 166–178.

Borgman, C. (1996). Why are online catalogs still hard to use? *Journal of American Society for Information Science, 47*(7), 493–503.

Bowker, G., & Star, S. (1999). *Sorting things out: Classification and its consequences.* Cambridge, MA: MIT Press.

Broughton, V. (2004). *Essential classification.* New York, NY: Neal-Schuman.

Buckland, M. (1999). Vocabulary as a central concept in library and information science. In T. Arpanacetal (Eds.), *Digital Libraries: Interdisciplinary Concepts, Challenges, and Opportunities:* Proceedings of the 3rd International Conference on Conceptions of Library and Information Science (CoLIS3) (pp. 3–12). Zagreb, Croatia: Lokve.

Buizza, P., & Guerrini, M. (2002). A conceptual model for the new Soggettario: Subject indexing in the light of FRBR. *Cataloging & Classification Quarterly, 34*(4), 31–45.

Cochrane, P. (1985). *Redesign of catalogs and indexes for improved online subject access: Selected papers of Pauline A. Cochrane.* Phoenix, AZ: Oryx.

Cochrane, P. (1986). *Improving LCSH for use in online catalogs.* Colorado Springs, CO: Libraries Unlimited.

Cochrane, P. (2000). Improving LCSH for use in online catalogs revisited: What progress has been made? What issues still remain? *Cataloging & Classification Quarterly, 29*(1/2), 73–89.

Coyle, K. (2010, November 20). Re: changes to FRBR? [Electronic mailing list message]. Retrieved from http://infoserv.inist.fr/wwsympa.fcgi/d_read/frbr/FRBR_Listserv_Archive.rtf.

Cutter, C. (1904). *Rules for a dictionary catalog.* (4th ed.). Washington, DC: Government Printing Office.

Delsey, T. (2005). Modeling subject access: Extending the FRBR and FRANAR conceptual models. *Cataloging & Classification Quarterly, 39*(3/4), 49–61.

Farradine, J. E. L. (1970). Analysis and organization of knowledge for retrieval. *ASLIB Proceedings, 22*(12), 607–616.

Gemberling, T. (2010). Thema and FRBR's Third Group. *Cataloging & Classification Quarterly, 48*(5), 445–449.

Greenberg, J. (2003). Metadata and the World Wide Web. In M. Drake (Ed.), *Encyclopedia of Library and Information Science* (pp. 1876–1888). New York, NY: Marcel Dekker.

Guerrini, M. (2009). In praise of the un-finished: The IFLA Statement of International Cataloguing Principles (2009). *Cataloging & Classification Quarterly, 47*(8), 722–740.

Hjørland, B. (1997). *Information seeking and subject representation: An activity-theoretical approach to information science.* Westport CT: Greenwood Press.

Hjørland, B. (1998). Theory and metatheory of information science: A new interpretation. *Journal of Documentation, 54,* 606–621.

IFLA Working Group on the Functional Requirements for Bibliographic Records. (1998). *Functional requirements for bibliographic records: Final report.* Munchen, Germany: K. G. Saur. Retrieved from http://www.ifla.org/files/cataloguing/frbr/frbr.pdf

IFLA Working Group on the Functional Requirements for Bibliographic Records. (2008). *Functional requirements for bibliographic records: Final report* [As amended and corrected through February 2008]. Retrieved from http://www.ifla.org/files/cataloguing/frbr/frbr_2008.pdf

IFLA Working Group on Functional Requirements and Numbering of Authority Records. (2009). *Functional requirements for authority data—a conceptual model.* Munchen, Germany: K. G. Saur.

IFLA Working Group on Functional Requirements for Subject Authority Records. (2010). Functional Requirements for Subject Authority Data. Retrieved from http://nkos.slis.kent.edu/FRSAR/index.html

International Organization for Standardization. (1985). *Documentation: Methods for examining documents, determining their subjects and selecting indexing terms.* Geneva, Switzerland: International Organization for Standardization.

Jackson, S. (1958). *Catalog use study: Director's report.* Chicago, IL: American Library Association.

Jansen, B., Spink, A., & Koshman, S. (2007). Web searcher interaction with the Dogpile.com metasearch engine. *Journal of the American Society for Information Science and Technology, 58*(5), 744–755.

Jansen, B., Spink, A., & Pedersen, J. (2004). The effect of specialized multimedia collections on Web searching. *Journal of Web Engineering, 3*(3/4), 182–199.

Joint Steering Committee for Development of RDA. (2010). *Resource description & access: RDA.* Chicago, IL: American Library Association.

Koshman, S., Spink, A., & Jansen, B. (2006). Web searching on the Vivisimo search engine. *Journal of the American Society for Information Science and Technology, 57*(14), 1875–1887.

Krikelas, J. (1972). Catalog use studies and their implications. *Advances in Librarianship, 3,* 195–220.

Langridge, D. (1989). *Subject analysis: Principles and procedures.* London, United Kingdom: Bowker-Saur.

Larson, R. (1991a). Between Scylla and Charybdis: Subject searching in online catalogs. *Advances in Librarianship, 15,* 175–236.

Larson, R. (1991b). The decline of subject searching: Long-term trends and patterns of index use in an online catalog. *Journal of the American Society for Information Science, 42*(3), 197–215.

Lee, H. (2003). Information spaces and collections: Implications for organization. *Library & Information Science Research, 25*(4), 419–436.

Lipetz, B. (1970). *User requirements in identifying desired works in a large library: Final report.* New Haven, CT: Yale University Library. Retrieved from http://www.eric.ed.gov/PDFS/ED042479.pdf

Lubetzky, S. (1960). *Code of cataloging rules: Author and title entry—an unfinished draft.* Chicago, IL: American Library Association.

Markey, K. (2007, March 8). *Users and uses of bibliographic data: Presentation.* Library of Congress Working Group on the Future of Bibliographic Control Meeting, Mountain View, CA.

Matthews, J., Lawrence, G., & Ferguson, D. (Eds.), (1983). *Using online catalogs: A nationwide survey—a report of a study sponsored by the Council on Library Resources.* New York, NY: Neal-Schumann.

Maxwell, R. L. (2008). *FRBR: A guide for the perplexed.* Chicago, IL: American Library Association.

Morgan, E. L. (2006). A "next generation" library catalog [Web log message]. Retrieved from http://litablog.org/2006/07/a-next-generation-library-catalog-executive-summary-part-1-of-5

Oliver, C. (2009). *FRBR and RDA: Advances in Resource Description for Multiple Format Resources.* Retrieved from http://www.collectionscanada.gc.ca/obj/005002/f2/005002-2200-e.pdf

Peters, T. (1993). The history and development of transaction log analysis. *Library Hi Tech, 11*(2), 41–66.

Riesthuis, G., & Žumer, M. (2004). FRBR and FRANAR: Subject access. In I. McIlwaine (Ed.), *Knowledge organization and the global information society.* Proceedings of the 8th International Conference of the International Society for Knowledge Organization (ISKO '2004) (pp. 153–158). Würzburg, Germany: Ergon.

Šauperl, A. (2002). *Subject determination during the cataloging process: Observation.* Lanham, MD: Scarecrow Press.

Spink, A., Jansen, B., Wolfram, D., & Saracevic, T. (2002). From e-sex to e-commerce: Web search changes. *IEEE Computer, 35*(3), 107–111.

Svenonius, E. (2000). *The intellectual foundation of information organization.* Cambridge, MA: MIT Press.

Tagliacozzo, R., & Kochen, M. (1970). Information-seeking behavior of catalog users. *Information Storage and Retrieval, 6,* 363–381.

Taube, M. (1953). *Studies in coordinate indexing.* Washington, DC: Documentation Incorporated.

Taylor, A. (2006). *Introduction to cataloging and classification: Part V. Subject access* (10th ed., pp. 301–368). Westport, CT: Libraries Unlimited.

Tillett, B. (2011, May 20). *Chapters 12–16, 23, 33–37 (Group 3 entities and "subject").* Memorandum to Joint Steering Committee for Development of RDA. 6JSC/LC rep/3. Retrieved from http://connect.ala.org/files/35265/www_rda_jsc_org_docs_6jsc_lc_rep_3_pdf_15150.pdf

Urban, R. (2010, October). *Principle violations: Revisiting the Dublin Core 1:1 principle*. Poster presented at the 73rd American Society for Information Science and Technology Annual Meeting, Pittsburgh, PA.

Weinberg, B. H. (1995). Why postcoordination fails the researcher. *The Indexer, 19*, 155–159.

Wilson, P. (1968). *Two kinds of power: An essay on bibliographic control*. Berkeley, CA: University of California Press.

Wilson, T. D. (2000). Human information behavior. *Information Science, 3*(2), 49–55.

Zavalina, O. (2007). Collection-level user searches in federated digital resource environment. *Proceedings of the American Society for Information Science and Technology, 44*(1), 1–16.

Zeng, M., & Salaba, A. (2005). *Toward an international sharing and use of subject authority data*. FRBR Workshop, OCLC, 2005. Retrieved from http://www.oclc.org/research/events/frbr-workshop/presentations/zeng/Zeng_Salaba.ppt

Zhang, Y., & Salaba, A. (2009). What is next for Functional Requirements for Bibliographic Records (FRBR)? A Delphi study. *Library Quarterly, 79*(2), 233–255.

Reconsidering Universal Bibliographic Control in Light of the Semantic Web

GORDON DUNSIRE
Independent Consultant, Edinburgh, UK

DIANE HILLMANN and JON PHIPPS
Metadata Management Associates, Jacksonville, New York, USA

The article discusses the future of universal bibliographic control in the context of the Semantic Web. Resource Description Framework RDF), the basis of the Semantic Web, allows the replacement of attempts at one-size-fits-all schema, rules and other international/global standards with what might be termed an all-sizes-fit-one approach, as shown by the example of VIAF (Virtual International Authority File). This approach can support a much richer ecology of bibliographic communities and their standards, achieved by establishing the semantic mapping of individual properties, and sets of properties (or RDF graphs), to form a connected web into which legacy metadata and newly-minted statements can be deposited. Such deposits are made at the natural level of the source standard, preserving local granularity, semantic focus, context, and the data itself, using one-to-one RDF representations of the standard. The web of semantic links then allows this data to be readily assimilated into a universal, web-scale environment which connects all bibliographic metadata as "library linked data". The article is illustrated with examples drawn from IFLA standards such as FRBR and ISBD, and other international standards such as Dublin Core and RDA.

INTRODUCTION

The goal of universal bibliographic control (UBC) as a worldwide system for the control and exchange of bibliographic information acknowledges the resource discovery metadata requirements of modern, global-scale users of information. The first decade of this millennium has seen a significant change in thinking about the functions of UBC and how they can best be realized.

This is illustrated by the case of VIAF (Virtual International Authority File). VIAF links authority records from multiple national and regional agencies to form clusters of data labeling the same person, corporate body, or other entity. The service developed after the abandonment of attempts by the International Federation of Library Associations and Institutions (IFLA) to establish a framework that ensured that each entity of interest was referenced by a single, unambiguous name, "authorized heading," or similar label, to be used by all agencies creating bibliographic metadata. Decisions on what form the label should take proved difficult to make when local users required displays conforming to their cultural norms for language, script, and form. Initiatives by IFLA and other organizations to replace the single human-readable label with a language- and script-independent numerical identifier have also failed in the context of top-down UBC (Tillett, 2008).

Although new and ongoing projects such as the International Standard Name Identifier (ISNI) continue such endeavors, there is still no general agreement amongst the world's cataloguing communities to prefer any single system or type of identifier. Yet VIAF "expands the concept of (UBC) by ... allowing national and regional variations in authorized form to coexist; and ... supporting needs for variations in preferred language, script and spelling" (VIAF, 2011, para. 7). VIAF achieves this by retaining the authority data supplied by each agency and treating it equally; it is allowed to speak for itself. As well as offering locally preferred forms and local identifiers, the service also offers an identifier for the cluster of matched headings. This can act as the identifier for an aggregation node in a UBC system of linked identifiers; there is no need to provide a human-readable UBC label for a cluster because local forms are available.

VIAF shows that UBC for bibliographic authority data can be achieved from the bottom up, from local to global, by linking identifiers for local data to an aggregator identifier without transforming or discarding the local data. We believe that this approach can be extended to other types of bibliographic metadata by using a wider range of linkages to relate and map the data. In particular, we have been looking at the potential of the distributed architecture and "reasoning" capabilities of the Semantic Web to provide a future for UBC.

THE RESOURCE DESCRIPTION FRAMEWORK AND THE SEMANTIC WEB

During the last few years, interest and understanding of the role of the Resource Description Framework (RDF) and the Semantic Web environment based on it have begun to percolate through the library community. Among those who speak and write about these technologies and changes in thinking they represent, Karen Coyle has been among the most visible and prominent. Her recent publications for Library TechSource are particularly helpful for those looking for solid background reading on these issues from a library point of view (Coyle, 2010). The RDF Primer (Manola & Miller, 2004) provides a good technical introduction. In essence, RDF is a language read not by people but by applications and it is read in such a way as to not lose information.

In contrast to the record-based approach of traditional library metadata, in the RDF data model the focus is on individual metadata statements represented by three-part data triples in the form subject-predicate-object; for example "This website (subject) has a creator (predicate) with the name 'Smith' (object)." To allow unambiguous manipulation by machine, RDF requires each subject and predicate to be a Uniform Resource Identifier (URI); the object can also be a URI, or it can be a string of characters known as a "literal." Linking the object of one statement to the subject of another, via URIs, results in a chain of linked statements, or linked data. This avoids the ambiguity of using natural language strings as headings to match statements. As a result, a literal object terminates a linked data chain, and literals are generally used for human-readable display data such as labels, notes, names, and so on. A set of URIs assigned to specific RDF properties and classes using a single management infrastructure is called a "namespace." The RDF approach is very different from the traditional library catalog record exemplified by MARC21, where descriptions of multiple aspects of a resource are bound together by a specific syntax of tags, indicators, and subfields as a single identifiable stream of data that is manipulated as a whole. In RDF, the data must be separated out into single statements that can then be processed independently from one another; processing includes the aggregation of statements into a record-based view, but is not confined to any specific record schema or source for the data. Statements or triples can be mixed and matched from many different sources to form many different kinds of user-friendly displays.

The data content of a statement is kept separate from its semantic content, which is expressed through one or more statements using ontological predicates, or RDF properties. The bottom-up view of a bibliographic record becomes a set of data triples with the same subject URI using classes and properties from bibliographic element namespaces. The bottom-up view of a metadata schema is a set of ontological triples, or RDF ontology, using the same classes and properties as their subject URIs. Thus the ontology triples are about the classes and properties used in data triples about bibliographic entities.

RDF is immediately relevant to UBC because an RDF triple actually stores a linkage or relationship between two identifiers or an identifier and a label, and the identifiers are designed for global scale. Because the property used for the relationship has its own URI, it can be linked or related to another property as well as to an RDF class or literal. This "property of properties" or ontological property mechanism is very useful for relating properties from namespaces for different metadata schemas.

Among the ideas Coyle and others have articulated is that the ability to associate different data triples from various sources and using different metadata schema is one of the most important benefits of this new environment.

> It's an unfortunate fact that many systems combine data from different sources using only the "dumb down" method, reducing the metadata to the few matching elements and resulting in the least rich metadata record possible. This results in a tremendous loss of data and an inferior user experience. The "smart up" method uses all or most of the data from the different sources, resulting in enhanced information. For example, the Open Library record is able to link to any number of information sources both from its pages for books and its pages for authors, in part because it can store linkable data from any source without having to be concerned about fitting that data into a particular record format. It also means that it can create a display that is richer than any one data source. (Coyle, 2009, p. 11)

The notions of "dumbing down" and "smartening up" are critical to understanding the differences between top-down and bottom-up views of data relationships and mapping. Rethinking the notion of UBC in this environment requires that both viewpoints be kept in mind when defining relationships as well as maps.

> Despite the fact that some metadata developers do not think of the relationships as a form of mapping, the DCMI "dumb-down" principle is an example of a pre-defined semantic mapping that retains great value in a mapping environment, particularly when the level of granularity between schemas is very different. One of the core principles behind the notion of dumb-down is a requirement that the more refined of two related properties must be considered to be a subset (subproperty) of the more broadly defined property. Even though the loss of specificity may mean less clarity of understanding, the data does not lose meaning when "dumbed down" to its broader relative. Of equal and perhaps even greater value, broader properties defined by Simple DC may be

"smartened up" to provide increased specificity when possible. (Dunsire, Hillman, Phipps, and Coyle, 2011, p. 30)

The RDF environment provides basic ontological properties that are used by software "reasoners" to make logical inferences. This effectively results in the automatic generation of new data triples, a mechanism that provides interoperability of data when an RDF ontology is based on a map between properties and classes from two or more metadata schemas.

LINKED DATA: INTEROPERABILITY FROM THE BOTTOM UP

Most of the major bibliographic metadata schemas used by libraries are at some stage in the process of representation in RDF as properties and classes (Dunsire & Willer, 2011). Real examples are used in the following discussion.

The Figures use RDF graphs to represent triples. An arc represents the predicate or RDF property of a triple, connecting two elliptical nodes representing the URIs of the subject and object. The arrow of an arc points to the object. An object that is a literal is shown as a rectangle pointed to by only one arc; values without identifiers cannot form merged nodes in an RDF graph and, therefore, terminate the linked data chain. Arcs and nodes have labels based on their URIs. For the sake of readability, URIs are given in modified Compact URI (CURIE) format, with the namespace in an abbreviated form called a qname separated by a colon from the associated English label in quotes. For example, the URI http://iflastandards.info/ns/isbd/elements/P1004 has the CURIE isbd:P1004, modified for display on a graph as the label isbd:"has title proper."
Some frequently-used properties are abbreviated further:

d (domain) = rdfs:domain
eP (equivalent property) = owl:equivalentPropertyOf
r (range) = rdfs:range
sC (subclass) = rdfs:subClassOf
sP (subproperty) = rdfs:subPropertyOf

The qnames used are

dc = http://purl.org/dc/elements/1.1/
dct = http://purl.org/dc/terms/
ex (Example instance namespace)
frbrer = http://iflastandards.info/ns/fr/frbr/frbrer/
isbd = http://iflastandards.info/ns/isbd/elements/
owl = http://www.w3.org/2002/07/owl#
rdact = http://rdvocab.info/termList/RDACarrierType/
rdafrbr = http://rdvocab.info/uri/schema/FRBRentitiesRDA/

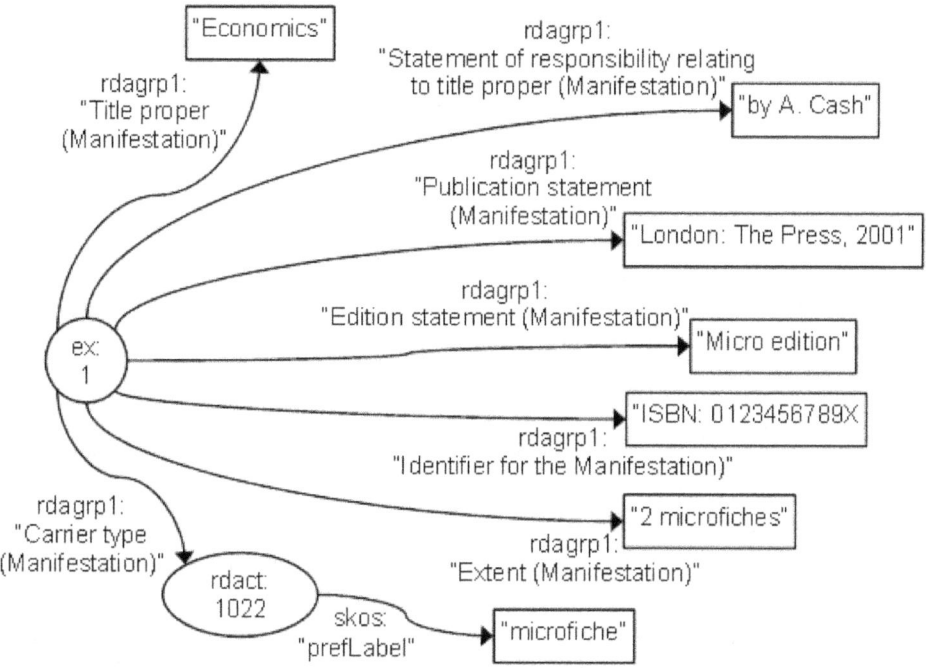

FIGURE 1 RDF graph of core attributes of a specific RDA manifestation.

rdagrp1 = http://rdvocab.info/Elements/
rdaopen (RDA unconstrained by FRBR; under construction)
rdfs = http://www.w3.org/2000/01/rdf-schema#
skos = http://www.w3.org/2004/02/skos/core#

Figure 1 shows the RDF graph of a set of triples using properties representing the RDA core attributes for a manifestation. Most triples have the same subject URI, ex:1, and a literal object. The exception is the object of the carrier type, which is linked to an RDA controlled vocabulary represented in RDF/SKOS. It is worth noting that the publication statement is an aggregated statement (Hillmann, Coyle, Phipps, & Dunsire, 2010). It can be replaced with or broken down into a more refined set of triples with attribute properties such as place of publication, publisher's name, and date of publication, some of which can be linked to further triples.

The graph in Figure 1 contains more information than the specific instance data represented in its triples. Each property has a URI, which is itself the subject of a set of triples specifying properties of that property, including a human-readable label. The label "Title proper (Manifestation)" is such a triple; another literal with the same subject is the definition "The chief name of a resource (i.e., the title normally used when citing the resource)." A property can also be related to another property or class via a triple using various special ontological properties. Of particular interest to mappings are

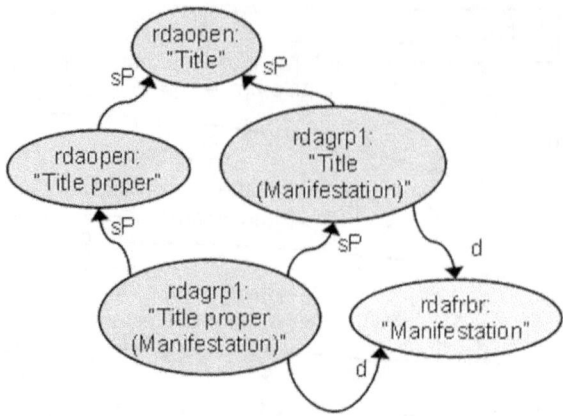

FIGURE 2 RDF graph of the ontology of rdagrp1: "Title proper (Manifestation)."

properties from the RDFS namespace with labels "domain," "range," "subclass of," and "subproperty of." Figure 2 is the RDF graph of the set of ontology triples of the RDA property labeled "Title proper (Manifestation)." It contains triples that say that this property is a subproperty of two other RDA properties, each of which is a subproperty of yet a fourth RDA property. It also says that the original property and one of the related properties have a domain of the RDA class labeled "Manifestation." This ontology is derived from an RDA entity-relationship diagram and the addition of general versions of the RDA properties (Hillmann et al., 2010).

The important feature for mapping is that ontological triples can be used to infer, or entail, new data triples. For example, a data triple using a property that has a domain entails another data triple saying that the subject is a type or member of the class specified as the domain.

For example, the resource identified by the URI of the subject of a triple using the "Title proper (Manifestation)" property can be inferred to be an instance of the class "Manifestation" because the domain of the property is specified as that class. In other words, the statements "<This resource> <has title proper (manifestation)> 'A Title'" and the property "<has title proper (manifestation)> <has domain> 'manifestation'" imply the statement "This resource is a manifestation." This is important because, from an RDF point of view, inferring that a resource is a type of thing, and directly stating that it is a type of thing, are fundamentally equivalent. This differs from XML where, unless you explicitly declare a resource to be a type of thing, you can't know what type of thing it is. This has great value in metadata aggregation because it allows a resource to be described from the perspective of many different communities as many, usually similar, types of thing.

The "range" property similarly entails that the object of a data triple using the property is an instance of the class specified as the range. The "subclass" property entails that a URI, which is an instance of the subclass,

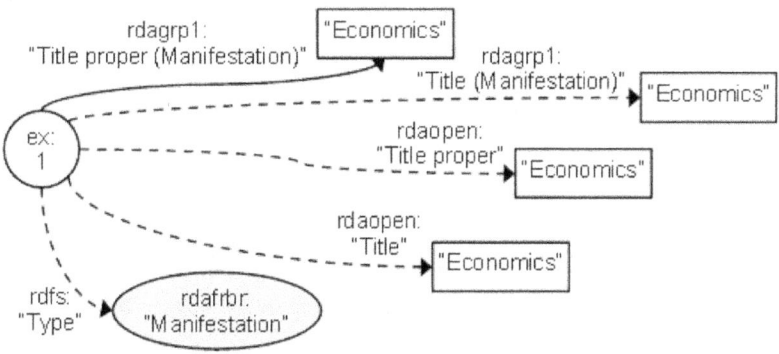

FIGURE 3 RDF graph of entailed triples.

is also an instance of the superclass. If "This is a Border collie" and "'Border collie' is a subclass of 'Dog'," then "This is a dog."

The "subproperty" property is very useful for the interoperability of data from different metadata schemas. Using a property that has a "subproperty" property entails a triple using the specified superproperty with the same subject and object. We can state that a property is a subproperty of a second property if it is determined that the definition of the first property is entirely subsumed by the definition and meaning of the second property. In Figure 2, "Title proper (Manifestation)" is a subproperty of "Title (Manifestation)" because a title proper is a type of title. So a data statement using the "Title proper (Manifestation)" property, say "This resource has title proper (manifestation) 'That title'" entails the new statement "This resource has title (manifestation) 'That title'."

Figure 3 is an RDF graph of the triples that can be entailed from the "Title proper (Manifestation)" triple in Figure 1 using the ontology in Figure 2. The new triples are shown with dashed line arcs. Any of the triples can be used in any other linked data graph. Entailed triples can be generated once and stored as instance data triples or generated on the fly as an application requires them.

The same RDF ontological properties can be used to link properties and classes from different namespaces, allowing two ontologies to be mapped and combined into a superontology.

Figure 4 shows the RDF graph of the ontology of the ISBD property labeled "has title proper." It is a subproperty of another ISBD property, and both have the ISBD class "Resource" as a domain.

A combined ontology for the RDA and ISBD "title proper" properties can be developed if ontological relationships can be determined between any of the RDA properties in Figure 2 and any of the ISBD properties in Figure 4. This requires careful analysis of the property definitions to determine if they are equivalent or if one subsumes the other. Semantic incoherence must be avoided in any entailments that result from linking the ontologies; for

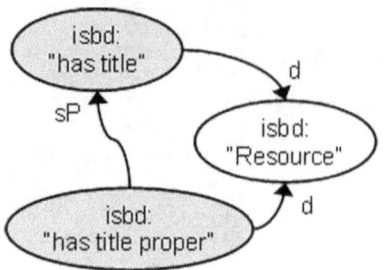

FIGURE 4 RDGF graph of the ontology of isbd "has title proper."

example, the RDA class "Manifestation" is not a subclass of the ISBD class "Resource," and this should not be entailed inadvertently from the combined ontology.

Figure 5 is the combined ontology of Figure 2 and Figure 4. It identifies two pairs of related RDA and ISBD properties. ISBD's "has title proper" is a subproperty of the general RDA property "Title proper" to avoid linking the classes "Resource" and "Manifestation" and generating a false entailment. ISBD's "has title" is linked to the general RDA property "Title" using the OWL (web ontology language) property "equivalent property," indicating that the definitions, while different, have the same semantic meaning. Thus a data triple using one of the properties entails a triple using the other property, with the same subject and object.

This process can be repeated to link properties and classes from any namespace, ontology, or general RDF graph. Figure 6 is the RDF graph of Figure 5 combined with properties from the Dublin Core namespaces.

These combined ontologies effectively constitute mappings between the attributes, represented as RDF properties, of one metadata schema and another. The mappings are instantiated through entailed instance data triples. Figure 7 shows RDF graphs of three instance data triples based on RDA,

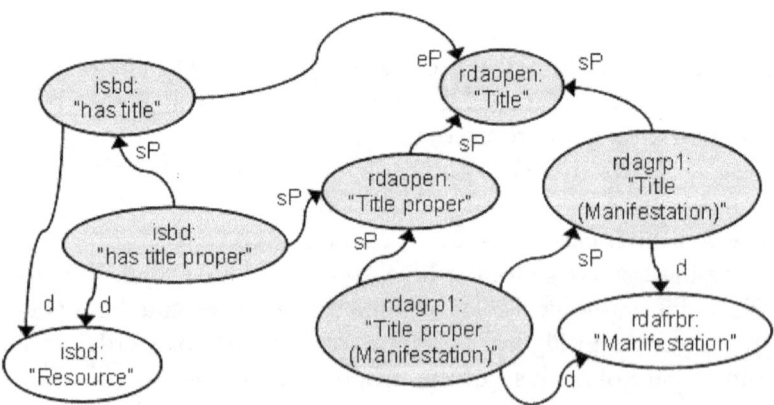

FIGURE 5 RDF graph of combined ontology of the ISBD and RDA "title proper" property.

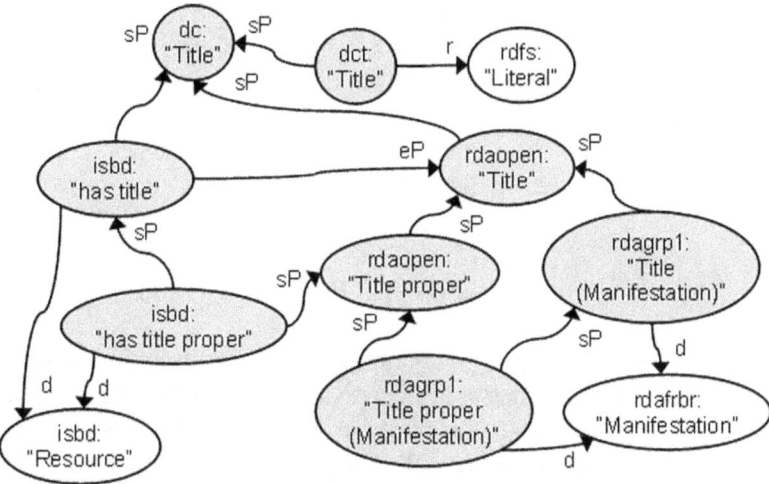

FIGURE 6 RDF graph of ontology of ISBD, RDA, and DC "title" properties.

ISBD, and DC Terms properties respectively, with triples for RDA general and DC properties entailed from Figure 6.

These entailed triples can be used by applications generating "title proper" and general title indexes from instance data derived from different metadata schema for a range of types of information resource.

This approach has several important features:

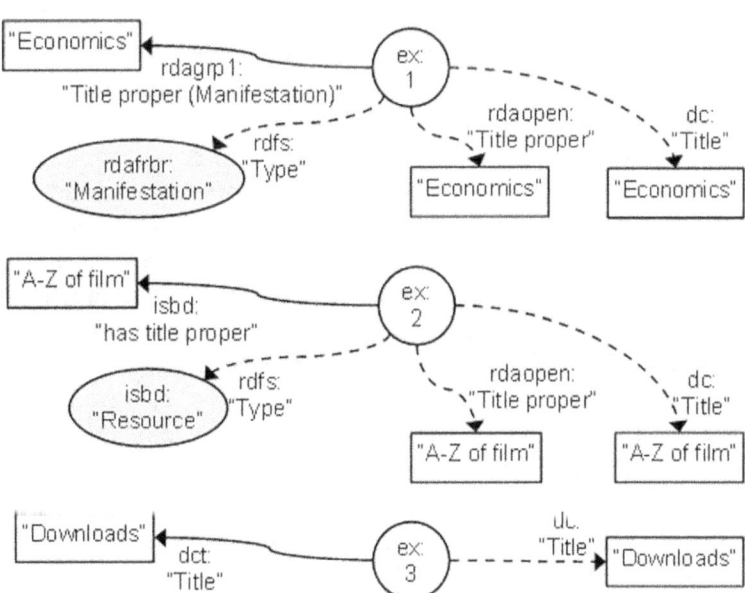

FIGURE 7 RDF graphs of RDA, ISBD, and DCT instance triples with selected entailments.

- The original data triples remain intact and available to any application.
- The entailed data triples are available to any application.
- The values of the objects in the original triples remain unchanged in the derived triples.
- Multiple levels of semantic granularity are supported with entailments derived from subproperties available for all less specific, "dumber" properties.

FUNCTIONAL FUTURES

In the library world, "mapping" has been synonymous with "crosswalking." However, much of the crosswalking research of the last decade or so focuses less on the creation of the maps and more on the resulting transformational process. In this traditional world, maps are developed, ingested, and maintained as documents (usually spreadsheets) that are not necessarily actionable outside of applications. Thus a further, but separate, step beyond the intellectual process of creating a map is the creation of programs that implement the mapping and transform data based on the decisions made during the creation of the maps. Because of the centralization of the traditional library metadata world, this focus has led to a situation in which only a few large organizations with significant development resources have thought much about—or built—crosswalks or programs to use them.

The meaning and implications of "mapping" changes radically when moving from a database and record-based approach to an open, multidomain, global, shared environment based on linked data technologies—where anybody can say anything about any topic, validity constraints are not acknowledged, a nearly infinite number of properties can be defined to describe an infinite number of entities, and authority is multidimensional and often ephemeral. The classic approach to such apparent chaos is to attempt tighter control over the creation process, more filtering, additional restrictions, and less access. This approach hinders appreciation and use of the broad diversity of perspective that comes with a world of open data.

Mapping through linked data semantics does not have the same result as mapping through crosswalks. Crosswalks are generally managed through applications that not only translate values stored in one metadata schema to another but also transform the values themselves. In the new environment, without the necessity of considering a transformative end process, the idea of one "best" map (or collection of maps) no longer seems relevant. Limiting mappings to close-match equivalences also seems outdated. A more useful approach would define a mapping strategy that is open, extensible, and built using technology that goes beyond the spreadsheet.

In an RDF-based data environment, transformation can still take place within an application, but as a separate operation from mapping. Transformation performed in a semantically mapped environment removes some of the anxiety surrounding potential degradation when round-tripping the contents of data elements because it is done without loss of information about the original semantics. Without the necessity of defining an "authoritative" or "best" mapping, a metadata element can have more than one set of semantics at the same time; this means it should be a simple matter to move from different but compatible definitions as needed within an application.

RDF permits and encourages the publishing and aggregation of metadata statements rather than records that describe a bibliographic resource. Thus, RDF "records" represent arbitrary collections of statements. These statements may be defined and validated by any number of metadata "formats," and a collection of such statements can be composed of properties selected by the publisher of the metadata. Systems aggregating this published data are free to choose the properties from this record that the system "understands." Properties defined by MARC21 can be freely mixed with properties defined by RDA, or any other vocabularies. RDF "records" can vary widely in terms of overall content and there are no constraints on what a system may publish. For example, the DC Application Profile framework (Coyle & Baker, 2009) provides a means of specifying the components of a "description set" to be used to aggregate statements for an application. This is distinct from the creation, validation, and storage of resource descriptions. The process of metadata creation benefits greatly from the current notion of bounded and constrained records in order to enforce rational limits on how data is validated and managed.

This bottom-up approach to UBC allows the functions of bibliographic metadata curated by the library community to remain focused on the requirements of that community. Expressing the schemas and data that support those functions in the open framework of RDF-linked data allows other communities to reuse the data to meet similar requirements in their own environment. But it also allows the data to function for any purpose imaginable. What those new functions might be, and how well library metadata serves them, should trouble libraries no more than how a patron uses the information from their collections. The true worth of library linked data lies in its consistency and completeness, of high value when it is mixed into the uncontrolled environment of the Semantic Web.

CONCLUSION

Looking forward and backward as the authors have above is only part of the picture. Libraries are at a period of great change, driven to a large extent by technology. The transition we face as we look toward the future requires that we understand the environment before us, and those librarians with one foot in the world of cataloging and another in the emerging metadata space have particular issues to address. Before we begin making decisions about how our future will look, we need to understand the burdens of our prior modes of thinking, and where they must change. What the term *bibliographic control* means is a critical place to start.

The lessons of the past and the opportunities facing us combine to suggest strongly that continuing to interpret bibliographic control as a monolithic, top-down effort designed to achieve universality—as the library world has traditionally done—is not going to allow us to take advantage of new technologies or new ways of thinking about and building metadata. A new paradigm of bottom-up allows "control as co-ordination" through semantic mappings—making the essential shift from controlling the data to controlling the semantics that will allow us to move forward, taking our legacy data with us.

REFERENCES

Coyle, K. (2009). Metadata mix and match. *Information Standards Quarterly*, *21*(1), 9–11. Retrieved from http://kcoyle.net/isqv21no1.pdf

Coyle, K. (2010). Understanding the Semantic Web: Bibliographic data and metadata. *ALA Techsource*, *46*(1). Retrieved from http://alatechsource.metapress.com/content/p3022442071g7655/fulltext.pdf

Coyle, K., & Baker, T. (2009). Guidelines for Dublin Core application profiles. Retrieved from http://dublincore.org/documents/profile-guidelines/

Dunsire, G., Hillmann, D., Phipps, J., & Coyle, K. (2011). A reconsideration of mapping in a semantic world. *Proceedings of the International Conference on Dublin Core and Metadata Applications, North America, August 2011.* Retrieved from http://dcevents.dublincore.org/index.php/IntConf/dc-2011/paper/view/52/6

Dunsire, G., & Willer, M. (2011). Standard library metadata models and structures for the Semantic Web. *Library Hi Tech News*, *28*(3), 1–12.

Hillmann, D., Coyle, K., Phipps, J., & Dunsire, G. (2010). RDA vocabularies: Process, outcome, use. *D-Lib magazine*, *16*(1/2). Retrieved from http://www.dlib.org/dlib/january10/hillmann/01hillmann.html

Manola, F., & Miller, E. (2004, February 10). RDF primer. In B. McBride (Series Ed.), *RDF Primer W3C Recommendations*. Retrieved from http://www.w3.org/TR/rdf-primer/

Tillett, B. (2008, July 1). A review of the feasibility of an International Standard Authority Data Number (ISADN). Prepared for the IFLA Working Group on Functional Requirements and Numbering of Authority Records. Retrieved from http://archive.ifla.org/VII/d4/franar-numbering-paper.pdf

VIAF. (2011). VIAF (the Virtual International Authority File). Retrieved from http://www.oclc.org/research/activities/viaf/

Serials, FRBR, and Library Linked Data: A Way Forward

LAURA KRIER
California Digital Library, Oakland, California, USA

This article proposes a new way of cataloging serials using linked data and Resource Description Framework (RDF), as well as how the concepts of Functional Requirements for Bibliographic Records (FRBR) can be expanded to apply to journal content at both the journal level and the article level, all with an eye toward ease of access and understanding for users.

The practice of cataloging has not changed significantly over the last century. Catalogers still create records that describe objects in the library's collection. Libraries maintain local databases that attempt to detail the circumference of the knowledge the library possesses. But as information resources become ever more complicated, these practices begin to feel constrained. The traditional functions of the cataloger might not be sufficient to bring libraries into a world where resources are networked and scholarly communication is a changing practice. Library ownership of objects is giving way to licensing of digital resources. Scholarly communication is slowly shifting to an open-access model, wherein the library no longer needs to be a financial and digital gateway for research. More and more, libraries are moving into a world where traditional descriptive cataloging will not meet users' needs. The functions of cataloging will likely change significantly: Instead of providing descriptions of static resources, catalogs will provide links to a dynamic world of digital information, helping patrons make connections and explore. Serials management is one area that could specifically benefit from a change in the function of bibliographic control.

In the early 20th century librarians made the decision not to catalog the articles published in scholarly journals. The business of creating article-level metadata was given over to abstracting and indexing services like H. W. Wilson, and library metadata was thereafter split between different library systems: the catalog and published abstracts and indexes. This made some degree of sense when librarians were the parties responsible for locating resources for patrons, but with the advent of the Web, and the increasing ease of access to networked resources, patrons have begun to take their information searching into their own hands. The split between catalogs and journal databases is not intuitive to patrons, and librarians have been trying for the past few decades to figure out how to unify these resources in ways that are easier to understand and navigate. Federated search engines have been implemented, but they present problems around the quality of searches (Baer, 2004). Discovery layers like VuFind and AquaBrowser were built to provide access to library resources across multiple systems, but their effectiveness depends on the existence of rich metadata in a variety of environments.

In recent years, Web-scale discovery systems, including EBSCO's Discovery Service and Serials Solution's Summon, have appeared in the library environment, promising to solve data silo problems by providing a single point of access to all library materials. But these systems rely on unstable means of bringing together diverse resources. Data is aggregated into a discovery system based on the vendor's agreements with publishers and the vendor's ownership of abstracting and indexing services. A library's ability to access the entirety of the resources owned or licensed through the discovery system is dependent upon the whims, deep pockets, and negotiating abilities of the vendor. Current discovery systems are not built using a standard for aggregating article-level and traditional bibliographic metadata, and our existing metadata doesn't adequately serve this purpose.

In order to effectively develop library discovery systems that incorporate article-level, journal-level, and monograph resources, developers and catalogers need to start thinking about how we represent these resources and the relationships between them in new ways. Librarians have long struggled with how to present these relationships to users and represent them in bibliographic and authority records. Many articles have been written that explore the relationship between a print journal and its digital counterpart, the relationship of a particular journal title to volumes published under a previous title, and the relationship of an article to the journal in which it was published. For decades catalogers have searched for answers to the problem of multiple versions or format variation. Graham (1990) presented a paper at the Multiple Versions Forum in which she identified the developments that have led to the "crisis" of multiple versions. The proliferation of new formats and the need to create new records for each format have resulted in cataloging bottlenecks, and this has confused patrons trying to access resources and libraries involved in resource sharing. Graham argues that existing cataloging practices "have hopelessly intertwined the terminology for the physical pieces and the ideas they contain" (p. 11). Although Graham gives some recommendations for differentiating between works and versions, she doesn't suggest any significant cataloging changes that might effectively solve the problems.

Oliver (2004) explores the impact of the Functional Requirements for Bibliographic Records (FRBR) on the format variation issue by detailing the single record and the separate record approaches: in the single record approach, a cataloger would create a single MARC record in which all manifestations of the work are described; the separate record approach requires each format to be described by its own record. Oliver discusses how these different approaches for serials might work with the FRBR model and concludes that "FRBR offers another way of looking at the same problem and indicates a way to resolve it," and proposes that notes, linking fields, and uniform titles might be sufficient to pull together different manifestations of a title (p. 35).

Riva (2004a) also details the ways in which FRBR can help solve the multiple versions dilemma by suggesting that linking entry fields can be put to use to collocate manifestations. She points out, however, that there are significant differences in the scope of the "three distinct categorizations of bibliographic relationships" that FRBR details (p. 138). Riva suggests that "understanding how precisely MARC 21 coding maps to theoretical taxonomies of bibliographic relationships can be a consideration in future format development" (p. 138).

The solutions and ideas suggested by these authors all assume that libraries will continue to operate in a record-based data environment. Each presents solutions for a MARC-based library system, but this is a system that will always struggle to adequately deal with networked library resources. In their examinations of the multiple version problem, they all acknowledge the difficulty, if not the impossibility, of adequately resolving the problem in the current MARC-based cataloging environment. However, there is an open and reliable way to pull together disparate sources of bibliographic metadata through the use of Resource Description Framework (RDF) and linked data. RDF is a Web language used to represent information about resources "that can be *identified* on the Web, even when they cannot be directly *retrieved* on the Web" (Manola & Miller, 2004a, para. 1).

Linked data practices may offer a way to answer some of these questions, and to change cataloging practices by defining relationships between entities, instead of creating discrete records for static displays of data. It can be used to build links between many different types of metadata and to manipulate that metadata in ways that work best for users at any given point in time. However, shifting to this model entails a radically different concept of library resources and library data.

This paper looks at the use of linked data in libraries and how it can be used to catalog serials in order to bring together all library resources in Web-scale discovery systems. It looks at some of the ways people have tried to incorporate serials into the Functional Requirements for Bibliographic Records (FRBR) model. FRBR can be expanded to apply to journal content not just at the journal title level, but also at the article level. These problems are examined with an eye toward ease of access for patrons and openness of metadata for widespread use and reuse. Finally, the paper explores the ways that linked data can be used to show the relationships between various library resources and allow patrons easier access to the information they need, and proposes some ideas about the kinds of discovery systems that might be built to best meet both librarian and patron needs.

Linked data refers to structured data and metadata that are published in a way that allows links to be created between various data sets, element sets, and value vocabularies. It allows data to be read by computers, and to be reused and extended in a variety of ways. Linked data challenges traditional models of bibliographic metadata, because the data model differs markedly. Traditional library data live in discrete records: Each record contains a set of elements (e.g., MARC tags) and their associated values, and each record describes a unique resource. Linked data is not record based; it is based on a graph data model. The graph data model centers around statements, not records. According to Baker et al. (2011), "In a graph-based ecosystem an organization can supply individual statements about a resource, and all statements provided about a particular uniquely identified resource can be aggregated into a global graph" (para. 9).

In a linked data ecosystem, each resource, element, and vocabulary term is assigned a unique identifier, a Uniform Resource Identifier (URI) that will allow a resource to be accessed using the protocol of the Web: Hypertext Transfer Protocol (HTTP). These identifiers allow a resource to be used unambiguously in a variety of different places on the open Web.

In RDF, "statements may be either URI refs, or constant values (called literals) represented by character strings, in order to represent certain kinds of property values" (Manola & Miller, 2004b, para. 7). Statements are in the form of subject, predicate, and object. These statements can be in the form of a graph or, when not convenient, "each statement in the graph is written as a simple triple of subject, predicate, and object, in that order" (para. 8). For example, Figure 1 below shows both a graph example and a typical "triples" for a fictional journal named "Serials Catalogers" constructed in the same manner as the examples found in the RDF Primer.

The English statement would read:

http://www.exampleURL.com/index.html has *a title* whose value is *Serials Catalogers.*

What does this mean for bibliographic metadata? An item to be cataloged as a resource is assigned a URI that is available on the open Web. A cataloger would then use element sets such as the Dublin Core Metadata Initiative terms, the International Standard Bibliographic Description (ISDB) terms, or FRBR concepts in RDF to describe that resource by making statements about it. Value vocabularies like the Library of Congress Subject Headings (LCSH) and Getty Union List of Artist Names are used, as they are

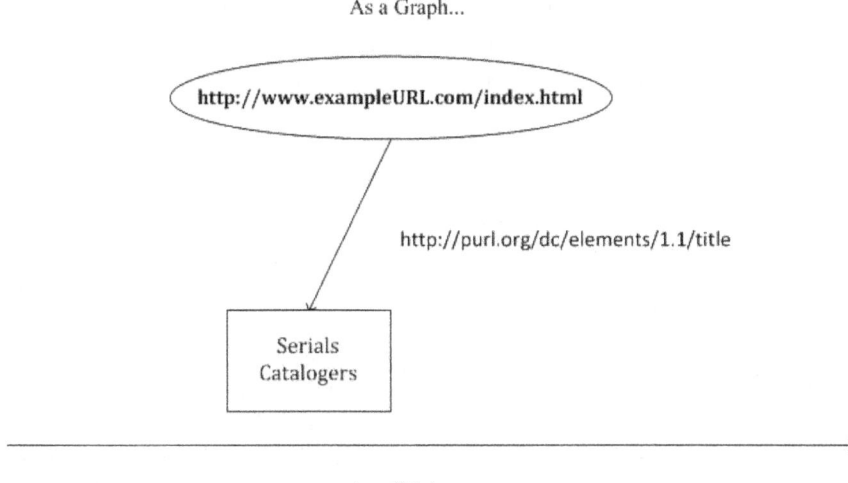

FIGURE 1 Example of linked data with RDF statements.

in traditional cataloging, to ensure uniformity in bibliographic description and to help collocate items. Many bibliographic resources, elements sets, and vocabularies have already been published in RDF on the Web and are ready for use in bibliographic descriptions.

The significant difference between traditional record-based cataloging and cataloging in a linked data model revolves around the existence of discrete records in local databases: In a linked data model, records largely disappear. Rather than downloading and editing, or creating, a new record for each item added to the collection, a cataloger would find data already available about an item, and make statements that link the item to the library, indicating that it is held in the library's collection. The cataloger could also publish any locally specific notes as additional RDF statements. Library systems would in turn pull data from many places on the Web to dynamically assemble a display for a user. Different data elements could be pulled together depending on the need of the user; no single, consistent record exists, but a "record" is created at the point of need. In this model, Integrated Library Systems would cease to consist of databases storing records locally and would instead become editors and servers of RDF statements. Rather than maintain redundant sets of records at every library, librarians could store bibliographic data in centralized databases, maintained collectively and used as needed by individual libraries and users.

The linked data model works especially well for serials, where the relationships are some of the more complicated in the bibliographic universe. Even before the advent of electronic journals and the multiple versions (or

MulVer) problem, serials presented issues for catalogers through frequent title changes, publisher changes, and shifts in scope (Everett Allgood, 2006). When serial titles began to be published in multiple different formats, the problem became more intractable, and existing cataloging practices were "contorted" to try to accommodate users' needs. Catalogers went back and forth between creating single records for each serial title, attaching holdings records for each unique manifestation, and creating a new bibliographic record for each format available. The changes in cataloging practice over time resulted in catalogs containing inconsistent metadata, where user confusion was practically guaranteed.

A shift away from the record data model for bibliographic metadata could more readily accommodate the serials environment that exists today. As resources become more and more available in an electronic format, description becomes less important than identification, and the relationships between resources become crucial (Antelman, 2004). Users need links to resources more than they need descriptions of those resources.

The International Federation of Library Associations and Institutions (IFLA) recognized the importance of bibliographic relationships when it drafted the FRBR model. FRBR is centered around identifying relationships between bibliographic resources and the metadata that help people to discover those resources. The Group 1 entities of work, expression, manifestation, and item are intended to allow different versions of a particular bibliographic resource to be more easily collocated. However, it was clear from the start that the FRBR model works well for monograph resources but not necessarily for modeling continuing resources. Over the past decade, several people have proposed changes to the FRBR model to incorporate serials. Adams, Santamauro, & Blythe (2008) draw on the work of Frieda Rosenberg and Diane Hillman, and suggest that in the serials world, there might be three levels, rather than four, in the Group 1 entities. They suggest that work and expression might be combined into a *superworkspression*, as "an umbrella record that collects the bibliographic information relating to a serial's content ... serving all its manifestations in different formats" (p. 195). This record would change infrequently; the manifestation record would reflect the data specific to different formats. Riva (2004b) suggests relationship-based clusters created at the work level to show the relationships between serials as they shift over time. Curran (2009) suggests that perhaps each serial change is itself a new manifestation.

The problem with the FRBR model for serials is that serials publications contain two related entities that could both be identified on the work level: the journal itself, and each individual article within a particular issue. The separation between the journal and the articles it contains has been deeply embedded in cataloging practices for over century, and current ideas about bibliographic relationships haven't adequately addressed the issue of trying to bring these two work-level resources together.

However, if FRBR is viewed as a conceptual model for defining relationships, rather than a strict template, the model can expand in several directions. If the relationships between resources are reconceptualized as the central component of cataloging, then the links between resources created using the RDF model become the engine that drives collocation and discovery. The journal and its articles can be brought back together in discovery systems, making it easier for users to find what they need no matter how they begin their search.

If the journal and article can both be considered as the "work," users can begin searches from any entry point, and displays of "records" can shift depending on the ways a user navigates through bibliographic metadata. Beginning at the article level, a particular article, in an abstract sense, is defined as a work. The expression of the work might be the article as written by the author, and in a particular language. The first manifestation of the article could be the print version as published in a particular journal and then a second if it was published as a digital version. If the article goes on to be republished in a monograph anthology, another manifestation (and possibly another expression) is created, and can be linked to the article as published in the journal.

The work can also be defined from the journal title level; a user can navigate from a journal title search to see all articles contained in individual issues of the journal. This introduces a new question: What is a serial work? How the boundaries of a particular journal have been defined has changed over time: the debate between latest-entry and successive-entry cataloging illustrates the shifts in thinking around this issue. Latest-entry cataloging, in which title and publisher changes for a particular journal are made in the main entry fields of a MARC record, with the previous title moved to a former title field and indexed in the library system, suggests that the serial as a whole constitutes the work, each part of its history contained within the work and subsumed to its current incarnation. The shift to successive-entry cataloging, in which a new record is created with each change in title, signified a different way of thinking about the serial as a work. The new title becomes a discrete resource, separate from its earlier incarnations. The gap between these two models could be bridged with the concept of the serial work in FRBR: If one considers the journal family, encompassing its whole history, as a work, each title change or change in scope becomes a new expression, and an expansion of the journal family. Each manifestation of the journal, with a new title or publisher, can be cataloged as a separate entity and linked to its previous incarnations through a unique identifier assigned to the journal family.

The concept of linking journals together as a family already exists in the MARC record, through the use of 76X-78X linking fields. However, attempting to create these links in an isolated library system is flawed because the single library might not hold the entirety of the journal family: The links are easily broken (Riva, 2004b). If bibliographic data is shifted away from the isolated library system and into a network of bibliographic data, these links can be maintained, and resources can be more effectively grouped for easier discovery. Data can be pulled in when needed, and disregarded when it is not, based on point-of-use needs.

The current record-based bibliographic model requires that the cataloger make a decision about what constitutes the work: the journal or the article. A linked data model will allow either article or journal to be positioned as the work, depending on the needs of the user at a given point in time. Rather than treating resources as static entities, the linked data model allows for a fluidity that reflects the real existence of these resources in a networked environment. The following example illustrates how this might work in a discovery system.

A user has a citation in hand for a particular journal article: "Sweet Revolution" by Adam Gopnik, published in *The New Yorker* in 2011. If the user searches the article title, the search will treat the article as the work. The article has a unique identifier that has been linked to the identifiers for the publication *The New Yorker,* both in its electronic and print incarnations. This article was republished in a book called *The Table Comes First.* This book also has an identifier, and the article was linked to this book, as well, by way of that identifier. When the user searches for the article by the article's title, an on-the-fly display will be created that shows all of these versions. The electronic and print versions of the article as published in *The New Yorker* constitute one expression of the work, in two different manifestations. The library might own the print copy (identified by an item identifier: a barcode), as well as the electronic copy (which will have its own identifier based on the database in which it's published and on how the library has access to it). The article as reprinted in the book is another expression and manifestation. If there is an e-book available, then the book expression has two manifestations.

The user may not care which is the manifestation and which is the expression. She may simply want to know how she can read this article. The on-the-fly display will show that the article can be read online, either as originally published in *The New Yorker* or as published later in the e-book version of the anthology, and that print copies of these items are available.

If the user is interested in the print copy of *The New Yorker*, he or she may decide to see what else has been published in the journal. Clicking on the journal title will change the display, and the journal-as-work, rather than as expression, would become the organizing principle behind the display. The user could then see the history of the publication and click into any volume or issue of the journal to see which articles it contains. The user could also take the author name or subject heading as an entry point, and subsequent changes in the display could reflect information about the author or subject, as well as displaying what related resources are available. These displays could go beyond what is available through traditional authority records by pulling data about authors, places, and terms from outside of traditional library sources.

Once bibliographic data is shifted away from the record-based model, it no longer matters whether the article or the journal is considered the work, or whether a serial title is cataloged as a single item or as a group of successive, related items. Relationships are defined, and related resources are linked together by unique identifiers. The descriptive and access data that is required in a particular search can be pulled in and used at the point of need. If links are created between different format manifestations and different title variations of a publication, then they are easy to pull together in order to show the entire journal history, or just as easily pulled apart to find only a distinct issue or volume or article. Merely creating the links allows a user to see the data in whatever permutation or at whatever level is needed. If searching at the article level, then the user can see the different physical and digital formats that exist and the different modes of retrieval for that particular issue or article. If the user searches at the journal title level, he or she can be shown the "formerly published as" or "currently published as" links, as well as the journal title level metadata, and the options available for viewing content at an issue/volume level.

This model also allows bibliographic metadata to be used in new ways, beyond allowing a user to find a particular resource. Researchers may be interested in understanding publication history for a number of reasons: to understand a field of study in a new way or to see how scholarly communication has shifted over time. Publishing this information in an open, linked data form allows it to be used for any number of new purposes and can open up new avenues of scholarly understanding. As research in the digital humanities expands, this kind of data could prove very useful for new inquiries.

The shift to a linked data model would not only help users better understand the bibliographic universe; it would save immense amounts of time for catalogers, too. Rather than maintaining a whole catalog's worth of data, updating records with each publication change or deleting and reloading records every time a package of electronic resources is renegotiated, catalogers can work collaboratively to maintain bibliographic metadata, and take advantage of metadata released by publishers and vendors. The vision of collaboration that was begun with cooperative cataloging ventures like OCLC and RLIN can be truly realized.

This notion of a linked-data-based bibliographic ecosystem seems far away from a technical services perspective still mired in traditional MARC records. But there are signs of forward movement. The announcement in October 2011 by the Library of Congress that they are exploring the future of bibliographic metadata through the Bibliographic Framework Transition

Initiative (Marcum, 2011) and the work toward the adoption of Resource Description and Access are signs that catalogers are starting to think differently about bibliographic metadata. In the meantime, there are concrete projects librarians can undertake to make local data identifiable and usable in a linked data environment. Institutions that maintain institutional repositories can explore the release of that metadata on the open Web as RDF triples. Librarians who work with faculty to create data management plans and archive their research can ensure that identification systems like EZID are used to give data sets unique identifiers and allow them to be found on the Web. Most importantly, cataloging librarians can begin to learn about RDF and graph-based data models, and how they might be useful in their own context.

Current bibliographic systems were created to reflect a certain information landscape, one in which resources were discrete items, located and accessed in physical spaces. But today's librarians and patrons are not working in that landscape anymore, and library systems struggle to keep up and to reflect the new world of information resources. In order to create systems and provide access patrons can use and understand, we need to start thinking about our work very differently, and to imagine new possibilities unhindered by current practices. The fluidity of the linked data model offers a way out of the binds that we too often find ourselves in now.

REFERENCES

Adams, K., Santamauro, B., & Blythe, K. (2008). Successive entry, latest entry, or none of the above? How the MARC21 format, FRBR and the concept of a work could revitalize serials management. *The Serials Librarian*, *54*(3/4), 193–197. doi:10.1080/03615260801974099

Antelman, K. (2004). Identifying the serial work as a bibliographic entity. *Library Resources & Technical Services*, *48*(4), 238–255.

Baker, T., Bermès, E., Coyle, K., Dunsire, G., Isaac, A., Murray, A,... Zeng, M. (2011, October 25). Library linked data incubator group final report. Retrieved from http://www.w3.org/2005/Incubator/lld/XGR-lld-20111025/

Baer, W. (2004). Federated searching. *College & Research Libraries News*, *65*(9), 518–519.

Curran, M. (2009). Serials in RDA: A starter's tour and kit. *The Serials Librarian*, *57*(4), 306–323. doi:10.1080/03615260903218825

Everett Allgood, J. (2006). Serials and multiple versions, or the inexorable trend toward work-level displays. *Library Resources & Technical Services*, *51*(3), 160–178.

Graham, C. (1990). Definition and scope of multiple versions. *Cataloging & Classification Quarterly*, *11*(2), 5–32. doi:10.1300/J104v11n01_02

Manola, F., & Miller, E. (2004a). Introduction. In B. McBride (Series Ed.), RDF Primer W3C recommendations 10 February 2004. Retrieved from http://www.w3.org/TR/2004/REC-rdf-primer-20040210/#intro

Manola, F., & Miller, E. (2004b). 2.2 RDF Model. In B. McBride (Series Ed.), RDF Primer W3C recommendations 10 February 2004. Retrieved from http://www.w3.org/TR/rdf-primer/#rdfmodel

Marcum, D. (2011, October 31). A bibliographic framework for the digital age. Library of Congress. Retrieved from http://www.loc.gov/marc/transition/news/framework-103111.html

Oliver, C. (2004). FRBR is everywhere, but what happened to the format variation issue? *The Serials Librarian, 45*(4), 27–36. doi:10.1300/J123v45n04_02

Riva, P. (2004a). Mapping MARC21 linking entry fields to FRBR and Tillett's taxonomy of bibliographic relationships. *Library Resources & Technical Services, 48*(2), 130–143.

Riva, P. (2004b). Defining the boundaries. *The Serials Librarian, 45*(3), 15–21. doi:10.1300/J123v45n03_02

Effective Learning and Teaching of RDA: Applying Adult Learning Theory

NAOMI KIETZKE YOUNG
George A. Smathers Libraries, University of Florida, Gainesville, Florida, USA

Significant changes in both the cataloging code and our mode of recording metadata are slated to take place in the coming months and years. These changes give us an unprecedented opportunity to change our teaching strategies and our attitudes towards lifelong workplace learning for the better. In this study, we examine results of the U.S. RDA test, some basic principles of adult learning theory, and currently available training materials in order to consider what is most beneficial to practitioners in developing professional fluency and identity and what changes can be made to serve that end.

INTRODUCTION

Two large interdependent initiatives have the potential to radically change the nature and practice of metadata creation and editing in the 21st century: Resource Description and Access (RDA) and the development of an alternative bibliographic framework to replace the MARC formats. As a result of these initiatives, the effect of which will be further magnified by budget cuts and shifts in the availability and level of staffing, we will be presented with an unprecedented opportunity to examine our continuing education methodologies and our attitudes toward lifelong workplace learning in order to make changes for the better in form as well as content. This article presents an overview of the key findings of the Report and Recommendations of the U.S. RDA Test Coordinating Committee (2011) (hereafter referred to as the RDA Test Report) as they pertain to continuing resources, then gives a brief outline of what is known about adult learners, continuing education, and workplace learning. From this we can frame an instructional methodology and some suggested learning emphases that should be useful both for the transition to RDA and related attempts to establish and sustain a new metadata framework in a post-MARC environment.

EXAMINING RDA AND THE RDA TEST REPORT

Several of the recommendations in the RDA Test Report deal specifically with serials and integrating resources. (The umbrella term "continuing resources" as defined by Hirons and Graham (1998) does not appear in RDA, but their concept of seriality is to some extent represented by references to "mode of issuance"). Of particular interest is the following recommendation:

> A great deal of current training for RDA focuses on the cosmetic differences between the AACR2 [Anglo-American Cataloging Rules, 2nd Revised Edition] and RDA in a MARC environment. While this is an understandable approach to easily get staff up-and-running using the new rules, the Coordinating Committee believes this focus has led to a general misunderstanding about RDA and what it is intended to accomplish, leading to many comments from testers that it would be easier to just modify AACR2 with these cosmetic changes. The Coordinating Committee recommends that training material be developed that specifically focuses on the underlying principles of RDA which include not just FRBR concepts, but the idea that bibliographic descriptions be regarded as a set of reusable relationship information packets, rather than a monolithic set of individual and indivisible records. (U.S. RDA Test Coordinating Committee, 2011, p. 19–20)

The testers also reported that serials catalogers involved in the test were not in complete agreement about the efficacy of RDA for cataloging continuing resources. Many of the serials-specific comments were of a negative or guarded character, focusing on potential conflicts between the CONSER Standard Record (CSR) and RDA as written, particularly with regard to provider-neutral records. The report notes efforts by the CONSER community to reconcile these conflicts (U.S. RDA Test Coordinating Committee, 2011, p. 21–22). Indeed, the reconciliation process is well underway, and draft reports from various working groups to examine and recommend policies were in circulation at the time of this writing.

In terms of planning for future learning, it may be most interesting to consider the comments regarding error patterns in the common original set. Although the number of records in this set is relatively small, this paragraph of the report bears out the author's experience as a cataloging supervisor:

> Describing resources that continue over time is not well understood regardless of the rules used, as evidenced by numerous errors in providing correct start dates, relationships to earlier or later titles, and notes citing

which issue or iteration of the resource was used for the description and which was the most recent issue consulted. Online serials were especially challenging, and records for these resources were no less accurate under RDA rules than under AACR2 rules. The set of A/V resources was so diverse that no special patterns common to all of these resources were observed. (U.S. RDA Test Coordinating Committee, 2011, p. 52)

When serial and integrating-resource records were evaluated in more detail (U.S. RDA Test Coordinating Committee, 2011, p. 58–61), some error patterns concerning RDA records were found, a portion of which were attributed to the testers' experience with the CONSER Standard Record, with inappropriate generalization of those rules to the RDA environment. Interestingly, and perhaps bearing out the RDA decision not to incorporate serials and integrating resources into a single umbrella category, error patterns between these two types of resources differed in some ways.

As might be expected, material in a textual format was less problematic than nontextual materials (U.S. RDA Test Coordinating Committee, 2011, figure 37, p. 91). When mode of issuance is considered, multipart monographs were most problematic, then integrating resources, then serials (U.S. RDA Test Coordinating Committee, 2011, figure 38, p. 92).

When we turn to the journal literature, we see that most of what has been written so far concerning RDA and continuing resources cataloging has been of a very practical, nuts-and-bolts nature. Needleman (2008) explained the need for RDA as a new cataloging code based on FRBR concepts, rather than a revision of AACR2, and gave an outline of the structure of the proposed code itself. Curran (2009) presented a detailed overview of changes to AACR2 practice under RDA based on the most current existing draft at that time, a detailed list of issues yet to be determined in the final release, and an elements list shown both in natural language and MARC encoding. She followed this up (Curran, 2010) with a draft workflow for print serial as might be shown in the RDA Toolkit. El-Sherbini and Curran (2011) provided a general overview of RDA with some attention to the new 33X fields and Hawkins (2011) has examined those fields in depth.

ADULT LEARNERS AND WORKPLACE LEARNING

It is helpful to consider existing information about adult learners and workplace learning, as well as to examine some traits that may be more common in catalogers than in a broader population.

Malcolm Knowles (2011) pioneered the intensive study of the differences between adult learners and school-age learners. The chief characteristics of adult learners may be given as follows:

- They are self-directed and autonomous.
- They are goal oriented.

- They have life experiences that they more easily connect to the material being learned as compared to school-age learners.
- They value relevancy.
- They value practical information.

Building from Glazer's (1974) definition of the "minor professions," as well as his analysis of the distinguishing characteristics of a profession, Schön (1983, 1987) pioneered the concept of the *reflective practitioner*—an individual who is able to consciously reflect during workplace actions in order to meld theory and practice to form generalizable knowledge from information. Schön argues that the traditional view of professional activity as applying basic science to practical problems in order to solve them, or problem solving, ignores the additional and necessary process of framing the problem, or problem setting (1983, p. 39–40). Throughout the remainder of this discussion, the term "professional" is used as Schön used it: an individual who has attained competencies in problem setting and problem solving in the areas of cataloging/metadata creation and editing, regardless of the occupational rank of that individual or the means by which those competencies were attained, rather than limiting the term to those who have completed a specific academic course of study.

Anderson (1977) defined learning as the building of abstract mental frameworks called schemata. Any new concepts to which one is exposed must be built into an existing schema, a new schema created, or older schemata disassembled and reassembled into new frameworks. Bauer and Gruber (2007) build on these concepts to describe workplace learning as the establishment and modification of scripts and routines and the engagement in learning activities. They distinguish scripts from schemata by saying that scripts are behavioral and serve as default procedures thus roughly analogous to Schön's (1983, 1987) problem solving, whereas schemata are conceptual and abstract, more equivalent to problem setting.

In this model, learning takes place when the learner is able to see generalizations within similar situations and recognize and respond to deviations from what is expected. When a sufficiently large number of exceptions accrue, or when entirely new work tasks appear, learners must modify or abandon the scripts and schemata in order to respond correctly in novel situations (Bauer & Gruber, 2007, p. 681). Learners who are not able to discern a pattern in order to formulate generalizations will become frustrated and experience a loss of competency. This model of learning requires an accepting attitude toward error on the part of both the learner and the supervisor, as errors are an important indication of old scripts that must be discarded or of new scripts inadequately mastered. While this learning can take place without an intentional effort, conscious engagement in social learning activities will speed this modification process.

Wenger (1998) argued that these ongoing social learning activities result in "communities of practice," informal networks of expertise that create and sustain models of professional behavior and practice among those holding a common body of knowledge.

WORKPLACE LEARNING IN LIBRARY LITERATURE

Much of the library literature that highlights adult learning does so in the context of continuing education. Some of the best articles in this regard have been written specifically by and for medical librarians. In a foundational article, Mayfield (1993) examines many facets of continuing education for medical librarians, although there is little or nothing in it that would not be applicable to catalogers in all types of libraries. He outlines the four characteristics of competence, the distinctive characteristics of adult learners (and how pedagogic techniques based on formal schooling may not align with those characteristics), and evaluates options for creating and supporting self-directed learning. Key among his recommendations are the creation of "structured links among centers of excellence ... to exploit the potential for contextually relevant professional learning" and "alternative delivery systems for education and training ... that intentionally facilitate learner decision making and self-direction" (p. 430). Allen, et al. (2005) showed that an interactive workshop model involving both librarians and practitioners (nurses) had greater long-term benefit and learning for both groups, as well as promoting positive relationships between librarians and nurses.

Several articles (such as Paul, 2001; Pitts, 2003; Power, 2006; and Wenger, 1998) give general or personal narratives about the importance of and the process of succeeding in self-directed, ongoing professional development. O'Neill (1998) critiques the availability of formal continuing education, with a specific emphasis on acquisitions and collection development, and finds that professional organizations and practitioners need to fill the gap. Jizba (1998) defines various obstacles to professional development, contrasts formal and informal education structures, and underscores particularly the need for explicit institutional support in promoting continuing education, highlighting a variety of incentives and strategies for both individual and institutional progress in creating and sustaining opportunities. Although many of the articles on continuing education directly or implicitly target the degreed librarian, Gelber and Kandarasheva (2011) discussed the value of training their paraprofessional catalogers to catalog to the PCC standard. While their article primarily focused on the benefits to library patrons and the improvement of materials workflows, the personal satisfaction and skill development of the staff involved was also mentioned as a benefit.

As the modality of teaching moves increasingly into the Web environment, articles on continuing education have appeared online. Condron (2006) compiled a list of continuing education sites, both formal and informal; many of these sites are still operational. All of these articles deal primarily with the coursework or workshop model of continuing education, even if the intention is to demonstrate the shortcoming of those models.

KNOWING YOUR AUDIENCE: LIBRARIANS ARE DIFFERENT

Scherdin and Beaubien (1995) conducted a study of librarians' personality styles according to the Myers-Briggs Type Inventory (MBTI). They found that approximately 75% of technical services librarians were introverts: individuals who are more energized by reflection and solitude than interaction and communication. There is a good chance, then, that for a roomful of catalogers in a traditional group-participation workshop, both the instructor and a majority of the students will be uncomfortable, and actually less able to learn or teach effectively.

How can we adapt group learning to make it less stressful for a group composed mainly of introverts? The instructor may wish to try some of these techniques (even though they fly in the face of more conventional advice found elsewhere).[1] Keep in mind that using a variety of techniques in any given session makes learning possible for a wider variety of learning and personality styles.

- Arrange the room in a more traditional lecture style, rather than a circle or small clusters of seats.
- Minimize mandatory activities. Give everyone a chance to respond but also to pass.
- Collect feedback on student understanding by anonymous methods, such as clicker technology, boxes to collect written questions on slips, etc. Remote learning software generally offers personalized and aggregated (polling) response options.
- Offer generous breaks and thinking time for participants to build interior mental frameworks, and to work through in-class exercises individually.

Outside of a formal learning situation, how do we support different personality styles in the hands-on learning of everyday work? Cataloging is often considered to be an essentially lonely pursuit. Many catalogers do in fact prefer to work alone and undisturbed, while others prefer consultations with others and discussion of the choices they make regarding particular elements in the catalog record. Electronic discussion lists and bulletin boards such as those provided by the American Library Association's ALA Connect service have been invaluable as channels of discussion to clarify uncertainties about practice, strengthen and challenge underlying theories, and provide expert help, especially for those whose preferred mode of communication is in writing.

IMPLICATIONS FOR TRAINING

As we have seen, adult learning theory suggests that adults prefer learning that is strongly under their own control, applicable to their own lives, and embodied in active concrete experiences (Westbrook, 2005, p. 30). Emphasis on these latter two aspects can lead to continuing education programs that are directed toward specific skill development and light on underlying theoretical concepts. Indeed, the teaching of such underlying concepts is often criticized in the name of efficiency, especially when dealing with paraprofessional staff or copy catalogers. However, we can see that time spent in teaching FRBR concepts will give catalogers the opportunity to create the schemata that will help them to act as reflective professionals rather than to work automatically through memorized rote practices. This is borne out by suggestions in the RDA Test Report itself.

Just as original cataloging is not needed for every item that crosses a cataloger's desk, no cataloging department trainer or supervisor will need to create complete instructional programs for the mastery of RDA. However, just as knowing cataloging rules allows a skilled cataloger to craft a record to individual needs, knowledge of instructional design will help those charged with instruction to adapt pre-packaged materials. Robin Neidorf's (2006) book, although primarily intended for distance education, is helpful for anyone who wants to create or adapt material for autonomous learning.

Much of the established training materials from the Program for Cooperative Cataloging (PCC) and the Serials Cataloging Cooperative Training Program (SCCTP) have been designed with the needs of adult learners for engagement and relevance in mind. These courses were primarily designed for small group instruction, whether remotely or in person. They may be an excellent launching pad for those who prefer a more social approach to skill development and problem solving. Once national policies are in place, these courses (with the obvious exception of the holdings course) will be extensively revised.

Two apparently opposite kinds of revisions may be helpful in improving instructional materials for the mastery of RDA. If, as Bauer and Gruber have suggested, the mental indexing of errors and exceptions is an important part of workplace learning, trainers should make certain that the examples given include, not only those that illustrate a rule or principle, but also those that show significant exceptions to it. Where such exceptions cannot be worked into a formal presentation without confusion, they should be part of the informal follow-up as described below. However, the finding that many catalogers are still confused about unique aspects of serial records suggest that those who revise these modules should consider adding more foundational and theoretical material on the nature of seriality and the significance of mode of issuance to decisions made in the metadata creation process. If the reason for this additional theoretical grounding is explained in terms of its serving the practical end of better understanding and retention of concrete procedures, then it should not be seen as veering into unnecessary trivia.

Most of the discussion this far has centered on formal training programs, workshops that range (in general) from 90 minutes to two or three working days. The needs of adult learners for immediately relevant, practical information may be better served by smaller instructional modules each of which cover a single concept or subprocedure. While this level of granularity is more difficult for the instructor, it allows learners to take greater control of their own instructional planning. In this way, it is no longer necessary for a cataloger to watch (or scan through) a 90-minute recording to review a single area of concern.[2] These smaller sessions are easier to fit into the workday on an ongoing basis, rather than blocking out multiple full days for a traditional training course.

In order to create the skill sets and mental frameworks that will bring long-term understanding and fluency to the professional who is part of a larger community of practice, learning cannot be limited to workshops and seminars. Catalogers must develop a sufficient grasp of formally presented concepts in order to apply them in the workday context. Informal "office hours" meetings with no set agenda can be set up for catalogers to bring troublesome items, such as questionable title changes, or items with ambiguous or multiple numbering systems. By observing the strengths and weaknesses of different employees, supervisors can identify local experts for certain aspects of the rules.

USING TECHNOLOGY TO BEST ADVANTAGE

The webcast or webinar—whether live or prerecorded—has become a staple of continuing education and training in libraries. The method has many advantages that have likely contributed to its rapid growth. Experts and well-known speakers from all over the world are available even to a one-person library, and the recorded editions can usually be replayed by individuals or groups over a period of time after the live showing (or even indefinitely).

Beck, Bross, and Hawkins (2010) have written a good introduction on how to teach well using remote-learning software. How to *participate* well in a webinar has garnered less attention. These tips, while they are largely common sense, are sometimes ignored to the detriment of the educational experience.

Group viewings of webinars should be held in a room with lighting that allows note-taking without projecting glare onto the screen or washing out the screen image. All screen savers, power-saving timers, and background programs (except virus and malware protection) should be turned off on the group viewing computer, although someone watching individually may wish to have an additional program open to take personal notes. A volunteer from the group viewing the presentation, or someone from the library's training team (if one exists) should be present throughout the event to adjust volume, relay chat or voice questions and commentary to the presenter during a live presentation, and troubleshoot or remedy local technical problems. (This role may enhance the learning of a more extroverted participant.) If there is a lengthy "housekeeping" introduction designed to acquaint users with the interactive software, or during which the presenters grapple with their own technical difficulties, this section should ideally be removed from the archived presentation. If not, the local support person should fast-forward through this portion.

Individuals participating alone should not be interrupted and privacy should be ensured. This may mean viewing the webinar away from one's own workstation, especially in a "cubicle farm" technical services environment. If a headset with microphone is required for individual live participation, the learner should take time to run audio checks provided by the software and become comfortable with features of the headset such as the volume adjustment and the microphone mute setting. Learning how to use remote instructional technology and learning the actual content of RDA are separate tasks, and it is important for the former not to interfere with the latter. A recorded presentation meets the test of relevance and direct applicability, but active engagement may be more difficult to ensure, unless the viewing is paired with opportunities for discussion and practice with a local expert after the presentation takes place. Recordings may be the self-education tool of choice for the introverted cataloger, but there must still be a mechanism for each learner to interact with the material and receive feedback in ways that help cement learning.

ATTITUDINAL SUPPORT FOR WORKPLACE LEARNING

This discussion would not be complete without a brief mention of administrative attitudes and expectations that can help or hinder workplace learning. Cataloging managers may have personal expectations about the amount of interaction catalogers should have with others in the course of their work, and the rate at which work is completed. Time spent in learning how to manage new software packages and equipment that supports the learning process is as well-spent as time spent mastering rules and principles. While the RDA Test Report showed that catalogers rapidly increase their speed in creating RDA records, after adoption there will be an inevitable, albeit temporary, slowdown in work that must be accounted for in staff evaluations and departmental efficiency metrics. As mentioned above, reflection and making errors are essential parts of professional decision-making, and tolerating higher levels of error (although not without expecting them to be corrected) is the only way to ensure eventual mastery. Experienced catalogers who were used to performing "perfectly" may experience considerable discomfort at making mistakes or admitting confusion. Managers should be certain to model a sense of humor and acceptance of imperfection. Errors should be pinpointed and analyzed, not to rank workers or attach blame, but to determine faulty schemata and set out a plan for their revision. In cases where cataloging managers are also working catalogers, they may wish to consider having their own work reviewed by the persons they supervise, so that they can model an appropriate response to making and correcting errors. This will, of course, also aid managers in their own mastery of RDA.

CONCLUSION

As RDA and the new bibliographic framework are adopted, new communities of practice will form and reform among those who have come to an agreement on the correct application of the principles those standards describe. Policy-setting bodies such as the Library of Congress and PCC must make conscious efforts if they wish to remain vital centers for these communities of practice. The professional community as a whole should be aware that this time of upheaval will lead to the ascendancy of new experts and the decline of former ones, and the re-forming of alliances of various kinds. This adds to the uncertainty of the time of transition, but if the process is allowed to proceed naturally, then the networks established will be more successful and productive.

NOTES

1. The author is indebted to discussions with self-identified introverts for these suggestions.
2. The technology learning site http://lynda.com exemplifies the "bite-sized" approach to independent multimedia instruction.

REFERENCES

Allen, M., Jacobs, S. K., Levy, J., Pierce, S., Pravikoff, D., & Tanner, A. (2005). Continuing education as a catalyst for inter-professional collaboration. *Medical Reference Services Quarterly*, 24(3), 93–102. doi:10.1300/J115v24n03_08

Anderson, R. C. (1977). The notion of schemata and the educational enterprise. In R. C. Anderson, R. J. Spiro, & W. E. Montague (Eds.) *Schooling and the acquisition of knowledge*. Hillsdale, NJ: Erlbaum.

Bauer, J., & Gruber, H. (2007). Workplace changes and workplace learning: Advantages of an educational micro perspective. *International Journal of Lifelong Education*, 26(6), 675–688. doi:10.1080/02601370701711364

Beck, M., Bross, V., & Hawkins, L. (2010). Catalogers in (cyber)space: Glimpses into the starship's log of two online trainers. *Serials Review*, 36(1), 35–36. doi:10.1016/j.serrev.2009.11.001

Condron, L. (2006). Online continuing education. *Cataloging & Classification Quarterly*, 42(1), 3–5. doi:10.1300/J104v42n01_02

Curran, M. (2009). Serials in RDA: A starter's tour and kit. *The Serials Librarian*, 57(4), 306–323. doi:10.1080/03615260903218825

Curran, M. (2010). Print serials workflow in RDA: A draft workflow for RDA toolkit based on JSC's sample workflow for a simple book. *The Serials Librarian*, 59(3–4), 244–262. doi:10.1080/0361526X.2010.504918

El-Sherbini, M., & Curran, M. (2011). Resource Description and Access "RDA": New code for cataloging. *The Serials Librarian*, 60(1–4), 7–15. doi:10.1080/0361526X.2011.556425

Gelber, N., & Kandarasheva, I. (2011). PCC training for copy catalogers: Is it worth the investment? The Columbia University Libraries experience. *Library Resources & Technical Services, 55*(3), 163–171.

Glazer, N. (1974). The schools of the minor professions. *Minerva, 12*(3), 346–364. doi:10.1007/BF01102529

Hawkins, L. (2011), Content type, media type and carrier type: MARC 21 fields related to Resource Description and Access. *Serials Review 37*(3), 205–206. doi:10.1016/j.serrev.2011.05.012

Hirons, J., & Graham, C. (1998). Issues related to seriality. *Principles and future of AACR2* (pp. 180–213). Ottawa, Canada: Canadian Library Association.

Jizba, L. (1997). Everyone's job. *Technical Services Quarterly, 15*(1), 119–131. doi:10.1300/J124v15n01_10

Knowles, M. (2011). *The adult learner: The definitive classic in adult education and human resource development*, (7th ed.). (Amsterdam, The Netherlands: Elsevier).

Needleman, M. (2008). The Resource Description and Access standard. *Serials Review 34*(3), 233–234. doi:10.1016/j.serrev.2008.06.006

Mayfield, M. K. (1993). Beyond the classroom: Self-direction in professional learning. *Bulletin of the Medical Library Association, 81*(4), 425–432.

Neidorf, R. (2006). *Teach beyond your reach: An instructor's guide to developing and running successful distance learning classes, workshops, training sessions and more*. Medford, NJ: Information Today.

O'Neill, A. L. (1998). What's for dinner? Continuing education after the MLIS. *Library Acquisitions: Practice & Theory, 22*(1), 35–40. doi:10.1016/S0364-6408(97)00149-X

Paul, K. (2001). P.D.A.S.: Professional development avoidance syndrome—the career killer. *School Libraries in Canada, 21*(2), 2.

Pitts, S. (2003). Working while going to school online. *Public Libraries, 42*(6), 355–356.

Power, G. (2006). Workplace learning for busy information professionals. *Legal Information Management, 6*, 260. doi:10.1017/S1472669606000867

Scherdin, M. J., & Beaubien, A. K. (1995). Shattering our stereotype: Librarians' new image. *Library Journal, 120*(12), 35–38.

Schön, D. (1983). *The reflective practitioner: How professionals think in action*. New York, NY: Basic Books.

Schön, D. (1987). *Educating the reflective practitioner*. San Francisco, CA: Jossey-Bass.

U.S. RDA Test Coordinating Committee. (2011). *Report and recommendations of the U.S. RDA Test Coordinating Committee*.

U.S. RDATest Coordinating Committee. (2011). *Report and recommendations of the U.S. RDA Test Coordinating Committee*. Retrieved from http://www.loc.gov/bibliographic-future/rda/source/rdatesting-finalreport-20june2011.pdf

Wenger, E. (1998). *Communities of practice: Learning, meaning, and identity*. Cambridge, United Kingdom: Cambridge University Press.

Westbrook, L. (2005). Problem-based learning: A staff development model for tight budget times. *Technical Services Quarterly, 21*(1), 27–33. doi:10.1300/J124v23n01_03

Charting a Course With NOMAP: Integrating Metadata Workflows Into a Traditional Cataloging Unit

TERESSA M. KEENAN

Maureen and Mike Mansfield Library, The University of Montana, Missoula, Montana, USA

The life of a cataloger today is in a state of flux; as libraries continue to transition from a predominately print world to a digital one, catalogers need to secure a functional future. To do so catalogers must change their mental models to stay flexible and pertinent in an ever-changing information environment. A recent digital project undertaken at the University of Montana provides an example of how research and developments in the area of metadata and bibliographic control have influenced cataloging and metadata workflow integration.

Cataloging workflows are in a state of flux as libraries continue to transition from a predominately print world to a more digital world. Catalogers can no longer simply rely on the Anglo-American Cataloguing Rules, Second Edition revised (AACR2rev) for guidance; they must now choose between AACR2rev, Resource Description and Access (RDA) and a host of other metadata schemas such as Dublin Core (DC), Metadata Encoding and Transmission Standard (METS), Metadata Object Description Schema (MODS), Encoded Archives Description (EAD), etc. Additionally, catalogers now need to be aware of and understand the difference between metadata schema, or rules, and syntax. While syntax has not always been clearly differentiated from data entry, nor has its importance been consistently highlighted in the mind of the traditional cataloger, it is, nevertheless, essential to creating useable data. Proper encoding allows the data to be understood and processed by a computer. To secure a functional future, catalogers must change their mental models and develop their skills to allow them to work with multiple encoding schemes such as Machine Readable Cataloging (MARC), Resource Description Framework (RDF), eXtensible Markup Language (XML), and Hyper-Text Markup Language (HTML). A recent digital project undertaken at the University of Montana provides an example of how research and developments in the area of metadata and bibliographic control have influenced cataloging and metadata workflow integration in the real world.

During the summer of 2009, the Maureen and Mike Mansfield Library (ML) joined forces with Native American scholars to provide access to previously identified resources pertaining to the indigenous peoples of Montana. Led by Dr. David Beck, professor and chair of the Native American Studies Program (NAS) at the University of Montana, and Dr. JoAllyn Archambault, director of the Native American Program at the National Museum of Natural History, Smithsonian Institution, the Natives of Montana Archival Project (NOMAP),[1] is a collaborative project to collect primary source documents related to the various tribes of Montana. Collections from the National Archives, National Museum of Natural History, and the Smithsonian were targeted with the intention of making them digitally accessible to researchers without direct access to the original physical documents.

Prior to the library's involvement, NAS researchers used the Southwest Oregon Research Project (SWORP) as a model (Southwest Oregon Research Project, 2006; Younker, 2009). An inventory of major archival collections and a key word identifier index were created. This research uncovered more than two million relevant documents within a single record group at the National Archives (RG 75 CCF 1907–1939). From this work a priority list for coordinating the digitization of the original documents was created. The digital-collections librarian then worked with a team of graduate students to establish best practices and to provide training in the use of cameras and software. The students traveled to Washington, DC, and spent a month taking digital photos of the original documents. Raw images were saved to an external portable hard drive, which was then sent to the library. Library staff and faculty provided post-processing of the digital images, metadata creation, and public access to the digitized materials.

To date there have been more than 35,000 documents digitized, all of which are hosted on the Montana Memory Project, Montana's Digital Library and Archives web site (MMP).[2] The library portion of the project has been split into three phases, each phase requiring approximately a year to complete. Future phases are contingent upon continued funding. Phase 1 consisted of approximately 13,000 images collected in 2009 (published in 2010). Phase 2 involved collecting more than 22,000 images during the summer of 2010 (published in 2011). Phase 3 is in process with metadata currently being completed for the approximately 19,000 images collected during the summer of 2011 (publication expected in spring 2012).

Prior to implementing a plan for integrating metadata creation into the workflow of traditional copy catalogers, relevant literature was consulted in an effort to gain guidance in assimilating new concepts and practices into established routines. Presentations by researchers about future directions in metadata (Coyle, 2010d) combined with research on the expansion of cataloging to include digital objects (Riemer, 2010) were helpful in providing context for the incorporation of metadata into Bibliographic Management Services (BMS). While research on the Semantic Web and the future of cataloging were thought provoking and provided a theoretical background for project planning and for establishing a basis for explaining the job-priority changes to staff, actual case studies such as those conducted at the Georgia Institute of Technology Library (Hudgins & Macklin, 2000) provided a better framework for establishing local workflows and creating training opportunities.

Literature on future directions for metadata clearly indicates that libraries need to take a different approach to maintaining the data that is available to them, suggesting that data needs to be used, reused, and shared openly (Coyle, 2010a, 2010b, 2010c; Hartig, Zhao, & Mühleisen, 2010; Knight, n.d.; Zeng et al., 2010). However, not all libraries are in a position to follow such a course at this point in time. Small- to medium-sized organizations without the financial and intellectual resources to restructure their legacy data and that rely on "out-of-the-box" software for presentation and preservation of digital collections may have to postpone updating their library's infrastructure to accommodate a system of linked data. Current cataloging research corroborates this fact by pointing out that "converting legacy metadata to linked data will require a team of experts, including MARC-based catalogers, specialists in other metadata schemas, software developers, and Semantic Web experts to design and test normalization/conversion algorithms, develop new schemas, and prepare individual records for automated conversion" (Bowen, 2010). That same research, however, also provides reassurance that such changes are possible and that tools and standards are being developed that will assist all libraries in the future (Bowen, 2010; Hartig et al., 2010). Because of these continuing developments, libraries should monitor current best practices when embarking on new projects in an effort to make future data conversion as straightforward as possible.

The amount of literature that addresses the integration of non-MARC metadata functions into the workflow of traditional catalogers is continuing to grow. Much of this literature focuses on the benefits of involving catalogers in metadata functions and the need to keep skills of technical services personnel current and competitive (Feltner-Reichert & Veve, 2007; Hudgins & Macklin, 2000; Riemer, 2010). Other studies focus on the perceptions of catalogers (Feltner-Reichert & Veve, 2007; Veve & Feltner-Reichert, 2010), and some provide detailed descriptions of preparation and training necessary for the integration of non-MARC metadata into traditional cataloging workflows (Feltner-Reichert & Veve, 2007; Hudgins & Macklin, 2000; Valentino, 2010).

THE SETTING

The University of Montana (UM) is a multicampus university with four affiliated campuses located in Dillon, Helena, Butte, and Missoula. The Missoula campus is a satellite College of Technology (COT). UM is a medium sized coeducational, doctoral institution and is classified as a research university. Established in 1895, the Maureen and Mike Mansfield Library (ML) serves a student population of more than 14,000. ML holds the largest collection of books and media in the state of Montana with collections exceeding 1.5 million volumes. ML also serves as the Federal Government Depository for the state. Over the last 10 years, ML has increased access to electronic literature and now has more than 30,000 journals (print and electronic), hundreds of electronic databases, and 77,000 electronic books (Mansfield Library Collection Development Group, 2011).

Within the last five years, ML has begun to develop and build digital collections, making more than 114,000 digital objects available to the public. Digitization takes place within both the Archives and Special Collections Department and the Bibliographic Management Services Department (BMS). BMS provides all of the acquisitions, cataloging, and processing of library materials for ML and COT. BMS comprises 13 paraprofessional staff and two professional faculty organized in teams based on primary work focus. Five staff members focus on acquisitions and copy cataloging monographs and media; two focus on acquisitions and access for serials and e-resources; five staff members focus on cataloging (monographs, media, serials, music, maps, and government documents); and one staff member focuses on digitization. The head of BMS is one of two professional catalogers in the department. The administrator/cataloger's time is split between administering the unit and providing original cataloging and metadata guidance. The responsibilities of the other professional cataloger include original cataloging and oversight of acquisitions and e-resource processes.

NOMAP AND INTEGRATING METADATA

Integration of metadata creation into the workflows of copy catalogers within BMS has been an evolving process. Each phase of the NOMAP digitization project incorporated additional personnel into the general workflow. Figure 1 illustrates the changes in workflow as the project evolved.

Phase I

Phase 1 of this project was completed without the involvement of BMS staff. The digital projects librarian worked closely with individual faculty and graduate students from NAS to ensure adherence to current best practices for

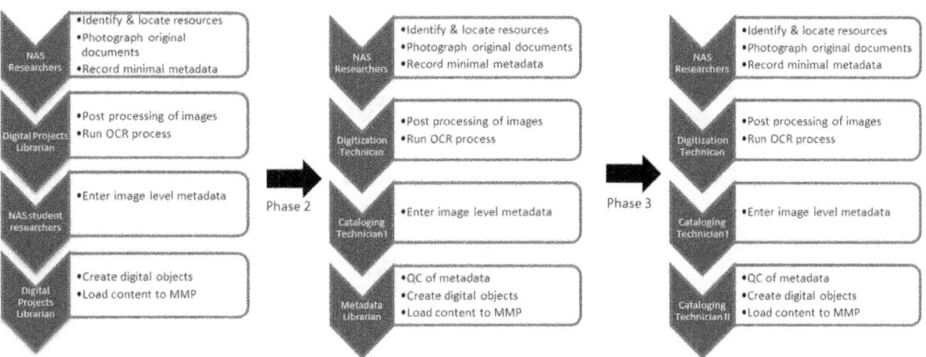

FIGURE 1 Illustration of workflow changes through each phase of the project.

digitization of the original materials. He assisted with training and provided all the post-processing of the raw images into a useable format for distribution. Working with NAS students and faculty, the metadata librarian subsequently determined that dates, names, and geographic locations were the metadata elements of primary importance to the researchers. Research about metadata quality and issues related to management and access of digital assets provided guidance in the creation of an application profile[3] that would work within the parameters of the software/presentation platform (CONTENTdm) currently in use by the library, while still providing for concerns by project stakeholders. Additional research on quality control of metadata stressed the importance of accuracy and consistency in metadata creation (Chapman, Reynolds, & Shreeves, 2009; Park, 2009; Park & Tosaka, 2010) and provided guidance in planning for training and reviewing the work.

The metadata librarian provided one of the NAS graduate students with an introduction to Dublin Core and an overview of how to record the data in Microsoft Excel in order for it to be transferrable to CONTENTdm. The librarian emphasized the importance of consistency in data entry. Figure 2 presents a portion of the Excel spreadsheet used by the student to record metadata. After the metadata were created, the digital projects librarian established the collection within MMP, matched the metadata to the appropriate image files, and loaded all of the digital objects to CONTENTdm. While this approach to the project worked, it was obvious to both the metadata librarian and the digital-projects librarian upon final review that the process was not scalable and that improvements were needed to enhance and ensure the quality of the metadata. Moreover, the expectation of the acquisition of a larger number of images during phase II suggested that additional personnel would be needed to provide metadata creation within a reasonable time frame. Producing metadata as part of the regular operations of BMS would also make the most of the skilled expertise of catalogers. Using controlled vocabularies for names and subject headings, combined with the natural

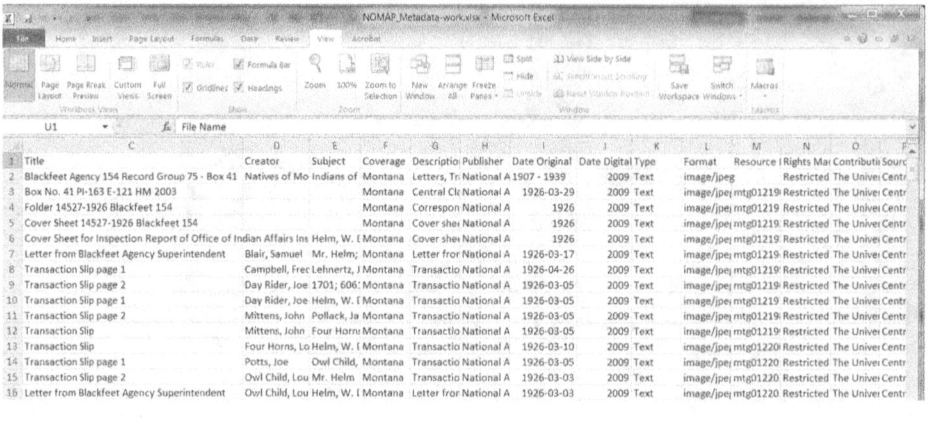

FIGURE 2 Illustration of a portion of the Excel spreadsheet used to record metadata during phase I of the project.

language keywords already being entered would provide better overall access to the collection.

Phase II

While the NAS students were in Washington, DC, collecting new digital images, library staff in BMS were introduced to the project. The general background and goals were shared, and a call for volunteers was issued. A majority of individuals within the department expressed interest in participating in the project. A group training session was scheduled to introduce staff to Dublin Core in general and to the application profile and workflow for the NOMAP project specifically. Instructions and reference resources were added to a wiki,[4] providing a centralized location for tracking all aspects of the project.

Prior to staff involvement with NOMAP, a smaller digitization project involving newspapers provided the opportunity for volunteers to practice their new skills applying descriptive metadata to digital objects using the rules associated with the Dublin Core element set. Additional training was provided to specifically address entering metadata for this project. Eleven paraprofessional staff from the department participated in the initial metadata training, and ten participated in creating metadata for the newspaper project.

This smaller project used Microsoft Excel as a tool for compiling metadata. While Excel is a common tool used by specialists outside the library, catalogers do not generally have the same level of comfort working with the program (Valentino, 2010). Our experience verified this with the local population as well. Much time was spent by the metadata librarian with troubleshooting, training, and quality control of data entered into the Excel spreadsheet. To alleviate this issue for the NOMAP project, the metadata librarian worked closely with systems staff to create an Access database. The

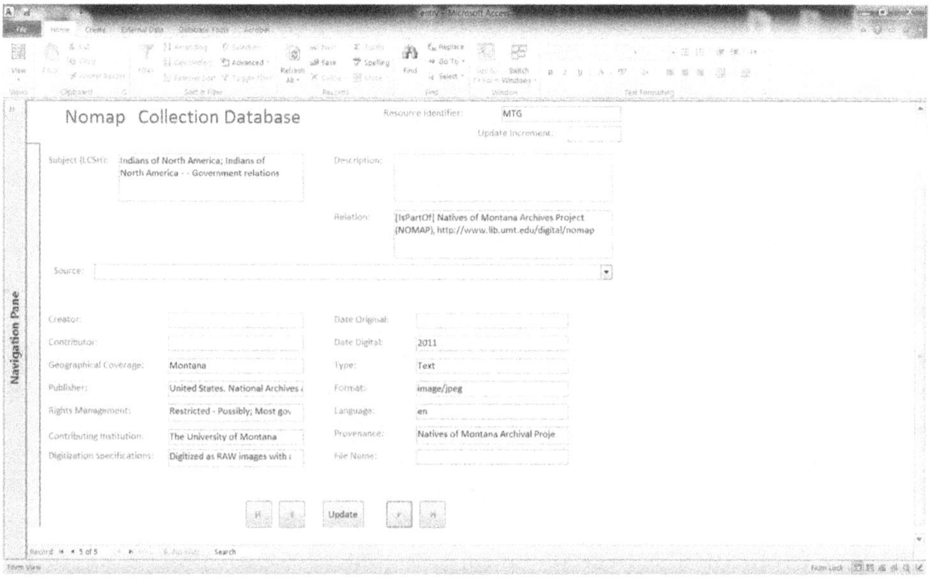

FIGURE 3 Example of the data entry form used by catalogers to record metadata into Access during phase II of the project. Default data is prepopulated in the form to increase efficiency and accuracy.

development of a data entry form (Figure 3) allowed catalogers to input metadata without having to learn the intricacies of the computer program in order to successfully complete the project.

Creation of the database was complicated by the fact that multiple individuals could potentially be working on the project at the same time. A master database was created and stored on the network, and individual databases were copied and loaded onto each cataloger's computer. A macro automatically transferred the data from an individual's hard drive to the master database upon completion of each data input session. An additional macro allowed information in the master database to be updated if changes were made to previously entered data. Training sessions for the catalogers were then scheduled to review the Dublin Core elements and to provide an introduction to entering the metadata via the new form. Of the eleven paraprofessional staff that attended the original training, eight worked on the project on a volunteer basis.

While periodic troubleshooting and review of the use of the Access form was needed at the beginning of phase II, until staff became comfortable using the new interface, this process was much more successful than using Excel for data entry as had been done with the newspaper project workflow. Once the metadata entry was completed by cataloging staff members, the metadata librarian used queries to retrieve and collocate the data and then export it to an Excel spreadsheet. The data were reviewed for quality control, and additional information was added to the spreadsheet to create the structure of the digital object. The final step by the metadata librarian involved loading the material into CONTENTdm for public access.

Phase III

After phase II and prior to the beginning of phase III of the project, cataloging staff was asked to review the data entry process. An informal discussion group was formed consisting of five of the paraprofessional catalogers and the metadata librarian. The Access form was modified and improved based on the suggestions made by the discussion group. Data that are often repeated were carried through from one image entry to the next, and dropdown menus (Figure 4) were added to improve consistency and ease of entry.

Because of the changes to the form and the fact that almost four months had passed since completion of phase II, instruction sessions were set up to provide general review of Dublin Core and to specifically examine common errors or problems discovered during the quality control process of phase

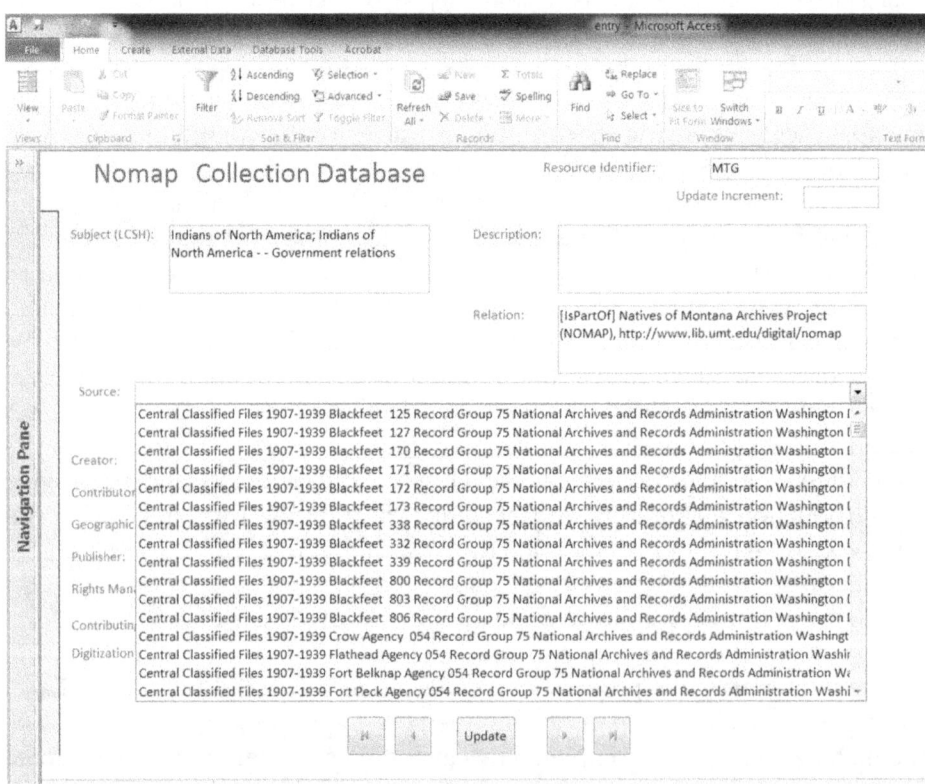

FIGURE 4 Screenshot of the dropdown menu that was added to the form for the source field prior to beginning phase III.

II. At the time of writing, six paraprofessional catalogers continue to create image-level metadata for this project, with the expectation that the digital objects will be publicly available in the spring. Preliminary quality control and ongoing discussions of the workflow with staff indicate that results are slightly better than phase II results. The staff is more comfortable with the Dublin Core element set and the revised Access form interface is leading to faster input and fewer errors. In particular, the use of the dropdown menus and the capability to auto-fill certain data elements has obviated some of the more common input errors encountered in phase II.

HURDLES AND SOLUTIONS

While the initial excitement and number of volunteers for the project was encouraging from a management prospective, a few obstacles needed to be overcome in order to seamlessly integrate metadata assignments into the normal workflows of the department.

Time, Productivity, and Perceptions

In spite of the large number of volunteers, it was evident that for phase II to be completed on schedule staff would need to dedicate more time to the project. A volunteer-only system was not producing the desired results. As with most organizations, the staff in the BMS department has a variety of tasks to perform. Adding the metadata creation to that list does not reduce the amount of traditional cataloging the staff is responsible for on a daily basis. Even with all the good intentions of the volunteers to work on the project, individuals felt they did not have the time to dedicate to the metadata entry. Informal discussions among staff members and comments by staff members to supervisors indicated that some believed the traditional cataloging responsibilities were a higher priority than were the new non-MARC metadata assignments. Thus the work was not progressing on the expected schedule.

In an effort to assuage this problem, catalogers and management worked together to improve the plan in action, resulting in better incorporation of metadata into traditional cataloging operations. Current trends in cataloging and libraries were described to staff and the overall goals of the project timeline were reviewed. Position descriptions were reviewed and updated to specify metadata as a regular job responsibility for four of the paraprofessional cataloging technicians. They were then asked to split their cataloging time equally between traditional MARC and non-MARC metadata work. Emphasis was placed on the fact that the expected result of this would be increased output of digital objects and reduced output of physical materials. This is part of the mindset that must change for catalogers to continue to have a functional future (i.e., that traditional cataloging is not necessarily our highest priority any more.) Catalogers may have to be flexible with priorities and reduce productivity in one area in order to increase it in another. Administrators and managers must also support this kind of flexibility.

In addition to the perception that non-MARC functions should take a back seat to MARC cataloging, informal remarks from staff indicated that there was a general feeling of inadequacy in regard to the use of Dublin Core. Some individuals felt that the metadata work was of a lower quality than they normally produced. Catalogers were used to following the AACR2rev. and MARC21 encoding at a much more granular level than was required of Dublin Core and the local application profile for the project. In order to assuage these types of concerns, management must communicate the end goals of the project, the difference between the standards, and why one standard is chosen over another. Professionals who are spearheading these types of projects need to be aware that these perceptions exist and work to help cataloging staff understand that their cataloging and indexing expertise is a valued component to the successful completion of any digitization project. Project managers need to highlight the fact that the schema and encoding schemes used will vary by project and catalogers must expect to be working with multiple options for best practice standards. Perhaps most important, project managers must emphasize that the work that catalogers do is still just as important as ever in providing access to resources.

Teaching New Skills

In addition to time management and clear expectations of productivity, effective training is essential. In completing the NOMAP project, it soon became apparent that the original group training would not be sufficient for complete integration of metadata into traditional workflows. Because of a wide variety in skills, education, and comfort with new technologies among staff, a more individualized approach to training was needed; some staff needed additional review and practice with the metadata while others needed to build general computer skills.

Four key staff members were identified as lead workers based on their advanced cataloging skills. It was thought that a strong understanding of AACR2 and cataloging practice would benefit individuals in learning the differences between traditional cataloging and creating metadata following standards such as Dublin Core. However, the reality was that a strong understanding of AACR2 both helps and hinders the process of transitioning to using multiple standards. It provided a shared context from which to base conversations and training; however, it was difficult for some staff to move from one standard to another. Habits developed over years of cataloging may be difficult to modify. One example involved confusion over the appropriate location for geographic information. Staff wanted to include geographic information in the subject field of a Dublin Core record just as they had traditionally done in the 650 field of a MARC21 record instead of exclusively in the Dublin Core geographic coverage field. A second example involved splitting out information that traditionally would be included in subfields of a single field such as the publisher information found in the 260 field of a bibliographic record encoded in MARC21. Rather than placing the publisher in one field and date information in another field, catalogers included delimiters and subfield codes into metadata fields, which were then not translated correctly by CONTENTdm. It became evident that training needed to provide more emphasis on distinguishing the difference between rules, syntax, and encoding. A better understanding of how these separate concepts work together to create access to a resource made it easier for catalogers to transition from one set of standards to another. Additional conversations with staff during regular cataloging meetings about the theory behind the use of Dublin Core brought to light that, while the concepts were understood, it was more difficult than expected to adapt to new cataloging procedures.

Furthermore, a strong understanding of AACR2 and traditional cataloging protocols did not guarantee comfort with working in a variety of computer interfaces. Computer skills and comfort varied widely, even among the four lead staff members assigned to the project. Review of file structure and naming, sorting principles, and the difference between local versus network drives was necessary for everyone to work effectively. Although the data entry form created by the System Department allowed staff to enter data with limited knowledge of Microsoft Access, some background in database structure and specific training on how to use the form was necessary. Most of this training needed to be done on an individual basis because of the differences in comfort and competence with computer applications among the staff. For some training was as simple as providing a reminder to click the update button so changes and/or additions would be included in the master database, while for others a more in-depth explanation of what a database is and the difference between storing information on their local computer versus a shared server was needed.

CONCLUSIONS

Overall, the outcome of the NOMAP project has been a success. Research materials were digitized and made available to the public. Work has been completed within the established timeline and budget allotted. At the completion of each phase of the project, workflows have been evaluated and redesigned to better integrate metadata creation into the general workflow of traditional cataloging within the department. Lessons have been learned that transcend the specific example of NOMAP and provide a foundation for future digital projects.

While the details of this case study will be of interest to other organizations that are looking for ways to modify existing or create new digital project workflows, lessons learned from this study have implications beyond that of general workflow design. NOMAP significantly impacted managers and staff in the technical services department of UM's Mansfield Library, and changes in philosophies and procedures have evolved in response to those lessons.

NOMAP project managers learned that clear direction to employees (catalogers) as to the goals of the project, time frames, and the mechanics of creating the metadata are essential. Managers must anticipate staff weaknesses and provide training where necessary within the constraints of budgets. The training can be a combination of educational opportunities, including one-on-one instruction, in-house seminars, webinars, or out-of-library short courses. Managers must also consider the necessity to keep moving forward with traditional cataloging and processing. They must determine the optimum balance between working with traditional materials and creating new metadata and clearly transmit their expectations to staff.

The NOMAP project demonstrated that staff members have different levels of comfort and competence with both the cataloging and the computer skills required to incorporate metadata creation into their workflows. An essential component of adding metadata to staff workflows was communicating the expectation that staff understand the changing nature of cataloging work and that they must be flexible and learn both new skills and how to apply existing skills to new situations. The atmosphere in technical services must be such that individual staff members are encouraged to review their own skill sets and communicate to their managers what skill sets need updating through additional training.

As part of the analysis of the skills required for projects such as NOMAP, managers and administrators must review the workflows related to digitization and metadata and assign responsibilities to optimize staff resources. For example, allowing the digitization technician and student employees to focus on technical aspects of creating and managing image files and relying on catalogers to add metadata allowed the library to make best use of the skills and abilities of personnel. From a broader perspective, the result of this analysis may be modification of the skill sets required for new employees. Graphic design, data structure, and experience with relational databases are becoming just as important to potential catalogers as are attention to detail and an understanding of cataloging and indexing.

Perhaps the most important lesson learned is that the incorporation of digital projects into the library's workflow is an evolving process. Minor modifications to the workflow may still be made based on lessons learned with phase III of NOMAP. For example, one recent minor modification to the project workflow is to inform the catalogers by email when a portion of the project has been added to MMP to encourage them to view the final product.

The hope is that seeing the end product will help them better envision what their efforts have produced and perhaps even formulate ideas as to how they might modify workflows to produce a better result.

Continued examination of various workflows and methods of integrating metadata into traditional cataloging departments of all sizes is needed. As libraries begin to transition to a system of linked data and digital collections, new tools are being developed that will assist with the creation, manipulation, and preservation of data. New models of information organization are being scrutinized and catalogers are learning new ways in which to apply their skills. Continued exploration and acceptance of these and other unforeseen changes will ensure a functional future for catalogers in the digital age.

ACKNOWLEDGMENTS

The author would like to express her sincere thanks to Marian Lankston, from the University of Montana, for her valuable suggestions during the writing of an earlier version of this paper. The author is also grateful to the reviewers of the Journal of Library Metadata for their useful comments.

NOTES

1. Natives of Montana Archival Project (NOMAP): http://www.lib.umt.edu/digital/nomap
2. Montana Memory Project, Montana's Digital Library and Archives web site: http://cdm16013.contentdm.oclc.org:80/, UM—Natives of Montana Archival project collection: http://cdm16013.contentdm.oclc.org/cdm/landingpage/collection/p15018coll44
3. The application profile that was created for NOMAP can be downloaded from the project documentation section of the library's digital projects wiki: http://wiki.umt.edu/library_digital/index.php/NOMAPS_Project_Documentation#Metadata_.2F_Data_Directories_.2F_Application_Profiles
4. NOMAP Instructions and Resources wiki: http://wiki.umt.edu/library_digital/index.php/NOMAPS_Instructions_%26_Resources

REFERENCES

Bowen, J. (2010). Moving library metadata toward linked data: Opportunities provided by the eXtensible Catalog. *Proceedings of the 2010 International Conference on Dublin Core and Metadata Applications*, DCMI '10 (pp. 44–59). Retrieved from http://dl.acm.org/citation.cfm?id=1891793.1891799

Chapman, J. W., Reynolds, D., & Shreeves, S. A. (2009). Repository metadata: Approaches and challenges. *Cataloging & Classification Quarterly, 47*, 309–325. doi:10.1080/01639370902735020

Coyle, K. (2010a). Chapter 1: Library data in the web world. *Library Technology Reports, 46*(?), 5–11

Coyle, K. (2010b). Chapter 2: Metadata models of the World Wide Web. *Library Technology Reports, 46*(2), 12–19.

Coyle, K. (2010c). *Understanding the semantic web: Bibliographic data and metadata*. Chicago, IL: ALA TechSource.

Coyle, K. (2010d, April 2). Archive: Directions in metadata webinar. *ALA TechSource*. Retrieved from http://www.alatechsource.org/blog/2010/04/archive-directions-in-metadata-webinar.html

Feltner-Reichert, M., & Veve, M. (2007, June 23). Integrating non-MARC metadata into a traditional technical services department: Perspectives from librarians at the University of Tennessee Libraries. Presented at the ALA Annual, Washington, DC. Retrieved from http://library.wichita.edu/techserv/CatNorms/Integrating_Non-MARC_Metadata.pdf

Hartig, O., Zhao, J., & Mühleisen, H. (2010, May). Automatic integration of metadata into the web of linked data. *Demo presented at SPOT 2010 at the 2nd Workshop on Trust and Privacy on the Social and Semantic Web,* Heraklion, Greece.

Hudgins, J., & Macklin, L. A. (2000). New materials, new processes: Implementing digital imaging projects into existing workflow. *Library Collections, Acquisitions, and Technical Services, 24*(2), 189–204. doi:10.1016/S1464-9055(00)00129-9

Knight, F. T. (n.d.). Break on through to the other side: The library and linked data. *SSRN eLibrary*. Retrieved from http://papers.ssrn.com/sol3/papers.cfm?abstract_id = 1815487

Mansfield Library Collection Development Group. (2011, May). Collection development policy. Retrieved from http://www.lib.umt.edu/files/Mansfield-Library_Collection-Development-Policy-2011–05.pdf

Park, J.-R. (2009). Metadata quality in digital repositories: A survey of the current state of the art. *Cataloging & Classification Quarterly, 47,* 213–228. doi:10.1080/01639370902737240

Park, J.-R., & Tosaka, Y. (2010). Metadata quality control in digital repositories and collections: Criteria, semantics, and mechanisms. *Cataloging & Classification Quarterly, 48,* 696–715. doi:10.1080/01639374.2010.508711

Riemer, J. J. (2010). The expansion of cataloging to cover the digital object landscape. *Cataloging & Classification Quarterly, 48,* 551–560. doi:10.1080/01639374.2010.496309

Southwest Oregon Research Project. (2006). Guide to the Southwest Oregon Research Project (SWORP) Collection 1850–1950. *NWDA.* Retrieved from http://nwda-db.wsulibs.wsu.edu/findaid/ark:/80444/xv14723

Valentino, M. L. (2010). Integrating metadata creation into catalog workflow. *Cataloging & Classification Quarterly, 48,* 541–550. doi:10.1080/01639374.2010.496304

Veve, M., & Feltner-Reichert, M. (2010). Integrating non-MARC metadata duties into the workflow of traditional catalogers: A survey of trends and perceptions among catalogers in four discussion lists. *Technical Services Quarterly, 27*(2), 194–213. doi:10.1080/07317130903585477

Younker, J. T. (2009). *Southwest Oregon Research Project: A model for large scale Native American archival reconnaissance missions.* Washington, DC: Native American Program, National Museum of Natural History Smithsonian Institution.

Zeng, M. L., Needleman, M., Oh, S., Phipps, J., Summers, E., Deridder, J., & Hodge, G. (2010). Linked data—Enabling standards and other approaches. *Proceedings of the American Society for Information Science and Technology, 47*(1), 1–2. doi:10.1002/meet.14504701053

Preliminary Training for RDA: A Survey of Cataloging Department Heads

ELYSSA M. SANNER
Lydia M. Olson Library, Northern Michigan University, Marquette, MI, USA

This study examined the preliminary training that has occurred and will occur in the future, as well as the perceptions of cataloging department heads toward RDA (Resource Description and Access) in American academic libraries. Previous research indicates that the successful adoption of new cataloging rules relies on the strength and elements included in the training offered to and required of individuals in the library cataloging community. This study found that many of the essential components for RDA training have been included in preliminary training. Now that a decision has been made by the Library of Congress, this study identified room for improvement in some areas of RDA training prior to adoption.

INTRODUCTION

Staff training is an oft-discussed topic in today's libraries, especially in academic libraries where change is felt more often and quickly than in other library settings. At its core, training seeks to make employees, a department, or even an entire organization more effective with regard to the task at hand. It is understandable, then, that many different types of training events are offered when change is imminent.

In the past, the introduction of new rules for descriptive cataloging have been met with a flurry of training sessions, including pre-conference events, workshops, in-house training, and courses. The newest version of international cataloging rules, RDA (Resource Description and Access), was released in July 2009 and recently completed a six-month testing period by 3 U.S. national libraries and 26 partner libraries. At the same time librarians in the test site libraries have undergone substantial training for RDA, training events have been offered to other individuals and libraries in preparation for the adoption of the new rules. This study examined the preparation of academic libraries in the United States for the assumed adoption of RDA.

LITERATURE REVIEW

Many books and articles discuss the issue of staff training in libraries. Blanksby (1988) advocates a systematic approach to training, stating that it is the "means of harnessing the individual's inherent curiosity, and their desire and ability to learn with the organisation's need for effective works" (p. 2). Although Blanksby speaks from the perspective of British libraries, she is correct to point out that those being trained must have a desire to learn in order for training to be successful. Therefore, training must simultaneously meet a need in the organization while encouraging the trainee to apply his or her newfound knowledge to the job.

Nearly every training resource details the essential steps taken within the staff training process. Blanksby (1988) enumerates these steps: the identification of needs, establishing the standard of performance required, choosing training methods that satisfy the learning objectives and best serve the trainee, and the evaluation of the training itself. The following describes what is meant by these phrases. The identification of needs is given as a statement of aims and objectives for the training, describing in broad terms what the training intends to cover and what the trainee should know or be able to do when the training has been completed (p. 11). The standard of performance required is simply a list of the tasks the trainee must be competent in or knowledge he or she must have. In choosing training methods that satisfy the learning objectives and the trainee, one must consider the training climate, the existing knowledge and capabilities of the trainee, the retention of information, and any limitations (for example, the location or preferred learning style of the trainer or trainee) that could affect the training design.

The training methods used can be any combination of the following: instruction: demonstrations; lectures; seminars; workshops; discussion groups; forum or panel discussions; courses; conferences; visits; case studies, simulations, and role plays; learning from previous experiences; projects and task forces; texts; manuals; tests; guided reading; check lists; technology-based methods; and structured group learning (Blanksby, 1988, p. 26–29). Evaluating the training method(s) used is critical because it examines the effectiveness of the training and provides information for future training and development needs (p. 35). Taking these steps in planning the training process ensures that the training will be a relevant, effective tool for distributing new knowledge to employees in order to successfully meet the needs of the library and skills of individual jobs.

Wells (1994) continues the discussion of training within the realm of system changes in the collaborative work *Academic Libraries and*

Training. When experiencing a significant change in the workplace, "a comprehensive, well-organized training program helps staff succeed in this rapidly changing environment by reducing the stress associated with ... changes" (p. 72). Wells emphasizes learning from previous experiences, knowing the staff, communicating, structuring training around existing knowledge, offering a variety of training opportunities, providing follow-up opportunities, and evaluating and redesigning training (p. 72–82). Specifically, training should involve staff members at all levels, include "detailed, written descriptions of new ways to accomplish present functions," and allow staff to connect new knowledge to existing skills and responsibilities (p. 78). It is possible to use these elements to provide a training program that best serves the individuals involved and creates assertive staff members capable of coping with change.

The steps in the training process and the planning for training based on system change are both translatable to training for changes to cataloging rules. The library community has already absorbed several transitions in cataloging rules, including the adoption of Anglo-American Cataloguing Rules (AACR) in 1967 and Anglo-American Cataloguing Rules 2 (AACR2) in 1978. The successful adoption of these rules largely lies with the Library of Congress' (LC) implementation of both sets of rules and the subsequent reliance of U.S. libraries on LC for copy cataloging. However, the transition from AACR to AACR2 was not as smooth as the adoption of AACR because many libraries and librarians feared the implementation of AACR2. As Hopkins and Edens (1986) state in *Research Libraries and Their Implementation of AACR2*, three factors were responsible for this fear:

(1) the content of the new code itself
(2) the decision of the Library of Congress to stop the practice of superimposition which it had adopted in 1967 to ease the adoption of AACR
(3) the growth of library participation in shared cataloging networks (p. 1–2)

Most of the research during and after the transition to AACR2 focused on the subject heading changes and the simultaneous transition to online catalogs. For example, Arlene Taylor Dowell's 1981 dissertation explored the impact of the Library of Congress's new policy for subject headings and projected the impact of these changes on cataloging in academic libraries. However, Hitchens and Symons (2009) observe:

> Catalogers ... prepared for AACR2 ... by comparing structure and sequence of operations, highlighting departures from the previous set of rules, and commenting on the use of more cataloger judgment. Some articles consisted of overviews of principles, structural changes, and philosophical changes, while others described planning and implementation at individual libraries. (p. 693)

Each of these elements, in addition to the steps in the training process and planning for training discussed earlier, were essential to the successful adoption of AACR2 and, based on past precedence, are also likely to be essential to the successful adoption of RDA.

Resource Description and Access (RDA), the proposed successor to AACR2, was released first as a full draft in November 2008 and was subsequently published in June 2009 after discussions about the future of AACR2 began in 1997. A recent survey by Sanchez (2011) solicited responses from catalog librarians and sought to "capture feelings toward RDA and AACR2 and its implementation, as well as facts and knowledge levels of respondents" (p. 23). The survey found that respondents were most commonly uncertain (62%) and curious (43%) about RDA, with only 39% self-identifying as possessing average knowledge of RDA, its creation, and why it is a necessary successor to AACR2. Sanchez also included questions regarding training staff members for RDA. Over half of the respondents had five or fewer staff to train. When asked to estimate how many training hours will be necessary for training librarians in RDA, 37% of respondents could not estimate the time necessary, while 23% estimated 30 or more hours. As Sanchez notes,

> This is a significant recognition of the training commitment that will be required for everyone to learn RDA, FRBR, and ILS functionality for the new cataloging code, the new bibliographic universe structure, and the changes they will evoke in integrated library systems (p. 28).

Despite calls from the Library of Congress Working Group on the Future of Bibliographic Control calling for suspension of work on RDA and a Memorandum Against RDA Test calling for re-coding of RDA test records in OCLC as "substandard" (Siemaszkiewicz, 2010), Hillmann (2009) states, "Yes, RDA is going to happen; is indeed happening" (p. 6). In 2010, the 3 national libraries (including Library of Congress) and 26 partner libraries completed a six-month testing period. In June 2011, they announced that they would adopt RDA with certain changes, but not before January 1, 2013 (Library of Congress, 2011, p. 2). In March 2012, LC announced that its "target RDA Implementation Day" would be March 31, 2013, while the other two national and other partner libraries would implement between January and March 2013 (Library of Congress, 2012). Although this date seems distant, training regarding the rules is imperative. Just as certain elements were essential for the comprehension and adoption of AACR2, Hitchens and Symons propose that the same elements will be essential to RDA training—the steps in the training process; planning for and implementing training; comparing the structure and sequence of operations; highlighting departures from the previous set of rules; commenting on the use of more cataloger judgment; overviews of principles, structural changes, and philosophical changes (Hitchens & Symons, 2009, p. 693).

RESEARCH QUESTION

Scholars and librarians have shown that training is essential to the effectiveness of the library as an organization and to the employee's ability to fulfill his or her job description. When new technologies alter how an employee's job is performed, training is necessary to facilitate the library and employee's transition. Little research exists examining the training options offered and used by catalog librarians, especially during times of significant cataloging rule changes.

The impending adoption of the RDA cataloging rules has sent the library cataloging community into a flurry of preparation activities. Training sessions, workshops, and courses are regularly advertised through newsletters, journals, and listservs. As the likely adoption of RDA constitutes the greatest cataloging development to occur since the debut of AACR2 in 1978, it is time to record what is being done to prepare catalog librarians for the rule change and whether those librarians find this training to be useful. At its core, this study sought to determine whether the elements Hitchens and Symons proposed in their 2009 article as being crucial to the successful adoption of RDA are being incorporated into current RDA training practices. Therefore, this study seeks to answer the question: *What training methods are being used to prepare cataloging department heads and cataloging departments in American academic libraries for the adoption of RDA and what are their perceptions of the usefulness of the training they have received?*

This research question includes the following subquestions:

Subquestion 1: What RDA training have cataloging department heads received? What RDA training will cataloging department heads receive in the future?

Subquestion 2: What RDA training have cataloging department heads offered their department staff? What RDA training will cataloging department heads offer in the future?

Subquestion 3: What are the perceptions of cataloging department heads regarding the usefulness and effectiveness of the RDA training they and their departments have received and offered?

METHODOLOGY

This study sought to examine the research question and subquestions by distributing a survey to cataloging department managers in academic libraries. The methodology used an online survey, created through the *Qualtrics* survey software (see Appendix 1 for complete survey). The survey was pilot tested by a select group of cataloging department heads in academic libraries in North Carolina and subsequently edited to include feedback offered by these librarians. Potential subjects were invited to participate in the survey via email. The email invitation included a URL that took participants directly to the survey web site, where they were able to complete and submit the survey.

This study selected its participants from the participating American academic Association of Research Libraries (ARL) because 8 of the 26 participating RDA testing sites libraries are American ARL members and it is assumed that due to their size and commitment to the future of academic libraries, the majority of ARL members will be preparing to some extent for the adoption of RDA. Since the focus of this study is on cataloging department heads in academic libraries, all participating ARL libraries that are Canadian national, U.S. national, or public institutions will be excluded from the selection criteria. This leaves 98 American academic ARL libraries as the population. The web sites of these libraries were examined for the contact information of each institution's cataloging department head.

The survey was divided into three sections: questions regarding training that has occurred, questions regarding training that will occur, and questions regarding individual perceptions and opinions. This arrangement allowed the participant to move logically and fluidly through the survey. A variety of responses were allowed from the survey's thirty-five questions: yes/no questions and questions that required a numeric response permitted only one answer per question; seven questions asked for free response answers; and all other questions asked respondents to choose all the options that applied. The survey was open on the *Qualtrics* web site for two-and-a-half weeks. The original email invitations were sent on Wednesday, February 16, 2011, and the survey closed on Friday, March 4, 2011. During this period, two reminder emails were sent asking cataloging department heads to consider participating and reminding them of the March 4 deadline.

Limitations for this study are primarily tied to the questionnaire format of the survey. While the pilot test determined that the questions were answerable and appropriate to the cataloging community, questionnaires do not have the ability to capture nuances that would have been discoverable through an interview or case study methodology. Sampling bias was introduced by the self-selection of the participants. As the sample population was chosen for its representation of the academic library climate in the United States, this study is partially generalizable to that population despite the small response rate and sampling method.

RESULTS

Responses

Ninety-eight heads of cataloging departments were sent invitations to participate in the survey. From this group, 38 surveys were returned, but only 32 surveys were completed and therefore usable for analysis. The completed survey response rate was 32.65%. The low survey response rate could be explained by the time demands placed on department managers, the continual discussions of RDA, or a number of other factors. As respondents to this study indicated, catalogers have been following the progression of RDA for years and have continuously questioned the standard's impact on their work. Note that each table presented throughout this report displays the visual representation of the results for each answer as percentages of the total number of respondents for each question.

The literature review for this study revealed that training, while always useful on the job, is especially necessary in rapidly changing environments (Wells, 1994, p. 72). A well-designed training program can not only provide employees with the knowledge to adapt to the latest change, but can also equip them to handle future changes in the work environment. As catalogers consider the inevitable adoption of RDA, it is important to know what preparation has already occurred, if any gaps in training can be identified, and what training must occur once the expected decision is made to adopt RDA. This section will discuss the results of the study in light of this information.

Types of RDA Training Sessions

The survey began with questions that focused on the cataloging department head and the RDA training he or she may have received. Sixty percent of respondents have not attended RDA training sessions intended for department heads only. The survey did not ask about training sessions attended that were not for department heads, as the survey was meant to gauge how department heads specifically were preparing for RDA. Of these respondents who indicated that they had attended RDA training sessions, the average number attended ranged from 2 to 20 sessions, with the median sessions attended being 7.5. Respondents received 0 to 50 hours of RDA training for a median of 15 training hours. As is demonstrated by these results, cataloging department heads have begun to train for RDA, but have not spent great amounts of time in training.

Respondents were asked about the types of RDA training sessions they have attended. Table 1 presents their responses. All respondents indicated that they had attended webinars for RDA training, with 86% attending national association workshops or presentations and 43% attending in-house group training sessions.

Overwhelmingly, respondents indicated that they were not required to attend RDA training sessions as a part of their job. However, many cataloging department heads have chosen to attend training sessions for RDA, implying that the time invested in training is currently at the complete discretion of the individual. The self-training methods reported by the respondents also

TABLE 1 Types of RDA Training Sessions Attended by Cataloging Department Heads

Answer	Response	%
Webinar	14	100
National association workshop or presentation	12	86
In-house group training session	6	43
Hands-on training (or practice)	4	29
Web-based course	3	21
One-on-one (or person-to-person)	2	14
Regional association workshop or presentation	2	14
In-house one-on-one	1	7
In-person course (i.e., through a library school)	1	7
International association workshop or presentation	1	7
Vendor workshop	0	0
Other (please explain)	0	0

suggest that many individuals make a conscious choice to invest time in training. Over 35% of respondents read articles and books to educate themselves on RDA, as well as followed listserv conversations, took the RDA test (which occurred August–December 2010), and reviewed presentations that had been posted online. Although cataloging department heads are seeking multiple ways to comprehend and internalize RDA, all of these activities suggest a very individualized approach to RDA training. In fact, only one respondent mentioned discussing RDA developments with colleagues. Also of note is the role that technology, especially online classes such as webinars, played in the results of this study. All of the respondents indicated that they had attended a webinar—which could indicate that convenience is a determining factor in what training is attended, that professional development budgets (at least for related travel) are low, or that the better training sessions are offered through webinars. Such individualized training methods can limit an individual's understanding of the topic at hand. As RDA is based on recently developed concepts such as the entity-relationship model Functional Requirements for Bibliographic Records (FRBR), discussing the many aspects of the new rules in a social setting could prove advantageous for comprehension.

Respondents were also asked about the RDA training he or she anticipated receiving in the future. Respondents indicated that they planned to attend RDA training sessions in the future, the most common types being webinars and national association workshops or presentations, as indicated in Table 2. Eighty-five percent of cataloging department heads will be expected, but not required, to attend RDA training sessions in the future, while 91% (in contrast with the 80% previously reported) of respondents plan to participate in self-training in the future. Figure 1 offers a visual comparison of the types of RDA training sessions attended and likely to be attended by cataloging department heads. These responses indicate that the majority of

TABLE 2 Types of RDA Training Sessions Likely to Attend in the Future

Answer	Response	%
Webinar	24	86
National association workshop or presentation	23	82
Regional association workshop or presentation	17	61
Group training session	12	43
Hands-on training (or practice)	8	29
Web-based course	8	29
Vendor workshop	5	18
International association workshop or presentation	3	11
In-person course (i.e., through a library school)	2	7
One-on-one (or person-to-person)	2	7
One-on-one training session	2	7
Other (please explain)	0	0

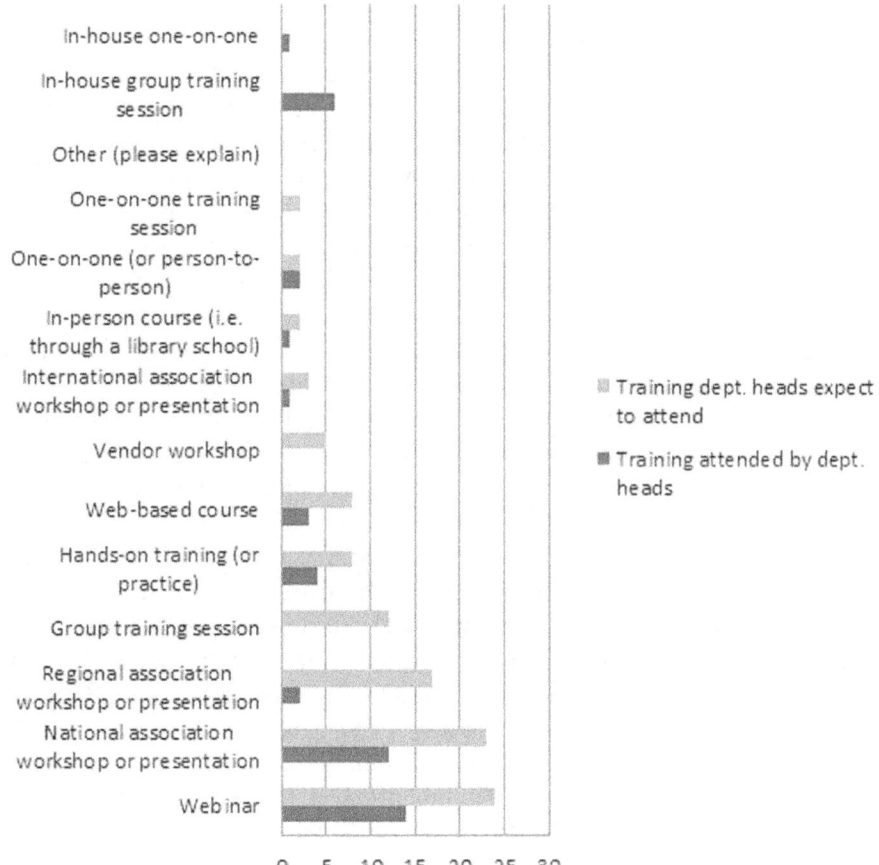

FIGURE 1 Types of RDA training sessions "attended" vs. "likely to be attended" by cataloging department heads.

TABLE 3 Type of RDA Training Sessions Taught by Cataloging Department Heads

Answer	Response	%
In-house group training session	9	90
In-house one-one-one	3	30
National association workshop or presentation	3	30
Hands-on training (or practice)	2	20
One-on-one (or person-to-person)	2	20
Regional association workshop or presentation	2	20
Web-based course	1	10
International association workshop or presentation	1	10
Other (please explain)	1	10
In-person course (i.e., through a library school)	0	0
Vendor workshop	0	0
Webinar	0	0

cataloging department heads anticipate training to become more important in the future, as the expected adoption of RDA becomes a reality.

Cataloging department heads were also asked about the RDA training sessions they have taught or offered to their department staff. The majority of respondents (71%) indicated that they had not taught RDA training sessions. Of the 29% that had taught sessions, the median number of sessions taught was 3. Estimates of sessions taught ranged from 1 to 50, and one participant mentioned having taught 2 in-person sessions but more than 30 online sessions.

The most common type of RDA training session taught by the respondents was in-house group training sessions. As can be seen in Table 3, 90% of the respondents had taught these sessions. Thirty percent of respondents had taught in-house, one-on-one sessions and national association workshops or presentations. No respondents had taught a webinar or vendor workshop.

Of the 74% of respondents who reported that they would teach training sessions in the future, 96% indicated that these training sessions would be held inside their own libraries. The types of training sessions likely to be used are reported in Table 4. In the "other" category, several respondents indicated that, while they would not personally teach training sessions for their staff, as they had prepared for another cataloger or outside instructor to train their staff in RDA. One respondent indicated that they had no idea what their department would "need to do if/when RDA is formally adopted." Again, cataloging department heads responses to RDA training sessions offered in the future indicates forethought toward the eventual adoption of RDA. Figure 2 shows a visual comparison of the types of RDA training sessions taught and the types of sessions likely to be taught in the future by cataloging department heads.

TABLE 4 Types of RDA Training Sessions Likely to be Taught by Cataloging Department Heads in the Future

Answer	Response	%
In-house group training session	21	60
Hands-on training (or practice)	17	49
In-house one-on-one	16	46
One-on-one (or person-to-person)	12	34
Regional association workshop or presentation	7	20
National association workshop or presentation	5	14
None	5	14
Other (please explain)	5	14
International association workshop or presentation	2	6
Web-based course	2	6
Webinar	2	6
In-person course (i.e., through a library school)	1	3
Vendor workshop	0	0

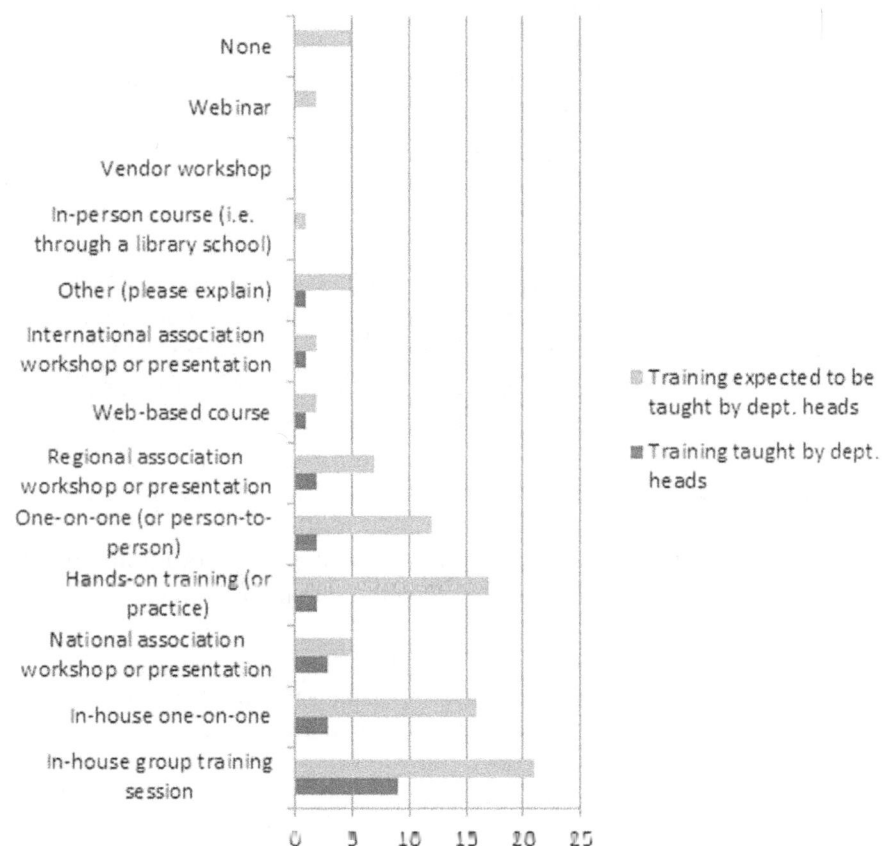

FIGURE 2 Types of RDA training sessions "taught" vs. "likely to be taught" by cataloging department heads.

TABLE 5 Types of RDA Training Sessions Received by Cataloging Departments

Answer	Response	%
Webinar	18	72
In-house group training	16	64
National association workshop or presentation	9	36
Web-based course	8	32
In-house one-on-one	6	24
Hands-on training (or practice)	5	20
One-on-one (or person-to-person)	4	16
Regional association workshop or presentation	4	16
Other (please explain)	2	8
Vendor workshop	1	4
In-person course (i.e., through a library school)	0	0
International association workshop or presentation	0	0

Respondents were also asked about the RDA training that their departments have already received. Almost three-quarters of respondents (71%) indicated that their departments have received informal or formal RDA training. The number of training sessions attended by departmental members ranged from 1 to 100, with one respondent stating, "It's hard to quantify [the number of informal or formal RDA training sessions attended]. Staff have been introduced to the concepts over a period of years; they also have been given the opportunity, but not required, to attend webinars."

As shown in Table 5, the types of training sessions commonly received by departmental members included webinars (18%) and in-house group training sessions (16%). In the "other" category, one respondent also indicated that Library of Congress' "RDA Train-the-Trainer" was used as a training tool for their department, while another mentioned that their in-house training sessions were only introductory explanations of RDA.

Overwhelmingly, 85% of respondents reported that departmental attendance at RDA training sessions has not been required because their respective institutions were waiting on a national decision on RDA implementation from the Library of Congress. As one respondent stated:

> We will make our adoption decision after hearing LC's decision, and at that point, I will begin aggressively pursuing training for myself and my staff. Also, I assume at that point that more training options will be available. I firmly believe that this kind of training needs to be in conjunction with changes in the workflow, not months and months in advance of such changes. I want my staff to go to the training and return to their desks and put it into practice.

Other respondents mentioned that they were staying abreast of developments with RDA and offering webinars and other training methods to staff

TABLE 6 Helpful Types of RDA Training Sessions for Cataloging Department Heads

Answer	Response	%
Webinar	21	75
National association workshop or presentation	13	46
In-house group training	10	36
Hands-on training (or practice)	7	25
Web-based course	6	21
Other (please explain)	5	18
One-on-one (or person-to-person)	4	14
Regional association workshop or presentation	3	11
In-house one-on-one	2	7
In-person course (i.e., through a library school)	1	4
International association workshop or presentation	1	4
Vendor workshop	0	0

members, but were not requiring attendance at training sessions until a formal decision regarding implementation had been reached.

Helpful Types of RDA Training Sessions

Respondents reported on the types of training sessions that were most helpful for their understanding of RDA. As shown in Table 6, the majority of respondents (75%) pointed to webinars as the most successful method of training. In the "other" category, one respondent indicated that they had only attended webinars, which reinforces the earlier observation that perhaps webinars are attended most often because of convenience, cost, preference, or a combination of all three. Reading, keeping up with listservs, and being a national RDA test participant were also listed as advantageous types of training for respondents in the "other" category. One respondent noted, "It [RDA] is such a radical new way of thinking about things that the more you can expose yourself to it over time, the better. Repetition really helps."

Of the training sessions offered to employees, 58% of cataloging department heads responded that webinars were the most helpful type; 46% reported that in-house group training sessions were also helpful, as shown in Table 7. This mirrors the findings of helpful sessions for cataloging department heads, as reported in Table 6. In the "other" category, one respondent noted that his or her department had only received RDA training via webinars thus far, and could not comment on the usefulness of one type of training session over another. Several respondents mentioned that their staff members had not used RDA in cataloging yet, that they were still in training, or that their staff members looked toward the new procedures instead of actually understanding why the procedures changed.

TABLE 7 Helpful Types of RDA Training Sessions for Cataloging Department Staff

Answer	Response	%
Webinar	14	58
In-house group training	11	46
In-house one-on-one	8	33
National association workshop or presentation	5	21
Hands-on training (or practice)	3	13
Web-based course	3	13
One-on-one (or person-to-person)	2	8
Other (please explain)	1	4
Regional association workshop or presentation	1	4
In-person course (i.e., through a library school)	0	0
International association workshop or presentation	0	0
Vendor workshop	0	0

Content Included in RDA Training Sessions

Cataloging department heads were also asked about the content of the RDA training sessions they have attended. As demonstrated in Table 8, all respondents indicated that training sessions included a discussion of the different structure of RDA, departures from previous rules, and FRBR (on which RDA is partially based). Most respondents have also received discussions about principles, structural changes, and philosophical changes as well as planning and implementation at the local level in the RDA training sessions they had attended. In the "other" category, one respondent indicated that he or she had received training in identifying RDA records.

The content included in RDA training sessions taught by cataloging department heads varied slightly from the content included in training sessions the department heads personally attended. As shown in Table 9, the focus in sessions taught was on departures from previous rules (100% of respondents).

TABLE 8 Content Included in RDA Training Sessions

Answer	Response	%
Departures from previous rules	14	100
Different structure of RDA	14	100
FRBR	14	100
Planning and implementation at the local level	13	93
Principles, structural changes, and philosophical changes	13	93
Cataloger's judgment	11	79
ISBD	10	71
MARC21	10	71
FRAD	8	57
Other (please explain)	1	7

TABLE 9 Content Included in RDA Training Sessions Taught by Cataloging Department Heads

Answer	Response	%
Departures from previous rules	14	100
FRBR	9	90
Principles, structural changes, and philosophical changes	9	90
Different structure of RDA	8	80
Cataloger's judgment	5	50
MARC21	4	40
Planning and implementation at the local level	4	40
FRAD	3	30
ISBD	3	30
Other (please explain)	0	0

In keeping with similar questions, Table 10 shows that 100% of respondents reported that the content of the training sessions for cataloging department members discussed departures from previous rules. Every other content category was included less often in training received by department staff than training received by cataloging department heads. Especially noteworthy is that the inclusion of FRBR, the basis of the new cataloging standard, was slightly less present in the training sessions for department staff as reported by cataloging department heads. This is in contrast with the 100% inclusion in sessions attended by cataloging department heads. Perhaps the RDA training offered to department staff members is encouraging attitudes that prefer procedural knowledge rather than the expectation that all individuals involved with the cataloging of library materials be able to comprehend, on some level, the underlying principles of RDA.

TABLE 10 Content Included in RDA Training Sessions Attended by Cataloging Departments

Answer	Response	%
Departures from previous rules	25	100
FRBR	23	92
Principles, structural changes, and philosophical changes	22	88
Different structure of RDA	21	84
Cataloger's judgment	17	68
MARC21	16	64
Planning and implementation at the local level	15	60
ISBD	14	56
FRAD	12	48
Other (please explain)	0	0

TABLE 11 Helpful Content of RDA Training Sessions for Cataloging Department Heads

Answer	Response	%
Departures from previous rules	22	79
FRBR	17	61
Principles, structural changes, and philosophical changes	16	57
Different structure of RDA	12	43
Planning and implementation at the local level	8	29
FRAD	7	25
Cataloger's judgment	6	21
MARC21	5	18
ISBD	4	14
Other (please explain)	2	7

Helpful Content of RDA Training Sessions

Again, the most helpful content of RDA training sessions for cataloging department heads was the inclusion of departures from previous rules, with discussions of FRBR and philosophical changes following as very helpful (see Table 11). In the "other" category, one respondent mentioned that s/he found none of the content to be helpful. The discussion of departures from previous rules is most likely the most discussed and most helpful content of RDA training sessions, because it establishes a point of reference and common ground for the attendees, from whence the discussion of RDA can take off and be understood.

As has been shown to be true earlier in the results, Table 12 shows that 88% of respondents reported on RDA training sessions that discussed departures from previous rules were most helpful for cataloging department employees. Also helpful were the inclusion of discussions of the different structure of RDA (58%); FRBR (58%); principles, structural changes,

TABLE 12 Content Included in RDA Training Sessions Perceived to be Helpful for Cataloging Department Staff Members' Understanding of RDA

Answer	Response	%
Departures from previous rules	21	88
Different structure of RDA	14	58
FRBR	14	58
Principles, structural changes, and philosophical changes	13	54
Cataloger's judgment	10	42
MARC21	5	21
FRAD	4	17
Planning and implementation at the local level	4	17
ISBD	3	13
Other (please explain)	0	0

and philosophical changes (54%); and cataloger's judgment (42%). These responses indicate that while training has had its benefits so far, more training needs to be done to overcome the obstacles preventing true comprehension of RDA and its components. Perhaps the understanding will come with more frequent and more detailed exposure, as it has for some of the cataloging department heads.

Perceptions Regarding RDA Training

To answer the final subquestion of this study, respondents were asked questions regarding their perceptions of the RDA training they and their departments had received so far. Nearly all respondents (93%) indicated that their RDA training has enhanced their understanding of RDA. Many listed additional benefits, such as a raised level of confidence, the ability to understand changes in the code, ability to discern the potential of RDA, gaining a wider-picture view of the code, understanding the reasons for considering a change from AACR2 to RDA, and understanding FRBR. However, 7% of respondents indicated that their RDA training had only somewhat or inadequately enhanced their understanding of RDA. As many respondents noted throughout the survey, RDA is best understood with frequent exposure and practice, and the amount of training that the 7% of respondents received is uncertain.

When asked if their RDA training lacked anything, a bare majority (52%) of cataloging department heads replied that their training was adequate. However, the other 48% of respondents mentioned several elements they had expected to receive: not enough training with RDA Toolkit; local implementation and workflow information; not enough hands-on experience; and RDA's effect on authority work. Others experienced frustration with inadequate regional association training, technological issues with some freely available online training, a local ILS incapable of displaying RDA tags, and a drop in enthusiasm because of the delay in announcing a decision regarding implementation. While these gaps in training and frustrations were small percentage-wise, they are still significant because they represent barriers to understanding RDA that could represent many catalogers' experiences. As the Library of Congress approaches the projected 2013 RDA implementation date, it will be more important than ever to ensure that the cataloging community is sufficiently prepared for cataloging library materials using RDA.

Respondents were also asked about their perceptions about the RDA training their department members had received. Overwhelmingly, 88% of cataloging department heads responded that RDA training has enhanced their employees' understanding of RDA. Eight percent of respondents stated that while their employees gained a better understanding of RDA, they had not yet used RDA in cataloging and could not determine whether their employees understood RDA in practice. Respondents also mentioned specific gains from RDA training, such as confidence, a firmer grasp of vocabulary and advantages, understanding RDA differences, and repeated exposure to FRBR principles increasing understanding of FRBR. One respondent stated that RDA training had not increased employees' understanding of RDA, while another respondent mentioned that her copy catalogers did not want to "'understand' RDA; they just want a list of changes or new procedures to follow."

CONCLUSION

Overall, this study serves only as a baseline for what training for RDA has occurred in academic libraries in the United States through March 2011. It shows that the library cataloging community is following Hitchens and Symons' (2009) recommendations for RDA training to ensure a successful adoption of RDA. The elements of planning for and implementing training; comparing the structure and sequence of operations; highlighting departures from the previous set of rules; commenting on the more frequent use of cataloger judgment; and overviews of principles, structural changes, and philosophical changes (Hitchens & Symons, 2009, p. 693) have all been included in the reported RDA training sessions, with a specific emphasis on departures from previous rules. These are all positive indications that a functional future, where catalogers and cataloging department staff are able to create library metadata that fulfills its role in connecting people to resources, is attainable. However, there are some gaps that should be addressed through training before RDA is adopted.

It is likely that most individuals in the cataloging community, whether librarians or paraprofessionals, are at least vaguely aware of RDA and its development. However, as the national libraries intend to fully adopt RDA between January and March 2013 (Library of Congress, 2012), the cataloging community cannot remain ignorant and must begin learning about RDA in order to avoid being left behind. Several respondents indicated that some professional librarians in their departments have chosen to remain uninformed about RDA until forced. While it may not make sense to require attendance at RDA training sessions until a specific adoption date is certain, it is not healthy for members to ignore developments in the community. Such individuals may, in fact, be holding their institutions and larger communities back from fully realizing the potential that RDA training has to aid the successful adoption of RDA in the future.

A second gap exists due to the differences in content in RDA training between cataloging department heads and their department staff members.

One respondent commented that her copy catalogers simply wanted to learn the new procedures to follow instead of understanding why the changes had been made. While this observation may be indicative of other institutions, the reported training content for department staff shows that every element is covered less in department staff training than cataloging department head training, except for the departures from previous rules. Although some department staff members are often responsible for the day-to-day activities involved in cataloging library materials and may be affected more by departures from previous rules, the relational model behind RDA makes the code significantly different from AACR2, and more attention must be given to the philosophical changes in future training than has been provided thus far. By including discussions of FRBR, FRAD, MARC21, and ISBD, these staff members might be able to better understand the reasons behind the change in rules, and not just the differences between the two sets of rules.

This study leaves room for future research into training for RDA and future cataloging codes. First, given the high usage of webinars for RDA training, further research could focus on the successfulness of this specific format. What attracts catalogers to this format? Is it better than other formats used for RDA training? If webinars continue to be heavily used in the future, what can be done to enhance their success? Secondly, the range of libraries surveyed in regard to RDA training should be expanded to include non-ARL libraries. Do any differences exist between the institutions? Can training methods or programs used at ARL libraries be used in smaller libraries or libraries with fewer financial resources? Thirdly, as one respondent mentioned, cataloging department heads are not always the individuals that provide training at their institutions. This survey could be expanded to include training librarians to gain a better perspective of department staff members' understanding of RDA. Lastly, surveying cataloging department heads again several months before an official RDA adoption date and six months after adoption would provide a broader picture of the actual effects and success of RDA training on implementation.

This study primarily exists as a snapshot of the cataloging community as it stands on the precipice of the adoption of the first new cataloging code in more than three decades. The cataloging community has been presented with an opportunity to shift from an admittedly outdated and inadequate model into a functional future. The new model, RDA, brings a mental shift that claims to match the dramatic explosion in information and subsequent shift in information organization since the prevalence of the Internet. As catalogers and cataloging department staff prepare for the adoption of RDA, the goal of a functional future should remain at the forefront of RDA training activities. This study provides insight into what RDA training is currently offered, leaves suggestions for changes to this training before the impending RDA adoption, and offers paths for future research.

REFERENCES

Blanksby, M. (1988). *Staff training: A librarian's handbook*. Newcastle-under-Lyme, UK: AAL Publishing.

Dowell, A. T. (1981). *A five-year project of the impact of the rules for form of heading in the Anglo-American Cataloguing Rules, second edition, upon selected academic library catalogs*. Retrieved from ProQuest Dissertations & Theses. (Document ID 303178103)

Hillmann, D. (2009). Getting there. *Technicalities*, 29(1), 6–9.

Hitchens, A., & Symons, E. (2009). Preparing catalogers for RDA training. *Cataloging & Classification Quarterly*, 47(8), 691–707.

Hopkins, J., & Edens, J. A. (1986). *Research libraries and their implementation of AACR2*. Greenwich, CT: JAI Press.

Library of Congress. (2011, June 13). Response of the Library of Congress, the National Agricultural Library, and the National Library of Medicine to the U.S. RDA Test Coordinating Committee. Retrieved from http://www.loc.gov/bibliographic-future/rda/source/rda-execstatement 13june11.pdf

Library of Congress. (2012, March 2). *Library of Congress announces its long-range RDA training plan*. Retrieved from http://www.loc.gov/catdir/cpso/news_rda_implementation_date.html

Sanchez, E. R. (2011). RDA, AACR2, and You: What Catalogers Are Thinking. In E. R. Sanchez (Ed.), *Conversations with catalogers in the 21st century* (p. 20–70). Santa Barbara, CA: Libraries Unlimited.

Siemaszkiewicz, W. (2010, November 2). November 2010 Memorandum Against RDA Test [Electronic mailing list message]. Retrieved from http://cdn.dltj.org/wp-content/uploads/2010/11/oclc-cat-rda.txt.gzip

Wells, M. R. (1994). Training library staff for system changes. In M. P. Glogowski (Ed.), *Academic libraries and training* (pp. 71–83). Greenwich, CT: JAI.

APPENDIX 1: SURVEY

(This survey was administered in an online format via Qualtrics. This document only serves as a representation of the online survey.)

This first page serves as the informed consent fact sheet.

University of North Carolina-Chapel Hill
Information about a Research Study

IRB Study # 11-0198   Consent Form Version Date: February 2011

Title of Study: Training for RDA: A Survey of Cataloging Department Heads

Principal Investigator: Elyssa Sanner
UNC-Chapel Hill Department: School of Information and Library Science
Faculty Advisor: Dr. Barbara Moran

Study Contact telephone number: 706-831-8001
Study Contact email: esanner@email.unc.edu

What are some general things you should know about research studies?
You are being asked to take part in a research study. To join the study is voluntary. You may refuse to join, or you may withdraw your consent to be in the study, for any reason, without penalty.

Research studies are designed to obtain new knowledge. This new information may help people in the future. You may not receive any direct benefit from being in the research study. There also may be risks to being in research studies.

Details about this study are discussed below. It is important that you understand this information so that you can make an informed choice about being in this research study. You should ask the researcher named above any questions you have about this study at any time.

What is the purpose of this study?
The purpose of this research study is to determine what training has been obtained and offered or will be obtained and offered by cataloging department heads in American academic libraries for the imminent adoption of the new cataloging rules, RDA (Resource Description and Access), and what training methods have proved most helpful to learning these new rules. The survey will ask you about your experience with RDA training and your opinions on the most effective training you have received.

How many people will take part in this study?
If you decide to be in this study, you will be one of approximately 100 to 150 librarians in this research study.

How long will your part in this study last?
Your participation in this study consists of filling out the survey questionnaire. You can expect to spend a total of 15 to 20 minutes completing the entire survey. Once you have completed the survey, your part of the study is complete.

What will happen if you take part in the study?
If you take part in this study, you will answer a questionnaire containing the types of questions described in the study purpose section above. You may skip any question you do not have an answer for or do not wish to answer. Your responses will be saved as you complete each page of the survey, but your responses will only be used if you complete the entire survey. The survey software will alert you when you have reached the end of the survey. Your participation will be complete at that time.

What are the possible benefits from being in this study?
Research is designed to benefit society by gaining new knowledge. You may also expect to benefit by participating in this study by receiving a copy of the study's final report, which will give you an indication of the RDA training that has occurred throughout the academic library community and what your peers consider to be the most effective training.

What are the possible risks or discomforts involved from being in this study?
We do not think you will experience any discomfort or risk from participating in the survey. If you do feel discomfort or risk from any of the survey questions, you are free to skip those questions or discontinue your participation in the survey. Every effort will be made to keep your responses confidential, as described in the next section. However, there is always a negligible risk that information sent over the Internet could be intercepted or information stored on a computer could be accessed by an unauthorized person, despite the researcher's best efforts to prevent such an occurrence and the great unlikelihood of such an occurrence. There may be uncommon or previously unknown risks. You should report any problems to the researcher.

How will your privacy be protected?
The only people who will have access to the answers you provide in the survey are you, through the link provided in this email and while the survey is in progress, and the principal investigator. While the survey is in progress, your answers will be stored on a secure server belonging to the Odum Institute for Research in Social Science at UNC. Only the principal investigator will have access to your answers at this time, through a password protected web account. Once the survey period has ended, the principal investigator will download all survey data to her laptop computer and remove all individual identifiers from the data set that linked you to your answers.

Participants will not be identified individually in any report or publication about this study.

Will you receive anything for being in this study?
You will receive a copy of the study's final report by email for participating in this study, so that you may know the results of this research.

Will it cost you anything to be in this study?
There are no costs for being in the study.

What if you are a UNC employee?
Taking part in this research is not a part of your University duties, and refusing will not affect your job. You will not be offered or receive any special job-related consideration if you take part in this research.

What if you have questions about this study?
You have the right to ask, and have answered, any questions you may have about this research. If you have questions, or concerns, you should contact the researcher listed above.

What if you have questions about your rights as a research participant?
All research on human volunteers is reviewed by a committee that works to protect your rights and welfare. If you have questions or concerns about your rights as a research subject you may contact, anonymously if you wish, the Institutional Review Board at 919-966-3113 or by email at IRB_subjects@unc.edu.

Thank you for helping me with this study.

The following is the body of the survey:

I. This section contains eight questions pertaining to RDA training sessions you (as a department head) have attended.

1. Have you attended any training sessions for RDA specifically for department heads?
   ___ Yes
   ___ No

   (If yes, go to Question #2. If no, go to Question #7.)

2. How many training sessions for RDA have you attended? (Please enter only numeric values.)
3. How many hours of RDA training have you received? (Please enter only numeric values.)
4. What kinds of training sessions for RDA have you attended? (Please check all that apply.)
   ___ One-on-one (or person-to-person)
   ___ Web-based course
   ___ Webinar
   ___ Hands-on training (or practice)
   ___ In-person course (i.e. through a library school)
   ___ In-house group training session
   ___ In-house one-on-one
   ___ Vendor workshop
   ___ International association workshop or presentation
   ___ National association workshop or presentation
   ___ Regional association workshop or presentation
   ___ Other (please explain) _____

5. Have the RDA training sessions you've attended discussed: (Please check all that apply.)
   ___ Different structure of RDA
   ___ Departures from previous rules
   ___ Cataloger's judgment
   ___ Principles, structural changes, and philosophical changes
   ___ FRBR
   ___ FRAD
   ___ MARC21
   ___ ISBD
   ___ Planning and implementation at the local level
   ___ Other (please explain)

6. Were you required to attend training sessions for RDA as a part of your job?
   ___ Yes
   ___ No

7. Have you participated in any self-training for RDA?
   ___ Yes
   ___ No

8. What specific self-training methods did you participate in? Please explain.

II. This section contains seven questions pertaining to RDA training sessions that you (as a department head) have taught.

9. As a department head, have you taught any formal or informal training sessions for RDA?
   ___ Yes
   ___ No

   (If yes, go to Question #10. If no, go to Question #13.)

10. How many formal or informal training sessions for RDA have you taught? (Please enter only numeric values.)

11. What kinds of formal or informal training sessions for RDA have you taught? (Please check all that apply.)
    ___ One-on-one (or person-to-person)
    ___ Web-based course
    ___ Webinar
    ___ Hands-on training (or practice)
    ___ In-person course (i.e. through a library school)

___ In-house group training session
___ In-house one-on-one
___ Vendor workshop
___ International association workshop or presentation
___ National association workshop or presentation
___ Regional association workshop or presentation
___ Other (please explain) _____

12. Have the RDA training sessions you've taught discussed: (Please check all that apply.)
    ___ Different structure of RDA
    ___ Departures from previous rules
    ___ Cataloger's judgment
    ___ Principles, structural changes, and philosophical changes
    ___ FRBR
    ___ FRAD
    ___ MARC21
    ___ ISBD
    ___ Planning and implementation at the local level
    ___ Other (please explain)

13. Were you required to teach any training sessions for RDA as a part of your job?
    ___ Yes
    ___ No

(If yes, go to Question #14. If no, go to Question #15.)

14. Has your RDA training prepared you to train members of your department? Please explain.

15. What kinds of formal or informal training sessions for RDA will you likely teach in the future? (Please check all that apply.)
    ___ None
    ___ One-on-one (or person-to-person)
    ___ Web-based course
    ___ Webinar
    ___ Hands-on training (or practice)
    ___ In-person course (i.e. through a library school)
    ___ In-house group training session
    ___ In-house one-on-one
    ___ Vendor workshop
    ___ International association workshop or presentation
    ___ National association workshop or presentation

___ Regional association workshop or presentation
___ Other (please explain) _____

III. This section contains six questions pertaining to the RDA training that your department has received.

16. Has your department received any formal or informal RDA training?
    ___ Yes
    ___ No

(If yes, go to Question #17. If no, go to Question #20.)

17. How many formal or informal training sessions for RDA has your department received? (Please enter only numeric values.)

18. What kinds of formal or informal training sessions for RDA has your department received? (Please check all that apply.)
    ___ One-on-one (or person-to-person)
    ___ Web-based course
    ___ Webinar
    ___ Hands-on training (or practice)
    ___ In-person course (i.e. through a library school)
    ___ In-house group training session
    ___ In-house one-on-one
    ___ Vendor workshop
    ___ International association workshop or presentation
    ___ National association workshop or presentation
    ___ Regional association workshop or presentation
    ___ Other (please explain) _____

19. Have the RDA training sessions your department has received discussed: (Please check all that apply.)
    ___ Different structure of RDA
    ___ Departures from previous rules
    ___ Cataloger's judgment
    ___ Principles, structural changes, and philosophical changes
    ___ FRBR
    ___ FRAD
    ___ MARC21
    ___ ISBD
    ___ Planning and implementation at the local level
    ___ Other (please explain)

20. Was your department required to attend formal or informal training sessions for RDA as part of their job duties?
   ___ Yes
   ___ No

21. If your department was not required to attend formal or informal training sessions for RDA, why not? (Please explain.)

IV. This section contains six questions pertaining to RDA training that you (as a department head) or your department will attend in the future.

22. Do you plan to attend any training sessions for RDA outside your library in the future? (Do not include sessions that you have already attended in answering this question.)
   ___ Yes
   ___ No

   (If yes, go to Question #23. If no, go to Question #25.)

23. What kinds of training sessions for RDA are you likely to attend? (Please check all that apply.)
   ___ One-on-one (or person-to-person)
   ___ Web-based course
   ___ Webinar
   ___ Hands-on training (or practice)
   ___ In-person course (through a library school)
   ___ In-house group training session
   ___ In-house one-on-one
   ___ Vendor workshop
   ___ International association workshop or presentation
   ___ National association workshop or presentation
   ___ Regional association workshop or presentation
   ___ Other (please explain) _____

24. Will you be expected to attend training sessions for RDA as a part of your job?
   ___ Yes
   ___ No

25. Will you participate in any self-training for RDA in the future?
   ___ Yes
   ___ No

26. Will you teach any formal or informal training sessions for RDA in the future? (Do not include sessions that you have already taught in answering this question.)
    ___ Yes
    ___ No

(If yes, go to Question #27. If no, go to Question #28.)

27. If yes, where will these training sessions be held? (Please check all that apply.)
    ___ Inside your library
    ___ Outside your library

(If you or your employees have not received training for RDA, you have completed your part of the survey. Thank you for your participation.)

V. *This section contains seven questions pertaining to the understanding of RDA that you and your department have received as a result of RDA training.*

28. Has your RDA training enhanced your understanding of RDA? Please explain.

29. Did your RDA training lack something that you were expecting to receive Please explain.

30. What kinds of training sessions for RDA have been most helpful for your understanding of RDA? (Please check all that apply.)
    ___ One-on-one (or person-to-person)
    ___ Web-based course
    ___ Webinar
    ___ Hands-on training (or practice)
    ___ In-person course (through a library school)
    ___ In-house group training session
    ___ In-house one-on-one
    ___ Vendor workshop
    ___ International association workshop or presentation
    ___ National association workshop or presentation
    ___ Regional association workshop or presentation
    ___ Other (please explain) _____

31. What aspects covered in the RDA training sessions you've attended have been most helpful for your understanding of RDA? (Please check all that apply.)
    ___ Different structure of RDA
    ___ Departures from previous rules

___ Cataloger's judgment
___ Principles, structural changes, and philosophical changes
___ FRBR
___ FRAD
___ MARC21
___ ISBD
___ Planning and implementation at the local level
___ Other (please explain)

32. Do you feel that your employees understand RDA better as a result of the training sessions they have attended? (This includes training when you have been the teacher.) Please explain.

33. What kinds of training sessions for RDA have been most helpful for your employees' understanding of RDA? (Please check all that apply.)
   ___ One-on-one (or person-to-person)
   ___ Web-based course
   ___ Webinar
   ___ Hands-on training (or practice)
   ___ In-person course (through a library school)
   ___ In-house group training session
   ___ In-house one-on-one
   ___ Vendor workshop
   ___ International association workshop or presentation
   ___ National association workshop or presentation
   ___ Regional association workshop or presentation
   ___ Other (please explain) _____

34. What aspects of the RDA training sessions your department has attended have proven most helpful for your employees' understanding of RDA? (Please check all that apply.)
   ___ Different structure of RDA
   ___ Departures from previous rules
   ___ Cataloger's judgment
   ___ Principles, structural changes, and philosophical changes
   ___ FRBR
   ___ FRAD
   ___ MARC21
   ___ ISBD
   ___ Planning and implementation at the local level
   ___ Other (please explain)

35. Is there anything else regarding RDA training that I have not asked?

Thank you for your participation! It is greatly appreciated. A final report will be ready in April 2011.

"Mind the [Trans-Atlantic] Gap, Please": Awareness and Training Needs of UK Catalogers

ANNE WELSH
Department of Information Studies, University College London, London, UK

CELINE CARTY
Cambridge University Library, Cambridge University, Cambridge, UK

HELEN WILLIAMS
LES Library Services, The London School of Economics and Political Science, London, UK

Methodology: Action research. Analysis of emails sent to an e-forum on RDA in the UK in April 2011. Emails were assigned tags based on contents. Email addresses were analyzed for sector. The resource list co-created by participants was analyzed for format and country of creator(s). Findings: More than 200 people subscribed and received 195 emails sent by 38 individuals about current actions; training; training needs; the hybrid catalog and cataloger judgment; implementation; productivity; the RDA Toolkit; MARC and FRBR. Topical concerns were found to be the same as for U.S. RDA testers, although accompanied by "vague concerns" about whether they were acting quickly enough.

INTRODUCTION

This article considers the UK cataloguing community's awareness of the new international cataloging code, *Resource Description and Access* (RDA) (Joint Steering Committee for the Development of RDA, 2010a) and the training needs concerning it expressed in an online discussion forum held in April 2011 (CILIP Cataloguing and Indexing Group, 2011c). It provides a discussion of RDA's importance within the future of bibliographic control, an overview of the current state of training and awareness of RDA, and a list of key topics identified in the Chartered Institute of Library and Information Professionals (CILIP) Cataloguing and Indexing Group (CIG) E-Forum on RDA, held on April 18 and 19, 2011.

RDA AND THE FUTURE OF BIBLIOGRAPHIC CONTROL

As the Library of Congress Working Group on the Future of Bibliographic Control pointed out in its report *On the Record* (2008), the library catalog is now only one route that users take to access data. The standards for library cataloging, currently the *Anglo-American Cataloguing Rules,* 2nd ed. (AACR2) (Joint Steering Committee for Revision of AACR2, 2005), and soon to be RDA, coexist alongside a range of other metadata standards:

> Today's metadata environment comprehends AACR2/RDA, MARC 21, MARC XML, the Metadata Object Description Schema (MODS), Dublin Core, and the Online Information Exchange format (ONIX), amongst others, while the retrieval protocol environment encompasses Z39.50, the Search and Retrieve services (SRW/U), the Metasearch XML Gateway (MXG), and the need to work with OpenSearch and other protocols. (Library of Congress Working Group on the Future of Bibliographic Control, 2008, p. 26)

AACR2 draws on a tradition of bibliographic control with roots in the work of Panizzi at the British Museum (1841), Cutter's *Rules for a Printed Dictionary Catalogue* (1876) and trans-Atlantic initiatives from the dawn of the 20th century, beginning with *Rules: Author and Title Entries* (Library Association and American Library Association, 1908; American Library Association and Library Association, 1908). It is often claimed to be "the most widely-used standard for descriptive cataloguing in the Englishspeaking [sic] world" (Kiorgaard & Kartus, 2009), although recent surveys focus on the use of MARC, the exchange format most commonly associated with AACR2, not on AACR2 itself, and so a level of inference is involved in these claims.

Ma's survey of Association of College and Research Libraries (ACRL) conducted in 2007 and reported in 2009 found that of the 68 libraries (55%) that responded, 61 (91%) were using MARC, followed by 56 (84%) using Encoded Archival Description (EAD). Other popular schema included Dublin Core (52 respondents, or 78%) and Qualified Dublin Core (45 respondents, or 67%), with other schema in use by less than 50% of the respondents including TEI, MODS, and VRA Core Categories (Ma, 2009, p. 5).

In the United Kingdom, a survey conducted by CILIP Cataloguing and Indexing Group (CIG) in 2010 found that 54 (90%) of the 60 respondents to the same question were using MARC21, with a further 9 respondents (15%)

using UKMARC and 1 respondent (1.7%) using UNIMARC. Dublin Core was used by 6 respondents (10%) with all other schema used by less than 10% (Danskin, 2010).

The usage reported in these surveys indicates that MARC cannot be ignored in a discussion of the future of bibliographic control, and since MARC21 as a communication format draws heavily on AACR2 for its content designation (Library of Congress Network Development and MARC Standards Office, 2006), we might infer that AACR2's successor, RDA, will be a major preoccupation for bibliographic control within the Anglophone library community.

The response to trainings offered by CILIP and CIG in 2010 and 2011 certainly indicates a high level of interest within the UK cataloging community and strategic managers.

RDA IN THE UK: TRAINING AND AWARENESS

The latest survey by CILIP CIG (Danskin, 2010) received responses from 78 members of the UK cataloging community. In the same year, there were 1,378 members of CIG (CILIP CIG, 2011b). The survey was open to members and nonmembers, and we do not know how many nonmembers were among the 78 respondents. Nor do we know how large a proportion of the entire UK cataloging community is represented in the 1,378 members. Any calculation of the representativeness of the survey can only be generally indicative, but with caution we can state that the 78 respondents equates to (but does not equal) just over 5% of CIG members (CILIP Cataloguing and Indexing Group, 2011b).

Many of the questions in the CIG survey were optional and so not all questions were answered by all respondents. Of the 66 who answered on their awareness of RDA, 39 (59%) had heard of it, but only 15 (23%) felt they understood it, and 9 (15%) said they would be confident to explain it. At the opposite end of the spectrum, 3 (less than 1%) respondents checked the box for "What is it?" in the survey.

Perhaps this last figure is less surprising than it first seems when we consider that of approximately 150 presentations about RDA listed on the web pages of the Joint Steering Committee, only 13 have occurred in the United Kingdom (Joint Steering Committee for the Development of RDA, 2010b, last checked 21 December 2011).

It is important to acknowledge that the availability of online courses and documentation make it increasingly possible for UK catalogers to follow developments in the United States: A series of webinars on RDA offered by the Association for Library Collections and Technical Services (ALCTS) were specifically recommended by two e-forum participants. The CIG e-forum itself was modeled on the ALCTS e-forum format.

It is equally important to remember that the links between UK catalogers and colleagues in the United States are largely informal: At the last survey of international members of the American Library Association available on the ALA web site, it was found that

> International members constitute nearly 3.5% of ALA membership. There are ALA members in 80 countries, though close to half of the non-U.S. members are in Canada (American Library Association, 2006).

Similarly, although the U.S. RDA Test Committee accepted test data from "informal testers" no matter their country of origin, application to become a formal test institution was not open to UK cataloging institutions. This is natural—the tests were convened by the U.S. National Libraries and aimed to provide information about the impact of RDA in the United States. There was not a similar national initiative in the United Kingdom.

The United Kingdom's own library association, CILIP, has so far reached the largest audience through its Executive Briefings on RDA. When the first of these was announced in 2010, it sold out in under a week—before it was even advertised in *Library + Information Gazette*, at that time the main published publicity organ for CILIP members (Welsh, 2010). In publicizing the 2011 briefing (RDA11), CILIP Events stated "Last year's two RDA briefings sold out with almost 180 attendees and were rated 93% Good to Excellent" (CILIP Events, 2011). The speed with which the events sold out could be said to reflect the eagerness of senior library staff to understand the potential impact of the new cataloging code on their institutions.

The 2010 briefing introduced attendees to RDA and addressed both transitional and future issues, as well as providing a live demonstration of the RDA Toolkit for the first time in the United Kingdom. Presentations included perspectives from the British Library; a library supplier; an experienced bibliographic services manager (based on the last comparably-sized transition, from UKMARC to MARC21); and three iSchool academics, Shawne Miksa, Anne Welsh and Keith Trickey (Taylor & Williams, 2010).

In 2011 Beacher Wiggins (Library of Congress and RDA Committee of Principals) travelled to the United Kingdom twice in the space of a month to address the UK cataloguing community on the progress of the U.S. National tests on RDA at CILIP's executive briefing. The agenda also included an overview of the British Library's preparation for RDA, two UK case studies of university libraries preparing for implementation and a supplier perspective on the transition to RDA (CILIP Events, 2011). CILIP has not publicly announced attendance figures for the two events, but they were high enough for another Executive Briefing on RDA to be planned for 2012 (Russell, 2011, December 14).

In addition to the Executive Briefings, CILIP organized two training courses, "Moving on in MARC21: Potential impact of RDA" (CILIP Training & Development, 2010) and "Getting started with RDA" (CILIP Training &

Development, 2011). Both were facilitated by well-known academic and trainer Keith Trickey and included practical cataloging work using the RDA Toolkit.

Courses such as these are an excellent resource, but are necessarily limited to those who have an employer willing to invest in RDA training or who can afford to attend themselves. As a benchmark on cost, the 2011 course was priced at £200 + VAT for CILIP members and £275 + VAT for nonmembers. In comparison, the last Cataloguing and Indexing Group event for which there were charges was priced at £75 for members and £85 for nonmembers (CILIP Cataloguing and Indexing Group, 2011d).

The Cataloguing and Indexing Group has always been active in educating members of the profession and keeping them up-to-date with developments in standards. Members of the CIG Committee sit on committees for standards bodies including the CILIP/BL Committee on RDA, and as well as organizing specific training sessions on topics of current interest, each year CIG holds its Standards Forum, which fulfills one of its stated objectives, "to disseminate information on current innovations, standards and practice within the Group's fields of interest." (CILIP Cataloguing and Indexing Group, 2011a).

Following the style of Association for Library Collections and Technical Services (ACLTS) forums in the United States, CIG held an e-forum on RDA specifically focused on the UK perspective. The current article provides an analysis of the discussion that took place during the forum's two days of email conversation between participants.

ANALYSIS OF EMAILS FROM THE CIG E-FORUM ON RDA 2011

Methodology

A spreadsheet was created and the 195 emails from the CIG E-Forum were entered into it. Basic analysis of the number of participants who contributed to the forum and the sectors in which they work was carried out. The emails' contents were analyzed and tagged using informal headings suggested by the body of each email (Table 1). Up to five topics were observed in each, with most emails displaying three or fewer topics. Most emails (53, or 27%) were concerned with training, although 20 emails (10%) shared current practice, and several participants took the opportunity to ask questions about RDA and its implementation (16 emails, or 8%), sometimes apologizing for their lack of knowledge about the new standard (3 emails, or 2%).

Overview

More than 200 people subscribed to the e-forum (Carty & Williams, 2011). Of these, 38 contributed at least one email to the forum. If we took the number of subscribers to be exactly 200, 38 would be 19% total subscribers.

TABLE 1 Email topic categories

Topic Categories	# Emails ($n = 195$)
Training	53 (27%)
Resources	24 (12%)
Hybrid catalog	21 (11%)
RDA Toolkit	21 (11%)
Current actions and sharing	20 (10%)
US RDA Tests	17 (9%)
RDA11	14 (7%)
Implementation	9 (5%)
MARC	8 (4%)
FRBR	8 (4%)
Rule changes	7 (4%)
Print RDA	7 (4%)
Productivity	6 (3%)
Cataloger judgment	5 (3%)
Authority records	4 (2%)
RDA10	1 (under 1%)

This represents a higher proportion than the general 1% rule of participation inequality, which states that 1% of participants in online discussions contribute the majority of the content, with a further 9% contributing intermittently and 90% reading or observing but without contributing (Nielsen, 2006). As Wu has pointed out, figures in support of the 1% rule are averaged out over a large number of statistics from a wide range of online communities (Wu, 2010).

In analyzing the opinions of this self-selecting group, we must remember that the majority of subscribers to the forum remained silent and did not choose to share opinions or ask questions. However, the emails sent by active participants can be seen to be representative of the UK cataloging community. A total of 38 people is also just under half the number that Danskin reported had answered one or more of the questions in the 2010 *RDA in the UK* survey, although we have no way of ascertaining whether all 38 active participants in the forum also took part in that survey.

However, if we consider that there were 1,378 members of CIG at the last count (CILIP Cataloguing and Indexing Group, 2011b) we can see that 38 equates to just under 3% of this figure and if we take there to be 200 people subscribed to the forum and receiving emails from it, that figure would equate to just over 14%. Observations made based on the emails in the e-forum are, therefore, no more than indicative of the opinions of the UK cataloguing community as a whole. On the other hand, we may assume that since the e-forum was free and not exclusive to CIG members, the self-selecting group who took part represents those members of the UK cataloguing community who were actively interested in RDA in April 2011.

As shown in Table 2, an overwhelming majority of active participants work in the academic sector: 27 participants (69%) had ".ac.uk" email

TABLE 2 Active participants

Participants	# (%)
Academic library	27 (69%)
Public library	3 (8%)
iSchool (academics)	3 (8%)
National library	2 (5%)
Vendor (LMS)	1 (2%)
Vendor (Records)	1 (2%)
Third sector	1 (2%)
Independent	1 (2%)

addresses but were not library academics. Academics in fact formed the second largest cohort—three participants (8%), jointly with three (8%) public library staff. Two participants (5%) worked in national libraries, while one participant (2%) belonged to each of the following sectors: vendor of cataloguing records; vendor of library management systems; the third sector (charities and voluntary organizations); and independent scholar.

Again, as seen in Table 3, the academic sector accounted for the majority of individual emails—133 emails (69%) were sent by academic librarians. Library academics sent 17 emails (9%), closely followed by 15 emails (8%) sent by public librarians. National library staff sent 7 emails (4%), while the participant from the vendor of cataloguing records sent 6 emails (3%). The LMS vendor sent 3 emails (2%) while the third sector employee sent only 1 email (rounded down to 0%). Meanwhile, the independent scholar contributed 11 emails, which was statistically high at 6%—only six emails fewer than the combined total of emails sent by library academics employed by iSchools.

In terms of individual contributions, it is unsurprising that the forum moderators, Carty and Williams, sent more emails than anyone else: 33 (17%) and 31 (16%), respectively. These emails incorporated "administrative" emails (introducing the forum, summarizing each day's activities and moving general discussion from one topic to another) and more substantive messages, describing the state of play in their home institutions—both large

TABLE 3 Participant emails

Participants	# (%) Emails
Academic librarians	133 (69%)
iSchool (academics)	17 (9%)
Public librarian	15 (8%)
Independent	11 (6%)
National library staff	7 (4%)
Vendor (Records)	6 (3%)
Vendor (LMS)	3 (2%)
Third sector	1 (0%)

academic libraries with strong research reputations. It is worth noting that at the time of the forum, Carty's institution was the only academic library in the United Kingdom known to have a full subscription to the RDA Toolkit, and as a result her emails provided answers to questions from forum participants.

There were 129 emails, excluding the moderators' postings. The average number of emails per participant was 3.5, but this average figure belies the long tail: 23 participants sent three or fewer emails, including 14 people who sent 1 email each. Only three people sent 10 or more emails: an iSchool academic (10), an independent scholar (11), and an academic librarian (13).

Topics

In reading the emails, there were several topics that emerged from the texts.

The forum took place a week after CILIP's Executive Briefing on RDA (RDA11), and as this paid event was priced, as its title suggests, for executives to attend, the moderators summarized its contents and answered questions about it. In total, there were 14 emails (7%) about RDA11 and 1 (under 1%) about RDA10. There was also interest in the U.S. RDA Tests (17 emails, or 9%). Another topic that was quite specific in nature was the RDA Toolkit (21 emails, or 11%) and, related to that, the availability of a print version of RDA (7 emails, or 4%).

Otherwise, topics were general and open:

- Current actions (20 emails, or 10%) and sharing knowledge (8 emails, or 4%)
- Training (53 emails, or 27%) and Resources (24 emails, or 12%)
- Implementation (9 emails, or 5%) and Productivity (6 emails, or 3%)
- MARC (8 emails, or 4%) and FRBR (8 emails, or 4%)
- The hybrid catalog (21 emails, 11%) and cataloger judgment (5 emails, or 3%)
- Authority records (4 emails, or 2%)

Seven emails (4%) also discussed specific rule changes from AACR2 to RDA.

The rest of this article analyses the forum emails on these topics, and contextualizes them within the wider United Kingdom and Anglo-American cataloging scene.

Current Actions and Sharing

The 20 emails on current actions were sent by 12 catalogers and one iSchool academic. Later emails in the forum discussed specific training actions and are discussed below in the section on training.

The catalogers who shared the current actions being taken by their institutions came from eight academic libraries and two public libraries. They all expressed a "wait and see" attitude, which was reinforced by an observation from the cataloger working in library supply.

The iSchool academic stated,

> One thing that really struck me last year and this year was how hard it was to fill the slot [in CILIP's RDA Executive Briefings] in which practitioners share their experience ... Similarly on RDA-L and AUTOCAT there are few UK practitioners sharing their current experience. I wonder why this is? (Welsh, 2011a)

Four catalogers responded to this query in 7 emails, giving reasons including wariness of discussing plans that are "still at a very changeable level" (Williams, 2011d); practical reasons such as lack of access to online tools like wikis, lack of copyright permissions to mount items such as title pages on the public web and the paper-based nature of many training materials (Jardine, 2011; O'Reilly, 2011); and cultural differences between the United States and United Kingdom (Carty, 2011b). Lack of access to the RDA Toolkit and the subsequent difficulty in referencing specific rules was also given as a reason for reluctance in sharing knowledge on general email lists (Williams, 2011d).

One of the outcomes of the e-forum was the production of a list of resources shared by participants (Williams, 2011a). This was the result of 24 emails (12% of the total number of emails) from 14 people (37% of the total number of participants). The contributors to the resource list were nine academic librarians (65% resource list contributors), three iSchool academics (21%), one public librarian (7%), and one independent scholar (7%). This list comprises 25 resources, supplemented by a separate document comprising 14 RDA references from the draft bibliography of a forthcoming book on cataloging (Welsh and Batley, 2012).

It is interesting to note that of the 38 unique citations on the resource lists, 9 (24%) were produced in the United Kingdom; 18 (47%) in the United States; 1 (3%) in Canada; and 10 (26%) by international organizations including the JSC and the European RDA Interest Group [EURIG]). A total of 24 (62%) resources were web sites (including blogs) and 11 (29%) were presentations (or web pages listing presentations). Only 1 (3%) book (Oliver, 2010), 1 (3%) book chapter (Tillett, 2007), and 1 (3%) article (Knight, 2011) were included in the lists. The preference for online resources may reflect a desire, at this stage in the introduction of RDA, for materials that are updated regularly. Certainly, Oliver's book was the only monograph on RDA available in the United Kingdom in April 2011, although other book chapters and articles have been published since RDA was first mooted in the mid-2000s.

All 12 catalogers who shared their current actions stated that they were following events in the United States led by the Library of Congress and were keeping up with reading on RDA. Although each of these practitioners demonstrated themselves to have current knowledge and to be following best practice, there were expressions of "vague concerns" about the timing of making policy decisions and offering training (cf. Perry, 2011; Francis, 2011).

The impossibility of ignoring RDA even in the short-term was also raised, with catalogers reporting RDA records in consortia downloads (cf. Perry, 2011; Taylor, 2011).

The Hybrid Catalog

The notion of the "hybrid environment" began to appear with some regularity toward the end of the U.S. RDA Test period. It featured in many of the RDA-related events at the ALA Midwinter meeting in San Diego, January 7–10, 2011, (LeBlanc, 2011) and was also an important part of the presentation given at the CILIP Executive Briefing on RDA by Beacher Wiggins in April 2011 (Carty, 2011a). In the context of discussions about the findings of the RDA Test, the term *hybrid* primarily concerns combining records created following AACR2 and those created using RDA within one database.

The Library of Congress Program for Cooperative Cataloging (PCC) offers a useful working definition in its Frequently Asked Questions:

> There are multiple meanings for this term: hybrid database, hybrid bibliographic records, and hybrid headings.
>
> At the database level, there is a hybrid environment when a database adds a new category of records that use a new/different set of rules. Usually over time, the number of records in that database that reflect earlier sets of rules gradually diminishes.
>
> At the bibliographic record level, a hybrid record might have headings reflecting one set of rules and bibliographic description a different set of rules.
>
> In authority records, a hybrid heading could be something like a corporate heading where part of the name is established under one set of rules, and another part uses a different set of rules; understandably, we want to avoid this situation.
>
> A hybrid environment could also be applied to the new types of discovery environments offered to our users today, where names from article metadata and digital library projects mix with formally controlled name headings. All of these meanings of "hybrid environment" apply as we think about RDA implementation. (Library of Congress Program for Cooperative Cataloging, 2011)

Just a few days before the e-forum took place, the Program for Cooperative Cataloging Policy Committee (PoCo) released a discussion paper on implementation alternatives looking primarily at implications of a hybrid environment where PCC members were creating records using both RDA and AACR2. Overall, the PCC concluded that "in any scenario, PCC must adapt to a hybrid environment" (Library of Congress Program for Cooperative Cataloging Policy Committee, 2011, p. 1).

Specifically, the committee found:

> The cataloging environment is already hybrid. OCLC WorldCat includes records created under AACR1, AACR2, RDA and a variety of other international rules. As OCLC continues to pursue global participation, particularly from national libraries, the environment will grow increasingly more diverse. (p. 2)

It also observed:

> It is likely that the JSC will continue to focus its attention on the development of RDA and that ALA will no longer revise AACR2. RDA will continue to evolve over time and will become increasingly divergent from AACR2. Perpetuating the hybrid environment long term will have a negative (and costly) impact on our catalogs and on all areas of bibliographic control. (p. 2)

Further, it offered this definition of the hybrid environment:

> One in which PCC libraries could chose to participate following either RDA or AACR2, and encoding in MODS, MARC or other schema. It is understood that while a library may choose to follow AACR2 or RDA, understanding of both cataloging codes will be required to interpret records correctly, to do record upgrades, and to perform appropriate bibliographic and authority file maintenance. All existing BIBCO, CONSER and NACO documentation will need to be reviewed. (p. 2)

Given the prominence given to the notion of a "hybrid environment" during the period prior to the e-forum, it is perhaps not surprising that this seemed to be a specific source of anxiety identified during the e-forum discussions. A total of 21 emails out of the total number sent to the forum by 13 participants (34%) from 12 different institutions pertained to this topic. All those involved in this discussion were practitioners coming from nine different academic libraries, one national library, one library management system provider, and one supplier of bibliographic records. It is notable that the topic was first raised at 11:12 on April 18 and ran throughout the two days, with the last email on the hybrid catalog timefranked 19 Apr 2011 15:58:24 +0000.

Overall, the hybrid catalog was a topic raised in response to eight different discussion threads within the forum:

1. AACR2 or RDA?
2. RDA in MARC
3. Incoming RDA records

4. AACR2 or RDA? What about the headings?
5. RDA workflows and productivity
6. Developing training for RDA/FRBR etc.
7. Welcome to CIG e-forum Day 2
8. National Libraries implementation

Participants highlighted their discovery of RDA records in consortia downloads (cf. Perry, 2011; Taylor, 2011); the lack of human intervention in the downloading of records (cf. Arens, 2011; Ryder, 2011); and the potential impact of RDA records on a non-RDA catalog managed by a non-RDA-trained cataloging team (cf. Ransom, 2011; Williams, 2011c).

Of course, the mixing of records within catalogs is nothing new, and this was pointed out by practitioners from institutions old enough to have been cataloging before the introduction of AACR.

It is always pleasing, when teaching MA LIS students about the hybrid catalog, to be able to point to one of Panizzi's own books as an example of a "hybrid record"—created under an earlier cataloging system and then amended in places to enable it to coexist with records created under newer systems. The British Library's record for Hosking's *Some Observations Upon the Recent Addition of a Reading Room to the British Museum*, with Panizzi's manuscript notes, is a case in point (British Library, n.d.). In it we can see that the pre-1968 format, pagination and publication details have been massaged through various data upgrades into the modern MARC catalog as

260 |**a** pp. 34. Pl. A-E. Edward Stanford: London, 1858.

300 |**a** fol.

We can see the drawbacks inherent in this record were it to be shared with another database using machine-readable cataloging with no human intervention (a *caveat* for the Semantic Web), but we can also see that for the human catalog user, there is no difficulty in understanding this hybrid record in our modern environment (AACR2 in MARC). This record is not only typical of many legacy records found in the British Library system but also those contained within comparable large libraries all over the world.

UK catalogers continue to look to the British Library for guidance on proceeding with the new cataloging standard. In the e-forum, Alan Danskin shared information based on the British Library's work so far with RDA:

> From a BL perspective we do expect to work in a hybrid environment. We have happily mixed RDA and AACR2 records in a development database on Aleph. We have linked bibliographic and authority data and haven't experienced any significant problems. We anticipate that there will be a long tail of AACR2 users and in the event that we adopt RDA we will continue to accept AACR2 records where these satisfy our quality criteria. We have had to make some changes to our "batch upgrade" routines.

> These routines are designed to automatically update records for which an LC CIP [Library of Congress Cataloging in Process record] is available and are quite complex (as the database record may not be the LC CIP, it is just flagged to indicate that a CIP exists). In order to avoid producing hybrid records when a full AACR2 record overwrites a preliminary RDA record, or vice versa we have revised the matching instructions; the merge profiles have been updated to take account of changes in RDA and some post processing fixes have been added to tidy up the final record. We would certainly like to see functionality in Aleph which would provide contextual links from the cataloger's worksheet to RDA which are similar to those currently enabled for MARC. (Danskin, 2011a)

The e-forum contributor from the LMS company was also reassuring:

> As a developer for a LMS, we're not expecting to see significant problems with a hybrid database of AACR2 and RDA records. Having worked for and with several system suppliers over many years, in the design of a catalog, one is much more concerned with the (logical) form of the data ... I think there are a few areas which may need some care—not least, the issue of possible changes to the form of, for example, personal names ... but this has been noted by others already. Another example is the handling of parallel titles, I think, where in RDA, parallel titles are included in full in 245, as well as, possibly, in tag 246 ... There are other changes which, I think, limit some of the functionality which we can currently provide (but fairly minor, I think) ... I see that several people have expressed some concern about the mixing and matching of RDA and earlier forms. I would be most interested to know if there are some objective problems which we're not aware of, or whether this is more a vague disquiet about the ability of vendors and LMS' to be able to support the situation. (Watson, 2011)

In fact, throughout the two days of the forum there were only 6 emails (3% total emails) discussing OPAC display, which is a surprisingly low figure considering the potential impact afforded by RDA's development using the FRBR model. Existing iterations of "FRBRized" catalogs include Variations/FRBR (Indiana University, 2010) and the RDA Sandbox (VTLS, n.d.), and both demonstrate alternatives to MARC-based catalog systems. Indeed, FRBR itself was the subject of only 8 emails (4%), and 3 of those were sent by iSchool academics.

RDA in MARC

Even MARC was the subject of only 8 emails (4%) out of the total emails sent. The forum took place a month before the Manchester Executive Briefing on RDA (RDA 11 Manchester), at which Beacher Wiggins circulated the press release for "Transforming our Bibliographic Framework" (Library of Congress Working Group on the Future of Bibliographic Control, 2011). This statement acknowledged that

> Spontaneous comments from participants in the US RDA Test show that a broad cross-section of the community feels budgetary pressures but nevertheless considers it necessary to replace MARC 21 in order to reap the full benefit of new and emerging content standards. (Library of Congress Working Group on the Future of Bibliographic Control, 2011)

The first of the stated objectives of the working group is to "determine which aspects of current metadata encoding standards should be retained and evolved into a format for the future. We will consider MARC 21, in which billions of records are presently encoded, as well as other initiatives" (Library of Congress Working Group on the Future of Bibliographic Control, 2011).

On 18–19 April, we did not know in the United Kingdom that this statement was being prepared on the other side of the Atlantic. The majority of the participants in the e-forum were silent about encoding format, and it is easy to see the common sense in Rosemary Stenson's view:

> Whilst I appreciate that there has to be a wider discussion on RDA beyond MARC, for those of us with busy cataloguing departments to run, our initial concern will be in training catalogers in RDA encoded in MARC (Stenson, 2011a).

RDA in the United Kingdom: Access to the Toolkit

As well as being unaware that the MARC format might cease to be the main format for bibliographic records, participants in the e-forum had limited experience of the RDA Toolkit. A total of 21 emails (11%) discussed the Toolkit and 7 emails (4%) were concerned about the availability of a print version.

In the *Report and Recommendations of the U.S. RDA Test Coordinating Committee* (2011) it emerged that U.S. catalogers had reported dissatisfaction with the RDA Toolkit during the U.S. test period. Difficulties in navigation (p. 85) and the lack of an index (p. 85) were both areas that had been criticized by those using the online product. By the time the RDA e-forum was held in the United Kingdom in April 2011, both of these issues had been addressed by the publishers and implemented into the Toolkit (Linker, 2011).

Although nonsubscribers could see these two new sections, which are freely available to everyone, at the time of the e-forum, participants discussed their difficulties in seeing the full content of the RDA Toolkit after the free access period in Summer 2010. At this stage the Toolkit was incomplete, so it is apparent that parts of the product had not been viewed at all by these members of the UK cataloging community. All but 2 emails regarding the Toolkit were concerned with lack of access. Two options for a free access period of 30 days have been released since the e-forum occurred.

Three emails stated the difficulties faced by small libraries in affording the RDA Toolkit, and while the print version was welcomed, its cost was seen as prohibitive, and small libraries were instead looking to their LMS providers for guidance, without obtaining access to RDA directly.

The fact that RDA is a closed standard was raised at RDA11, and has also been discussed on RDA-L and AUTOCAT and on UK cataloging blogs (cf. "Orangeaurochs," 2011). Part of the benefit of the Toolkit comes from the value of workflows contributed by users such as LC (http://www.loc.gov/bibliographic-future/rda/ full report, p. 84), but while the product remains closed, these will be lost to those who cannot afford to pay for access. Two participants reported owning a print copy of RDA, but generally it seemed to be accepted that the online version was easier to use, offered better value for money, was more straightforward to update, and had added value from workflows, mappings, and cross-referencing.

As so few have been able to investigate the complete Toolkit in detail, discussion was mostly limited to cost and access concerns. Only one participant was confident enough in the Toolkit to anticipate that the costs of it could be recovered by gains in productivity.

Productivity

Mid-afternoon on the first day of the e-forum, participants were asked how much thought they had given to productivity and workflows when introducing RDA. Discussion on this was quite limited (6 emails, or 3%) as it sparked a discussion on the hybrid catalog, but the productivity issues mentioned are nevertheless significant and worthy of brief discussion here.

Four participants (11%) highlighted a concern that productivity would be reduced while catalogers assimilated new rules, two of them mentioning that, particularly during a time of economic constraint, this would not be acceptable to senior management teams. The replies on this topic came from those at academic libraries, and at two of these institutions, catalogers also had responsibilities in both acquisitions and repository metadata, and consequently could not afford a slow-down or backlog in cataloging work, which would have a "knock-on" negative effect on other areas of their work. One respondent was reassured that RDA would be implemented in a MARC environment and that this familiarity would minimize some of the complexity of introducing a new standard, but overall the dominant feeling appeared to be one of concern.

Alan Danskin reported at CILIP's RDA April 2011 Executive Briefing that when considering "factors influencing the decision to implement RDA," discussions had concluded that "productivity must be sustained," and "key performance indictors must be satisfied," to the extent that there should be "no net increase in the amount of material routed to professional catalogers." (Danskin, 2011a, p. 8). At this stage it looked as if one possible way to achieve this would be to take RDA copy records where they were available, but to continue to accept AACR2 records where no RDA record was available and where the AACR2 record was considered fit for purpose (p. 15). This would allow material unlikely to have RDA copy records (such as theses, special collections, older donations, and gray literature), to be dealt with quickly using imported AACR2 records, which may help to offset the inevitable drop in productivity while RDA training and implementation is bedded in. A decision to produce such a policy, however, will lead to an environment in which the hybrid catalog increasingly becomes the norm.

RDA in the United Kingdom: Training

With 53 emails (27%) from 27 participants (71%), training was the topic discussed most often in the e-forum. It was raised for the first time at 11: 24 on April 18th, and topics discussed over the two-day period of the e-forum included whether it was too early to consider training (cf. Francis, 2011); the cost implications (cf. Ryder, 2011); and the timing of training (cf. Stenson, 2011b). Most catalogers were keen to see training developed by CILIP, CIG, and the consortia, and for training sessions to be equally available to people throughout the country.

By the evening of April 18th it had been suggested that the e-forum format might be adapted to offer a low-cost training option for those wanting to try some RDA cataloging (Welsh, 2011b). On April 19th expressions of interest were sought by the moderators and received from 17 participants (45%). Of the 14 people who contributed only one email to the forum, 6 (16%) commented to show interest in this idea.

The demise of CILIP Training and Development courses in July 2011 after a major review of all CILIP activities increasingly places CIG as the lead contributor to the RDA training scene in the United Kingdom. Overall, the e-forum generated many helpful suggestions for possible training. In response, CIG is preparing to run a practical e-forum in 2012, which will allow librarians and catalogers to share RDA records, air questions, examine problem areas, and discuss RDA options (Williams, 2011b).

One month in advance of the forum, 10 title pages will be circulated to participants along with a simple cataloging form for record creation and submission. Co-moderators will collate all the submitted records to present the most common issues or questions raised by each title (Welsh, 2011b). Participants will be able to ask any questions or bring up points of discussion for each record in turn. Subscribers can take part without submitting records personally, but the previous e-forum suggests that many people will be keen to take advantage of the opportunity to work with RDA. The more records received, the more the exercise will be able to teach about RDA and the current situation across the United Kingdom. CIG hope to make use of the collated data for further analysis or training.

From the analysis of the emails that form the e-forum discussion we can see that this self-selecting group of catalogers is interested in further training in RDA. Three specific rule changes were flagged as needing further work:

- the Rule of Three—currently an option to retain this rule in RDA
- the media, content, and carrier information now covered by recently introduced MARC fields 336–338
- the edition statement in RDA, particularly some confusion as to when an edition is a manifestation and when (if at all) it might be an expression

At a more general level, as discussed above, there was interest in training in FRBR concepts and how these are worked out in RDA.

CONCLUSIONS

It is clear from the emails within the e-forum discussion that in April 2011 this self-selecting group of catalogers in the United Kingdom were concerned about many of the same issues that were raised in the report of the U.S. RDA Tests two months later (U.S. RDA Test Coordinating Committee, 2011), especially:

- the hybrid catalog and its management
- training of staff
- the representation of RDA within MARC
- access to the RDA Toolkit and the cost of the print version
- productivity gains and losses
- timing of implementation
- rule changes

It was also evident that participants were looking to the Library of Congress as well as the British Library for guidance on all these issues.

As discussed in this article, participants in the e-forum expressed "vague concerns" about their current actions lest they should be doing more and had already fallen behind. They also gave clear reasons why it is unusual in the United Kingdom for cataloging training documentation to be published and made freely available on the open Web.

As discussed at the beginning of this article, an awareness of the current understanding of the main cataloging standards (AACR2 and RDA) is important when considering the future of bibliographic control. Success in change management depends to a certain extent on addressing the concerns of current practitioners.

In short, analysis of the emails that constitute the CIG e-forum on RDA in April 2011 reveals that the issues we identify are the same on both sides of the Atlantic, but without the culture of the annual ALA conference and the structured training provided by the U.S. RDA Test (which can now be cascaded from test institutions to other cataloging agencies), UK catalogers in these emails express themselves less confidently about their actions and observations so far. In developing future training, the UK cataloging community looks to the Library of Congress and other participants in the U.S. RDA Tests for materials and shared practice. We might conclude that the trans-Atlantic gap is not topical but emotional, but no less real for that.

ACKNOWLEDGMENT

Although the emails sent in the e-forum are available publicly in a JISCmail archive, the authors would like to thank the CILIP Cataloguing and Indexing Group Committee for permission to analyze the emails. This article is entirely the work of the authors and should in no way be seen to represent the opinions of CILIP, CIG, the CIG committee, individual participants in the RDA e-forum or the authors' employers.

REFERENCES

American Library Association. ([2006]). *International member survey. Summary.* Retrieved from http://www.ala.org/ala/aboutala/missionhistory/plan/international.cfm#;

American Library Association and the Library Association. (1908). *Catalog rules: Author and title entries* (American ed.) Chicago, IL: American Library Association.

Arens, E. (2011). Re: RDA in MARC Retrieved from https://www.jiscmail.ac.uk/cgi-bin/webadmin?A2=ind1104&L=CIG-E-FORUM&F=&S=&P=30010

British Library. (n.d.). Item details [for BL UIN BLL01001740501]. Retrieved from http://primocat.bl.uk/F?func=direct&local_base=PRIMO&doc_number=00174-0501&format=001&con_lng=prm

Carty, C. (2011a). Exec briefing on RDA summary [Email to CIG e-Forum, timefranked 18 Apr 2011 09:12:39 +0100]. Retrieved from https://www.jiscmail.ac.uk/cgi-bin/webadmin?A2=ind1104&L=CIG-E-FORUM&F=&S=&P=1265

Carty, C. (2011b). Re: Exec Briefing on RDA summary: Sharing practitioner experience [Email to CIG e-Forum, timefranked 18 Apr 2011 12:46:51 +0100]. Retrieved from https://www.jiscmail.ac.uk/cgi-bin/webadmin?A2=ind1104&L=CIG-E-FORUM&F=&S=&P=47176

Carty, C., & Williams, H. (2011, June). RDA in the UK: Reflections after the CIG E-Forum on RDA. *Catalogue & Index 163*, 2–4.

CILIP Cataloguing and Indexing Group. (2011a). About us. Retrieved from http://www.CILIP.org.uk/get-involved/special-interest-groups/cataloguing-indexing/about-us/pages/default.aspx

CILIP Cataloguing and Indexing Group. (2011b). *Annual report 2010: Prepared for the Annual General Meeting of CIG, September 2011*. Retrieved from http://www.CILIP.org.uk/get-involved/special-interest-groups/cataloguing-indexing/Documents/Annual%20Report%20(for%20CIG%202011%20AGM).pdf

CILIP Cataloguing and Indexing Group. (2011c). *CIG E-Forum* archives. April 2011. JISCMAIL. Retrieved from https://www.jiscmail.ac.uk/cgi-bin/webadmin?A1=ind1104&L=CIG-E-FORUM

CILIP Cataloguing and Indexing Group. (2011d, August 8). Reclassification Event. *Catalogue & Index Blog*. Retrieved from http://communities.CILIP.org.uk/blogs/catalogueandindex/archive/2011/08/08/cig-reclassification-event.aspx

CILIP Events. (2011, April 12). RDA: Resource Description and Access executive briefings, London/Wednesday 25 May 2011, Manchester. Retrieved from http://www.cilip.org.uk/rda2011/pages/default.aspx

CILIP Training & Development. (2010). *Training directory 2010. Autumn update*. Retrieved from http://www.cilip.org.uk/filedownloadslibrary/training/td_update-web.pdf

CILIP Training & Development. (2011). *Training directory 2011*. Retrieved from http://www.cilip.org.uk/SiteCollectionDocuments/pdfs/training/Training_Directory_2011.pdf

Cutter, C. A. (1876). *Rules for a printed dictionary catalogue*. Washington, DC: Government Printing Office.

Danskin, A. (2010). *RDA in the UK: Summary of results*. CILIP Cataloguing & Indexing Group Conference, 2010. Retrieved from www.cilip.org.uk/get-involved/special-interest-groups/cataloguing-indexing/Documents/CIG%20Conference%202010/2010DanskinA.ppt

Danskin, A. (2011a). *RDA in the British Library, UK and Europe: CILIP Executive Briefing, April 12th 2011*. Retrieved from http://www.cilip.org.uk/rda2011/Documents/Alan%20Danskin.pdf

Danskin, A. (2011b). Re: Welcome to CIG e-forum Day 2 [Email to CIG e-forum, timefranked 19 Apr 2011 10:16:25 +0100]. Retrieved from https://www.jiscmail.ac.uk/cgi-bin/webadmin?A2=ind1104&L=CIG-E-FORUM&F=&S=&P=90003

Francis, E. (2011). Re: RDA in MARC [Email to CIG e-forum, timefranked 18 Apr 2011 11:24:26 +0100]. Retrieved from https://www.jiscmail.ac.uk/cgi-bin/webadmin?A2=ind1104&L=CIG-E-FORUM&F=&S=&P=24127

Indiana University. (2010). Variations/FRBR: Variations as a testbed for the FRBR conceptual model. Retrieved from http://www.dlib.indiana.edu/projects/vfrbr/

Jardine, H. (2011). Re: Sharing practitioner experience and materials [Email to CIG e-forum, timefranked 18 Apr 2011 13:55:56 +0100]. Retrieved from https://www.jiscmail.ac.uk/cgi-bin/webadmin?A2=ind1104&L=CIG-E-FORUM&F=&S=&P=60215

Joint Steering Committee for the Development of RDA. (2010a). *RDA: resource description and access, RDA Toolkit*. Chicago, IL: American Library Association,

Canadian Library Association and CILIP (Chartered Institute of Library and Information Professionals). Retrieved from www.rdatoolkit.org/

Joint Steering Committee for the Development of RDA. (2010b). *Presentations on RDA*. Retrieved from http://www.rda-jsc.org/rdapresentations.html

Joint Steering Committee for Revision of AACR. (2005). *Anglo-American Cataloguing Rules* (2nd ed.). Chicago, IL: American Library Association, Canadian Library Association and CILIP (Chartered Institute of Library and Information Professionals).

Kiorgaard, D.& Kartus, E. (2009). *A rose by any other name?: From AACR2 to Resource Description and Access*. Canberra, Australia: National Library of Australia. Retrieved from http://www.nla.gov.au/openpublish/index.php/nlasp/article/viewFile/1169/1437

Knight, F. T. (2011). Resource Description and Access: from AACR2 to RDA. *Canadian Law Library Review, 36*(1), 8–12.

LeBlanc, J. (2011, January 22). Notes from the ALA Midwinter Conference. *Cornell University Library Conference Wiki*. Retrieved from https://confluence.cornell.edu/display/CULCONF/ALA+Midwinter,+2011+%28Jim+LeBlanc%29

Library Association and the American Library Association. (1908). *Cataloguing rules: Author and title entries* (English ed.). London, United Kingdom: Library Association.

Library of Congress Network Development and MARC Standards Office. (2006). *MARC 21 Format for Bibliographic Data. Introduction*. Washington, DC: Library of Congress. Retrieved from http://www.loc.gov/marc/bibliographic/bdintro.html

Library of Congress Program for Cooperative Cataloging. (2011). *Frequently Asked Questions: Program for Cooperative Cataloging and RDA*. Retrieved from http://www.loc.gov/catdir/pcc/PCC-RDA-FAQ.html#PCCandRDA5

Library of Congress Program for Cooperative Cataloging Policy Committee. (2011). *PoCo discussion paper on RDA implementation alternatives* (Original release 4/05/2011; revised 4/15/2011. Retrieved from http://www.loc.gov/catdir/pcc/PoCo-RDA-Discussion-Paper040511.pdf

Library of Congress Working Group on the Future of Bibliographic Control. (2008). *On the record: Report, January 9, 2008*. Washington, DC: Library of Congress. Retrieved from http://www.loc.gov/bibliographic-future/news/lcwg-ontherecord-jan08-final.pdf

Library of Congress Working Group on the Future of Bibliographic Control. (2011, May 13). *Transforming our bibliographic framework: A statement from the Library of Congress*. Retrieved from http://www.loc.gov/marc/transition/news/framework-051311.html

Linker, T. (2011, March 31). New content and functionality added to the RDA Toolkit. *RDA Toolkit Blog*. Retrieved from http://www.rdatoolkit.org/blog/119

Ma, J. (2009). Metadata in ARL Libraries: A survey of metadata practices. *Journal of Library Metadata, 9*(1–2), 1–14.

Nielsen, J. (2006, October 9). Participation inequality: Encouraging more users to contribute. *Jacob Nielsen' Alertbox*. Retrieved from http://www.useit.com/alertbox/participation_inequality.html

Oliver, C. (2010). *Introducing RDA: A guide to the basics*. London, United Kingdom: Facet.

"Orangeaurochs." (2011, March 23). RDA as a closed standard. *Aurlog*. Retrieved from http://www.aurochs.org/aurlog/2011/03/23/rda-as-a-closed-standard/

O'Reilly, B. (2011). Re: Sharing practitioner experience and materials [Email to CIG e-forum, timefranked 18 Apr 2011 13:47:23 +0100]. Retrieved from https://www.jiscmail.ac.uk/cgi-bin/webadmin?A2=ind1104&L=CIG-E-FORUM&F=&S=&P=59421

Panizzi, A. (1841). *Catalogue of printed books in the British Museum*. London, United Kingdom: British Museum.

Perry, J.-C. (2011). Re: RDA in MARC [Email to CIG e-forum, timefranked 18 Apr 2011 11:00:37 +0100]. Retrieved from https://www.jiscmail.ac.uk/cgi-bin/webadmin?A2=ind1104&L=CIG-E-FORUM&F=&S=&P=17556

Ransom, N. (2011). Re: Developing training for RDA/FRBR etc. [Email to CIG e-forum, timefranked 18 Apr 2011 14:57:17 +0000]. Retrieved from https://www.jiscmail.ac.uk/cgi-bin/webadmin?A2=ind1104&L=CIG-E-FORUM&F=&S=&P=81000

Russell, J. (2011, December 14). RDA in February 2012 [unpublished email from event organizer to Anne Welsh, event chair].

Ryder, J. (2011). Re: RDA in MARC [Email to CIG e-forum, timefranked 18 Apr 2011 11:20:41 +0000]. Retrieved from https://www.jiscmail.ac.uk/cgi-bin/webadmin?A2=ind1104&L=CIG-E-FORUM&F=&S=&P=39729

Stenson, R. (2011a). Re: RDA in MARC [Email to CIG e-forum, timefranked 18 Apr 2011 11:10:36 +0100]. Retrieved from https://www.jiscmail.ac.uk/cgi-bin/webadmin?A2=ind1104&L=CIG-E-FORUM&F=&S=&P=19576

Stenson, R. (2011b). Re: RDA in MARC [Email to CiG e-forum, timefranked 18 Apr 2011 13:26:14 +0100]. Retrieved from https://www.jiscmail.ac.uk/cgi-bin/webadmin?A2=ind1104&L=CIG-E-FORUM&F=&S=&P=53959

Taylor, H. (2011). Re: RDA in MARC [Email to CIG e-forum, timefranked 18 Apr 2011 11:18:14 +0100]. Retrieved from https://www.jiscmail.ac.uk/cgi-bin/webadmin?A2=ind1104&L=CIG-E-FORUM&F=&S=&P=21375

Taylor, W., & Williams, H. (2010). At the event: RDA (Resource Description and Access). *Ariadne 63*. Retrieved from http://www.ariadne.ac.uk/issue63/rda-briefing-rpt/

Tillett, B. B. (2007). FRBR and RDA: Resource Description and Access. In A. G. Taylor (Ed.), *Understanding FRBR: What it is and how it will affect our retrieval tools*. (pp. 87–95). London, United Kingdom: Libraries Unlimited.

US RDA Test Coordinating Committee. (2011). *Report and recommendations of the U.S. RDA Test Coordinating Committee, May 9, 2011, revised for public release June 20, 2011*. Retrieved from http://www.loc.gov/bibliographic-future/rda/source/rdatesting-finalreport-20june2011.pdf

VTLS. (n.d.) *RDA Sandbox*. Retrieved from http://www.vtls.com/services/rdasandbox

Watson, F. (2011). Re: Welcome to CIG e-forum day 2 [Email to CIG e-forum, timefranked 19 Apr 2011 11:21:01 +0100]. Retrieved from https://www.jiscmail.ac.uk/cgi-bin/webadmin?A2=ind1104&L=CIG-E-FORUM&F=&S=&P=96007

Welsh, A. (2010, February 11). RDA Briefing rerun on March 30. *Library Marginalia*. Retrieved from http://annewelsh.wordpress.com/2010/02/11/rda-briefing-rerun/

Welsh, A. (2011a). Exec Briefing on RDA summary: Sharing practitioner experience. Retrieved from https://www.jiscmail.ac.uk/cgi-bin/webadmin?A2=ind1104&L=CIG-E-FORUM&F=&S=&P=41129

Welsh, A. (2011b). Re: Developing training for RDA/FRBR etc. Retrieved from https://www.jiscmail.ac.uk/cgi-bin/webadmin?A2=ind1104&L=CIG-E-FORUM&F=&S=&P=85553

Welsh, A., & Batley, S. (2012). *Practical cataloguing: AACR2, RDA and MARC21*. London, United Kingdom: Facet.

Williams, H. (2011a). CIG e-forum resources list [Email to CIG e-forum, timefranked 19 Apr 2011 17:20:02 +0100]. Retrieved from https://www.jiscmail.ac.uk/cgi-bin/webadmin?A2=ind1104&L=CIG-E-FORUM&F=&S=&P=21375

Williams, H. (2011b, December 14). RDA practical e-forum [Unpublished email to e-forum moderators].

Williams, H. (2011c). RDA workflows & productivity [Email to CIG e-forum, timefranked 18 Apr 2011 14:50:02 +0100]. Retrieved from https://www.jiscmail.ac.uk/cgi-bin/webadmin?A2=ind1104&L=CIG-E-FORUM&F=&S=&P=64536

Williams, H. (2011d). Re: Exec Briefing on RDA summary: Sharing practitioner experience. [Email to CIG e-forum, timefranked 18 Apr 2011 12:33:58 +0100]. Retrieved from https://www.jiscmail.ac.uk/cgi-bin/webadmin?A2=ind1104&L=CIG-E-FORUM&F=&S=&P=43567

Wu, M. (2010, March 18). The 90–1-1 rule in reality. *Lithium lithosphere*. Retrieved from http://lithosphere.lithium.com/t5/Building-Community-the-Platform/The-90–9-1-Rule-in-Reality/ba-p/5463

Inadvertent RDA: New Catalogers' Errors in AACR2

JEAN HARDEN
Music Library, University of North Texas, Denton, Texas, USA

In Fall 2010, in the Music Library at the University of North Texas, a subgroup of the full-time music catalogers were both participating in the U.S. National RDA Test and overseeing the cataloging of a large gift of scores. Student workers (graduate students in music or librarianship) who had never cataloged before produced the records, using AACR2. The librarians actively working on RDA checked their work. This project provided a treasure trove of errors that suggest new catalogers will often produce RDA-compliant cataloging without ever reading an RDA rule but by merely doing what makes sense to them intuitively.

INTRODUCTION

In the fall of 2010 in the Music Library at the University of North Texas, several factors conspired to illuminate issues related to training catalogers for the new cataloging code, Resource Description and Access (RDA). This author was overseeing both a subgroup of the music catalogers participating in the U.S. National Libraries' RDA Test, and the cataloging of a large gift collection of scores, the Ben A. Brown Collection, using the current code, Anglo-American Cataloguing Rules, 2nd ed. (AACR2). During these months, on email lists such as AUTOCAT, correspondents persistently bemoaned the foreseen cost and difficulty of training catalogers to use RDA.

This confluence of circumstances produced the ideal situation for making a preliminary determination of how easy it would be to train catalogers to use the new cataloging code. The email lists kept the issue of training in the forefront of our minds. Our own experience in the RDA Test gave an indication of what it was like for experienced catalogers to learn the code. The large cataloging project that was going on at the same time and that was staffed chiefly by people who had never cataloged before provided a treasure trove of errors from which it was possible to deduce how readily new catalogers were apt to accept the new rules. This final point is the focus of this article.

LITERATURE REVIEW

Cataloging Teaching/Training in General

The voluminous literature on teaching or training of catalogers can be represented by two articles from the last decade that bring up the most prominent issues treated at great length in other writings. Intner (2002) discussed the major recurring issues, dividing them into three overarching themes: (1) the balance between theory and practice, (2) the optimal division in a curriculum of courses covering book cataloging and those covering the cataloging of everything else, and (3) the relative merits of formal courses and nonacademic routes, such as on-the-job training and continuing education. Intner pointed out that regardless of the teaching circumstance, it is always key to teach (or ask) why we do what we do, not only the actions to be taken. Otherwise, students will be unable to handle situations that are significantly different from the specific ones they have been taught. Intner's "why" is not answerable by "because this rule says so." Rather, it is asking learners to explore the purposes or principles that undergird the structure and handling of the bibliographic universe. These purposes or principles will only coincidentally be the same as those underlying any specific set of cataloging rules; exploring them is an attempt to discern the theory behind cataloging. In addition, the learning of cataloging must be seen as a process that continues throughout the cataloger's professional life; one begins with formal courses, moves to on-the-job training, and then keeps up-to-date with continuing education.

Hill (2004) provided a brief history of cataloging teaching or training, beginning before the time of Melvil Dewey, and moving to the situation that prevailed at the time her article was written. In Part I, which dealt chiefly with historical issues and with education for cataloging in library schools, Hill observed that many teachers of cataloging have concluded that it is better to introduce students to applying principles and rules across formats, rather than to teach separate courses about certain formats. Part II, generally about cataloging education/training outside library school, ended with hopes and admonitions. The author observed that libraries appeared at the time of writing to be at the start of a period of rapid evolution. As "AACR, MARC, the ISBDs, and bibliographic networks led to the end of isolation of libraries one from another, perhaps the next changes will break down the isolation of librarianship from the world at large." (p. 12) Because major changes in the field seem in large part to arise from and be based on cataloging and bibliographic control, if we are to achieve this melding of libraries with the rest of the world, we need librarians who understand cataloging, whether or not they themselves catalog, and who can view changes in cataloging codes or practices in the context of the whole field of librarianship, including its history and its goals. In short, Hill asserted, we need educated librarians. Although modes of instruction may have changed or, in some cases, may have become obsolete, education for cataloging is no more an obsolete concept than is education for librarianship.

Training for RDA

The Intner (2002) and Hill (2004) articles are only the proverbial tip of the iceberg of discussions of cataloging teaching/training in general. Far less has been written about teaching RDA specifically, since the rules are not even in the general application stages yet. Nevertheless, some informative articles have been published. Hitchens and Symons (2009) have provided a general introduction to ways to approach training on the new code. Their article includes a brief review of writings from the time of the change from AACR to AACR2, showing that the issues now are largely the same as then (for instance, concern with the proliferation of nonbook resources, a desire for greater internationalization and standardization, and a need to adapt to new technological advances). Welsh (2011) summarized how catalog teaching is done at University College London, namely, with a mix of theory and practice, incorporating RDA as an alternative when possible. She pointed out that the crux of the issue of how to teach remains whether to focus on theory or on practice. The underlying issue is the same as in all library school education: Does "training" have a place, especially in a graduate curriculum?

Bloss (2011) wrote about the experience of having a group of library school students at Dominican University participate in the RDA Test and incorporated practical advice on how to teach RDA in school. The article included specifics about what to teach, training materials that are already available, and student assessments of the new code. The author's observations were heavily weighted toward the problems of finding one's way around the RDA text and the RDA Toolkit, which were major stumbling blocks for the students during the test. Bloss put strong emphasis on the need for learners to understand FRBR (Functional Requirements for Bibliographic Records) (IFLA, 2009, and an earlier draft, IFLA, 1998) and, to a lesser extent, FRAD (Functional Requirements for Authority Data; IFLA, 2008), and to become familiar with RDA terminology. For these students, the experience of taking part in the test resulted in a highly positive view of RDA, although points of difficulty were not disregarded. The author asserted that for some time to come, students would need to know at least the basics of AACR2 in addition to RDA, in order to understand legacy data; over time, however, the need for teaching the older code will gradually diminish.

Several library school students have written short pieces on their recent experience learning to catalog, both in school and on the job. Howard (2011) discussed learning to catalog through courses in the United States and at University College London, plus on-the-job training during internships and volunteer placements. Learning to think critically, that is, understanding what lies behind the standards, played an important part. The author expressed excitement about the possibilities of RDA, citing specifically the improved handling of electronic resources in the new code, as well as its emphasis on user needs.

Mariner (2011) provided an intriguing insight in a short piece about catalog procedures in the small poetry library where she works. She discussed some specifics of that library's procedures that are closer to RDA than to AACR2, although they were developed prior to RDA's existence. The library uses an inexpensive, non-MARC online catalog in which it is customary to spell out place of publication in full; to include something similar to relator terms assigned to names, so that it is evident to the user what the person's role was in the particular publication represented by the catalog record at hand; and to disregard the "rule of three." The first two of these are prescribed in the new code, although the details differ from what Mariner's library currently does; the "rule of three" is not enshrined in RDA at all, in distinct contrast to AACR2. From observations of this sort, the author concluded that RDA seems to be trying to take small libraries and inexpensive (nonstandard and non-MARC) automated systems into account. This little article provides a salutary counterpoint to the insistence on listservs such as AUTOCAT that RDA is only going to be affordable to big, rich libraries and has taken only them into account.

THE GIFT-SCORES CATALOGING PROJECT AT UNT

The Collection

The Ben A. Brown Collection is the entire stock of scores from the New York City music store Music Exchange, Inc., which went out of business in the middle of the 1990s. This stock was held in storage for a number of years and was then donated to the University of North Texas Music Library. The collection as it arrived here consisted largely of 20th-century popular music, mostly in English, both in compilations (e.g., *The New Best of Lynyrd Skynyrd* or *A Souvenir Disney Songbook: Favorite Songs from Disneyland & Walt Disney World*) and individual song sheets (e.g., "I love Paris" by Cole Porter, "The original famous Mexican hat dance" by F. A. Partichela, or "Lover, come back to me" by Sigmund Romberg and Oscar Hammerstein II). Classical or semi-classical scores (e.g., a Dover score of the opera *The Abduction from the Seraglio* by Mozart, a Ricordi vocal score of *Simon Boccanegra* by Verdi, a Schirmer/Hal Leonard vocal score of *H. M. S. Pinafore* by Gilbert & Sullivan, a Boosey & Hawkes score of *The Age of Anxiety: Symphony No. 2 for Piano and Orchestra* by Bernstein) were a much smaller part of the gift.

With almost no exceptions, the classical and semiclassical scores were either added copies (i.e., we already had that exact edition at UNT, previously cataloged in full) or had high-quality copy on OCLC that needed little but routine work before being added to our catalog. In contrast, the popular music, particularly the individual song sheets, often required extensive editing or new input. Although popular music is far easier to catalog than art music, it still presents certain challenges. These are described later in this article.

Personnel

For the cataloging project that provided fodder for the observations recorded here, in Fall 2010 six graduate students from the College of Music or the College of Information (plus a seventh during September) supplemented the regular music cataloging staff. Student workers created or edited the records; full-time staff checked their work and provided feedback. All work was done online, using OCLC via the Connexion Client. The full-time cataloging staff involved with this project were also on the RDA Test team and consequently concentrated part of the day on the practical use of RDA, while some of the balance of their time went toward checking records that were being created according to AACR2.

Although this paper concentrates on the specifics of catalog records produced during this one season (Fall 2010, which coincided with the "actively-cataloging" portion of the RDA Test), the Ben A. Brown, or gift-scores, project as a whole lasted more than a year. Over the life of the project, the population of student workers was constantly in flux. Eleven student workers in total were involved and no single student worked throughout the entire project. However, the kinds of errors these project employees made were remarkably consistent across the entire time period, that is, Student A, working in Summer 2010; Student C, working in Fall 2010; and Student J, working in Spring 2011, would make the same sorts of errors. Particular types of errors that occurred frequently are discussed in the section Cataloging the Gift Scores.

Training

The student workers, the great majority of whom were completely new to cataloging, were trained in using the relevant documentation for AACR2 through *Cataloger's Desktop* and were instructed that their records were to be done according to that set of rules, in MARC, with ISBD punctuation. Each student followed our usual training regime, beginning with tutorials on Connexion Client and *Cataloger's Desktop*, followed by closely supervised searching and cataloging (both original and copy), which gradually changed to independent work as the student began to show mastery. This training was the responsibility of the project supervisor.

The student catalogers were able to contribute meaningfully to the project after roughly a dozen hours of training. Two features of the learning and cataloging environment contributed to this comparatively quick attainment of quasi-independence. First was the fact that questions and errors were *never* looked on as negative. All workers were told from the start to ask questions freely, whenever needed, and were assured that corrections to their catalog records were normal and expected. We emphasized that no one produces completely error-free records on the first try, or for quite a while after, and that students should not be discouraged if they received lengthy comments and numerous corrections. This assurance was repeated as it seemed appropriate for the individual worker. Narrative corrections routinely included AACR2 rule numbers or references to other rules or guidelines in *Cataloger's Desktop*; by looking up and reading the rule, with a specific case in mind, catalogers gradually learned enough about the current code and ancillary documents to create records that were correct or nearly so before they were first submitted for checking. It never happened that the error rate failed to diminish as the number of catalog records completed increased. That is, the assurance that errors were normal and expected did not produce a climate in which mediocrity prevailed, as might have been feared.

The second feature of the environment that contributed to relatively quick progress to quasi-independence was our use of Constant Data records in Connexion Client. These records simplified the cataloging task considerably, turning much of it into a fill-in-the-blanks exercise. With these records in place, students did not need to remember in the early stages what the various tags meant but were told by prompts what sort of information should go in each field or subfield. Nor did they need to remember the peculiarities of ISBD punctuation; all such punctuation and the related spacing were supplied.

The Constant Data for the descriptive part of the cataloging record is given in Figure 1. The prompts in angle brackets, such as <title proper>, would be overwritten by the information described by the prompt. Similarly, question marks would be replaced by information of the sort suggested by the context (indicators after MARC tags, numbers of pages or of centimeters in the 300 field).

Constant Data was available for each part of the cataloging record. During this project all students used these guides extensively, especially at the beginning. After only a small amount of coaching, these Constant Data records proved to be adequate guides to *what* should be put in each field. The training librarian could concentrate on more meaty matters, in particular why this information is important, why it appears the way it does on publications, and what we intend to accomplish by recording it.

040			INT ǂc INT
▸	020		<ISBN>
▸	024	?	<ISMN, EAN, other number>
▸	028	? ?	<publisher's or plate number> ǂb <publisher>
▸	049		INTM
▸	245	? ?	<title proper> : ǂb <other title information> / ǂc <statement of responsibility> ; <subsequent statement of resp.>
▸	250		<edition>.
▸	254		<musical presentation statement>.
▸	260		<city> : ǂb <publisher>, ǂc <date>.
▸	300		1 score (? p.) ; ǂc ? cm. (If the item is for a solo instrument or is not a score, say ? p. of music instead of 1 score (? p.))
▸	490	1	<series, as it is on the item> ; ǂv <series numbering>
▸	500		<source of title if not title page.>

FIGURE 1 Constant data for description.

Cataloging the Gift Scores

During this project, when students created a catalog record, especially the descriptive portion, the way they thought it "should" go, and without realizing that a specific rule existed to cover the case at hand, they usually guessed a solution that was in accord with RDA rather than AACR2. These students did not have ready access to the text of RDA; most were not even aware that it existed. They produced RDA-compliant cataloging not by reading rules but by entering data the way they thought it made sense. This effect was rather short-lived, however. After only a little experience, flavored with getting back many corrections to their records, most students began to follow AACR2 conventions. At times of fatigue or stress, though, most would revert to RDA-compliant descriptions.

This situation is entirely different from that described in the 2011 special issue of *Cataloging & Classification Quarterly* edited by Hall and Ellett and entitled *RDA Testing: Lessons Learned and Challenges Revealed*. The articles discuss the challenges and successes encountered, benefits accrued, and methods applied in trying to catalog according to RDA during the U.S. national test of the code. Although the UNT testers (three music catalogers) met with experiences similar to some reported in that issue, the student catalogers being discussed here were not trying to apply RDA, but were doing so inadvertently on frequent occasions.

What specifically did we see from the student catalogers? The following examples are from records created during Fall 2010, but they are consistent with what other beginning catalogers did during the rest of this project.

CAPITALIZATION

In titles, which the student catalogers readily understood to be transcribed, the issue of capitalization immediately came to the fore. Publications often capitalize each word of title-page information, or each word except minor ones. For instance, we were often confronted by titles such as

> Fallen Apples

The student catalogers persistently transcribed capitalization as found, except that when confronted by a title in all capital letters, they would capitalize each principal word, not each letter. AACR2 1.1B1 says that in transcribed fields one is to capitalize according to an appendix (Appendix A), which prescribes what amounts to sentence case in the language being transcribed. RDA 1.7.1-1.7.2 gives as the principal rule basically the same instruction, but alternative rules allow other conventions to be used, such as a style created by the cataloging agency. A Library of Congress Policy Statement (LCPS) creates such a style manual for the Library of Congress, instructing the cataloger to either "take what you see" or follow the appendix. Our student catalogers uniformly preferred the "take what you see" option, that is, transcribing literally, with the exception of substituting title case when the item had all capitals. In her portion of a report from Stanford University Libraries (Lorimer & de Groat, 2011), which took part in the U.S. National Test, and which has continued to catalog using RDA, Lorimer calls RDA's option of transcribing capitalization as given a strength of the code.

Noun Phrases

Noun phrases that come between the title proper and the statement of responsibility are treated differently in the two codes. For instance, we saw many title pages of this sort:

> The golden west, a silv'ry nest, and you
> > Waltz song
> > by Al Sherman & Al Lewis.

AACR2 1.1F12 tells us to "treat a noun phrase occurring in conjunction with a statement of responsibility as other title information if it is indicative of the nature of the work." This would produce (disregarding the issue of capitalization)

> The golden west, a silv'ry nest, and you: waltz song/by Al Sherman & Al Lewis.

RDA 2.4.1.8, in contrast, says to treat such a noun or noun phrase as part of the statement of responsibility. The result is what our student catalogers did:

> The golden west, a silv'ry nest, and you/waltz song by Al Sherman & Al Lewis.

A noun that is indicative of the nature of the work but does not appear in conjunction with the statement of responsibility continues to be included as other title information (RDA 2.3.4.1). This is not a change from AACR2 and, moreover, seemed to cause no confusion among the beginning catalogers at UNT.

Identifying Information Given With A Name

Identifying information given in conjunction with a name that will go in a statement of responsibility is treated quite differently in the two codes. Here is a typical example of what we saw on title pages:

words and music by Chris Yacich Sp. 2c U.S.C.G.R.

The identifying information in question is "Sp. 2c U.S.C.G.R.," which is everything after the surname of the creator. In other cases, identifying information might come before the name. In AACR2, most such information is omitted, unless certain quite restrictive conditions are met (AACR2 1.1F7). RDA 2.4.1.4, in contrast, tells the cataloger to transcribe the statement of responsibility as it stands on the source of information. This instruction is not conditional but absolute. Omission of inessential matter is an option, but the LCPS to this rule says not to apply the option.

The result in AACR2 would be

words and music by Chris Yacich.

If following RDA, we would put

words and music by Chris Yacich Sp. 2c U.S.C.G.R.

With considerable regularity, student catalogers transcribed the complete information given on the item, which results in a statement of responsibility correct according to RDA. This practice works beautifully in music materials of the sort cataloged for this project; Biella and Lerner (2011) point out that it is not so successful with all types of materials, however.

Publisher

Publishers or distributors usually are named on items as companies or other incorporated entities. Their names are normally something like T. B. Harms Company or Chappell & Co. AACR2 1.4D2 tells us to give the name in the shortest form that will be recognizable internationally. A Library of Congress Rule Interpretation (LCRI) allows us to shorten the name, or not, according to judgment, but absolves the cataloger from deciding how well the publisher is known internationally. The LCRIs also include other options, most of them coming down to the general principle of using judgment to decide what is inessential and therefore can be omitted. The practical result in the cases given above will most likely be

> T. B. Harms
> or
> Chappell

RDA 2.8.1.4 simply says to record the publisher's name as it is shown on the item. The result will be

> T. B. Harms Company
> or
> Chappell & Co.

Again, the student catalogers in our project would almost invariably produce the RDA version when they first began cataloging.

BRACKETED DATA

Information not from prescribed sources of information is normally enclosed in square brackets in catalog records. Student workers readily grasped this general concept. They had more difficulty, however, recalling exactly how to configure the bracketed statement.

According to AACR2 1.0C1, there should be one set of brackets around adjacent bracketed elements in one area. The RDA rules give the option of using brackets in such a situation but say nothing about precisely how to deploy them. The appendix on ISBD punctuation, in contrast to AACR2, calls for a separate set of brackets around each data element, even if it is contiguous with another bracketed element. This rule is stated in ISBD Consolidated, 2010 draft (ISBD Review Group, 2010), A.3.2.8, and also in RDA D.1.2.1.

Students might produce two variations that approximate this RDA/ISBD rule. Some bracketed each element separately, such as

> [New York] : [Chappell], [1976]

Others would do something like the following:

> [S.l. : s.n.], [1949]

The first of these examples reflects exactly what the RDA appendix and ISBD prescribe. In the second, we surmise that the student was thinking of the place and publisher as one string of information. The date is apparently being considered a separate piece of information; on most pieces of music, especially music from the period covered by this gift (chiefly early and middle 20th century), the evidence used to determine the date of publication is physically separate from that used to establish the place and publisher.

Only after some experience would a student produce the desired AACR2 version of either of these statements:

[New York : Chappell, 1976]
or
[S.l. : s.n., 1949]

Relationships

AACR2 is on the whole not greatly concerned about relationships among the various entities that appear in a catalog record. A few rules, particularly in Chapter 21: "Choice of Access Points," deal with giving access points, and sometimes explanatory notes, for related works or names (persons or bodies). The access points as prescribed in the rules do not say what the relationship is, although notes may do so. Although relationship designators on names have long been possible in MARC, they are optional in AACR2 (21.0D) and an LCRI to that rule says not to apply them. RDA, in contrast, is highly interested in relationships. The code includes six sections on recording relationships (out of ten sections total), plus four appendices about relationship designators (out of twelve appendices total). The appendices include extensive lists of the terms authorized for use in naming relationships.

A local practice in the Music Library at UNT produces headings that accidentally brought out a strong prejudice in favor of relationship designators among the student catalogers. The practice in question is rooted in our abhorrence of undifferentiated personal name headings. We do not want the items by the musician interfiling with the ones by the scientist, even if their names are the same and no information to differentiate them is available. As a consequence, we make heavy use of such modifiers as $c musician to differentiate names, even in situations where this modifier is not sufficiently supported to be added to the heading in a national authority record.

For instance, the Ben A. Brown Collection included a popular song with lyrics by Robert Bruce. There are many persons by this name in the LC authority file on OCLC. None are our lyricist, however. Because there is also an undifferentiated personal name heading for Bruce, Robert, we cannot simply use the name from the item without conflicting with this record. Consequently, we used Bruce, Robert, $c lyricist.

In our experience student catalogers are happy with this solution immediately. When they encounter the same person acting in another capacity (e.g., as a composer) however, they want to give the name a $c for that other capacity: Bruce, Robert, $c composer. That is, they see the $c as a relationship designator rather than as a distinguishing term to make the heading different from other headings. From this we surmise that using relationship designators will seem correct and easy to new catalogers. They will need to learn the precise format to use and how to locate the appropriate relationship designator in RDA, but the notion of supplying terms specifying roles will be comfortable.

SUMMARY: "INADVERTENT" RDA

From the preceding it is evident that our student catalogers would have little difficulty following many of the rules of RDA. Specifically, the descriptive rules, some punctuation rules from ISBD, and the general concept of recording relationships all seem to be the way these students would catalog if they were left simply to record information the way it makes sense to them. Moreover, this is the way they catalog when they are tired, preoccupied, or otherwise do not have their minds entirely on the task at hand.

While the sample population is far too small to allow drawing any firm conclusions, the fact that these beginning catalogers often produced RDA-compliant cataloging without ever reading an RDA rule is surely a hopeful sign that training new catalogers to use the new code will be relatively easy. If the basics of description, some punctuation, and the general idea of specifying relationships are likely to be understood immediately and done correctly with little more than a cursory introduction, then more time training and teaching can be on those aspects of RDA that are more difficult to grasp. In addition, supervisors and teachers will be able to put increased emphasis on the ever-important question of *why* the code is the way it is.

IMPLICATIONS FOR THE FUNCTIONAL FUTURE OF BIBLIOGRAPHIC CONTROL

What do these observations suggest about a "smarter" way to catalog in the future? First, if beginners get the descriptive part of a catalog record correct, according to RDA, almost automatically, then there is no reason that description of any but the knottiest of materials needs to be the function of a librarian. We will be able to use intelligent student workers or volunteers, probably guided by a fill-in-the-blank template, to do most bibliographic description. In fact, there is little reason in most cases to use humans at all. If the rules are sufficiently straightforward, machine-generated information (assuming intelligently written software) would suffice for this portion of the cataloging task for most materials.

There remain a few rules that require judgment, such as RDA 2.3.1.6, which prescribes that one should not transcribe words that serve as an introduction and *are not intended* as part of the title. Machines (or beginning catalogers) cannot reliably determine intent and thus cannot follow a rule such as this one. In RDA, this rule is followed by an "optional addition," which allows the title as found to be transcribed as a variant title if it is considered to be important. For the most streamlined application of this concept, perhaps the two rules should be reversed: The title as found should be the "title," and the version without introductory words could be the optional addition. If there is change in typeface, size of type, or other such visible characteristic between the introductory words and the title being introduced, even a machine generating the description could add the variant title. If no such characteristic is present, a human (perhaps a cataloger with some experience) would need to record the variant title. This procedure would not work for certain specialist communities, however, such as catalogers of Hebraica (Biella & Lerner, 2011).

The preceding brings out one view of the role of the cataloger in the future. Rather than spending time doing routine transcription, the cataloger would start with a skeletal descriptive record created by machine (or volunteer, or beginner) and flesh it out with those elements that require judgment, experience, and thought. To be sure, this is roughly what is done today with unenhanced vendor records in OCLC. The quality of the description in current vendor records varies greatly, however. Some require extensive cleanup before the cataloger can move to adding subjects, authority-controlled access points, and other nondescriptive material; moreover, deciding what needs to be cleaned up is not a task that could easily be automated or entrusted to beginning workers. In the hypothetical future being imagined here, the skeletal description would be the product of well-designed software and procedures, as some vendor records already are, and thus would need little, if any, cleanup.

What would be needed beyond the skeletal descriptive record, if that were indeed created intelligently, whether by a person or by an automated process? Chiefly the cataloger would add links to related works, persons, or bodies. For instance, if the "work record" for the intellectual product embodied in the manifestation being cataloged already indicated that this work was a symphony and was already linked to the "person" record for the composer, then the record for this specific manifestation would not need to repeat this information. If it were also linked to the appropriate expression information, the manifestation record would not need to specify that it was, say, the piano-four-hands arrangement of this symphony. The manifestation record itself would need very little beyond the descriptive information that could be created by machine or by a low-level worker, with links to records of related entities.

CONCLUSION

Our experience with the Ben A. Brown Collection tells us, not only that description under RDA turns out to be relatively simple and intuitive, at least for the types of material making up the bulk of this gift, but also that graduate student workers are entirely capable, with instruction and training, of doing a reasonably good job of identifying the works and persons connected with a composition. This collection consisted chiefly of popular music, which is far easier to handle than art music, but students still needed to be alert to such traps as songs published as independent works but actually being from musicals that are unmentioned on the publication, or songwriters with the same name as someone else who is already established in the authority file. With appropriate training, they usually found this information. Ferreting it out was not a task needing the insight of an experienced cataloger.

My role as the librarian in charge of this project, after the training stages, consisted mostly of checking that students had identified works and persons accurately (and had identified all the relevant people), correcting the occasional misidentification or adding someone who had been omitted, and, much less often, fixing occasional descriptive details, particularly where AACR2 and RDA differ. The majority of my time was focused on higher-level intellectual tasks. The routine work and the easier intellectual jobs were already done by the time records reached me.

In the future, under RDA, training for routine tasks should be far easier and quicker than it now is under AACR2. Automating descriptive work seems entirely possible. The time that need not be spent on teaching the minutiae of the current cataloging code can be devoted to training for the easier intellectual parts of cataloging. The experienced cataloger can concentrate on the more difficult (and usually more interesting) challenges of clarifying the links among the applicable FRBR entities. This will, in turn, result in an improved experience for library patrons, assuming that software becomes available to exploit these linkages to guide the patron to exactly the right publication to fulfill the need of the moment. This is one part of my vision of the future of bibliographic control.

REFERENCES

Biella, J., & Lerner, H. (2011). The RDA Test and Hebraica cataloging: Applying RDA in one cataloging community. *Cataloging & Classification Quarterly, 49*(7–8), 676–695. doi:10.1080/01639374.2011.616450 .

Bloss, M. (2011). Testing RDA at Dominican University's Graduate School of Library and Information Science: The students' perspectives. *Cataloging & Classification Quarterly*, *49*(7–8), 582–599. doi:10.1080/01639374.2011.616264

Hall, S. E., & Ellett, R. O. (Eds.). (2011). RDA testing: Lessons learned and challenges revealedd [Special issue]. *Cataloging & Classification Quarterly*, *49*(7–8).

Hill, J. S. (2004). Education and training and catalogers: Obsolete? Disappeared? Transformed? *Technicalities*, *24*(1), 10–15

Hill, J. S. (2004). Education and training and catalogers: Obsolete? Disappeared? Transformed? *Technicalities*, *24*(2), 9–13.

Hitchens, A., & Symons, E. (2009). Preparing catalogers for RDA training. *Cataloging & Classification Quarterly*, *47*(8), 691–707. doi:10.1080/01639370903203234

Howard, J. (2011). Learning to catalogue in 2010–11. *Catalogue & Index*, *163*, 10–11.

IFLA. (1998). Functional requirements for bibliographic records: Final report, 1998. Retrieved from http://www.ifla.org/files/cataloguing/frbr/frbr.pdf

IFLA. (2008). Functional requirements for authority data: A conceptual model. Final report, December 2008. Retrieved via *Cataloger's Desktop* at http://desktop.loc.gov.

IFLA. (2009). Functional requirements for bibliographic records: Final report as amended through February 2009. Retrieved from http://www.ifla.org/files/cataloguing/frbr/frbr_2008.pdf

Intner, S. (2002). Persistent issues in cataloging education: Considering the past and looking toward the future. *Cataloging & Classification Quarterly*, *34*(1–2), 15–28. doi:10.1300/J104v34n01_02

ISBD Review Group. (2010). International Standard Bibliographic Description (ISBD), (Consolidated ed.). Retrieved from http://www.ifla.org/files/cataloguing/isbd/isbd_wwr_20100510_clean.pdf

Lorimer, N., & de Groat, G. (2011). Stanford University Libraries reports on testing RDA. In R. Bothman (Ed.), Cataloging news. *Cataloging & Classification Quarterly*, *49*(4), 340–343. doi:10.1080/01639374.2011.571110

Mariner, L. (2011). RDA and the small specialist library. *Catalogue & Index*, *163*, 12–13.

Welsh, A. (2011). Teaching RDA in 2010–2011. *Catalogue & Index*, *163*, 5–9.

What Language Death and Language Planning Tell Us About MARC and RDA

SARAH THEIMER
Acquisitions and Cataloging Department, Syracuse University, Syracuse, New York, USA

The environmental and cultural factors that typically accompany language death are examined to determine if those traits are exhibited in the alleged death of MARC. In addition to measuring language prestige, usage, and change, we must also examine politics and identity. Politics impact languages as every nation creates and lives by a language policy. The role that language planning plays in creating, exacerbating, or minimizing MARC's death is examined. Through a basic review of the language death process, we identify where in the death process MARC is and what role language planning could and should play in future decision making.

INTRODUCTION

The number of rapidly dying languages is growing. Almost half of the estimated 7,000 languages spoken in the world today are in danger of extinction and are likely to disappear this century (Wilford, 2007). The last speakers of probably half of the world's languages are alive today (Harrison, 2007). Catalogers are often described as "speaking MARC" usually by reference librarians who can't understand what catalogers are saying. For decades machine-readable cataloging (MARC) has been the way catalogers communicate with online catalogs, the public, and with each other. There have been predictions, declarations, and audible wishful thinking regarding the demise of this cataloging language (though catalogers may wish to point out that the proper Library of Congress subject heading is actually "Language Obsolescence" not "Language Death"). In 2000, the American Library

Association (ALA) held a panel discussion entitled "Is MARC Dead"? Taking a more activist view, in 2002 Roy Tennant penned "MARC Must Die" followed by "MARC Exit Strategies," which apparently described how to flee from the police after killing it. Two other examples, "Will RDA mean the death of MARC?" (Cronin, 2011) and "Will RDA Kill MARC?" (Coyle, 2011), blame the death on inanimate rules. In May 2011, the Library of Congress, with international partners, announced a review of MARC to determine a "transition path," implying that dying MARC has seen the light and needs help crossing over (Library of Congress, 2011). With so many death declarations, there has been relatively little discussion of the death process. There are presently more than 1,800,000,000 MARC records in OCLC alone, with a new record being added to that database every 10 seconds. (De Rosa et al., 2012) These facts do not appear to depict a dying language.

To assess the alleged death of MARC, this paper examines environmental and cultural factors that typically accompany language death to determine if those traits are exhibited in MARC. Measuring language prestige, language usage, and language change requires looking at politics and identity, in addition to language, as all are intertwined. Politics impact languages as every nation creates and lives by a language policy and all languages are affected by them. This paper will also examine the role language planning played in creating, exacerbating, or minimizing MARC's death. Through a basic review of the language death process, we identify where in the death process MARC is and what role language planning could and should play in future decision making.

LANGUAGE POLICY AND PLANNING

Language policy develops language use principles and language planning puts policy into action. Policy is communicated through official documents, but can be inferred from people's language practices, ideologies, and beliefs. There are implicit and covert ways of regulating a language. This may be as simple as avoiding, delaying, and ignoring certain language issues or deliberately limiting the knowledge and learning of other languages. Such a strategy has been called the "invisible policy" (Giri, 2011). Visible or invisible, language plans are often used to maintain current power structure, influence public opinion, and allocate resources for the education and promotion of the chosen language. These policies often lead to benefits for some and loss of privilege status and rights for others.

However it is implemented, the planning process has three core activities. The first is status planning. Status planning involves planning the use of certain languages for particular purposes in certain domains. When the Library of Congress created MARC its intended purpose was the production of catalog cards via machine-readable records. In 1969 a task force changed MARC's use, declaring that the MARC Distribution Service should be expanded to include all languages and all material formats as rapidly as technology and resources would allow. MARC's status grew to include bibliographic, authority, and holdings data.

Corpus planning involves decisions about linguistic norms and forms. MARC standards went through many changes as its defined domain increased. After MARC usage grew beyond the Library of Congress, a process was developed to allow changes to the new MARC standards. Machine Readable Bibliographic Information (MARBI) is an interdivisional committee of the American Library Association (ALA), with representatives from the Association for Library Collections and Technical Services, the Library and Information Technology Association, and Reference and User Services Association. The mission of MARBI is to establish and maintain a mechanism for the development, review, and evaluation of needed standards. MARBI assists in coordinating, facilitating, and overseeing the evolution of the MARC format. Twice a year, proposal and discussion papers are discussed at the semiannual MARBI meeting and at the Canadian Committee on MARC meeting in Canada.

Content-related standards have also established supervisory committees for establishing and changing norms. AACR2 was the responsibility of the Joint Steering Committee for the Revision of AACR2 (JSC), consisting of members from the Library of Congress, the American Library Association, the Australian Committee on Cataloging, the British Library, the Canadian Committee on Cataloging, and the Chartered Institute of Library and Information Professionals. The JSC is responsible for reviewing the need for revision, consolidating, and preparing text. After receiving comments on the draft of AACR3, the committee decided a totally new standard designed for the digital age was needed. Resource Description and Access (RDA) is meant to change the nature and scope of rules. The senior management at the Library of Congress, National Agricultural Library, and National Library of Medicine created the RDA testing group to devise and conduct a national test of RDA. After a testing period, implementation was initially delayed, but in early March 2012 the Library of Congress stated that March 31, 2013, would be its target date for implementation (Wiggins, 2012).

Acquisitions planning requires deciding who will acquire the language and how it will happen. Initially the Library of Congress was in control of education and publicity. In 1968, the Library of Congress teamed with ALA's Information Science and Automation Division and held a series of MARC Institutes to introduce MARC. These workshops continued for several years. Along with LC and ALA, bibliographic utilities such as WLN and OCLC provided MARC documentation and education. Though not consciously documented as a formal language plan, the ALA and LC, with some international partners fulfilled the three core language planning areas.

LANGUAGE DEATH

Language planning does not ensure safety for a language. A change in the physical or cultural environment can create an unsurvivable ecosystem. Natural disasters such as floods or earthquakes can eliminate all speakers. In addition to population extinction, languages may die when overwhelmed by a more powerful culture. When this occurs the sequence of events affecting the endangered language seems to occur in three broad stages. First, there is pressure to speak the dominant language due to political, social or economic pressure. Later is a period of bilingualism, as people become proficient in the new language while still retaining competency in the old one. Often quite quickly bilingualism declines, leading to the final stage where the young generation becomes proficient in the new language, identifies with it, and finds the old one does not meet their needs (Crystal, 2000). Sometimes culture clash leads a government to try to kill a language in order to eliminate it as a sign of ethnic pride and national identity. A government may intentionally depict a language as ignorant, backward, or inadequate and relegated to culturally inferior and unimportant roles to accomplish its goal (Harrison, 2007).

MARC'S CULTURE CLASH

Though there was no flood or earthquake to decimate the cataloging population, there was a culture clash. MARC's culture clashed with the Internet. The clash was prefaced by a period of library automation during which MARC was vitally important. MARC enabled shared copy cataloging systems and online public access. The clash occurred when resources went electronic. Users grew frustrated with searches that ended in the identification of print material (Lynch, 2000). By the 1990s, the Internet and Web applications became the defining technology. A 2005 survey found that 93% of respondents agreed Google provides worthwhile information while 78% said the same of library web sites. Search engines were found to be the starting place for 84% of information searches, while 1% of searches began at the library web sites. The rise of Google also contributed to the assumption that formal cataloging is not necessary for access. (De Rosa et al., 2005)

PRESTIGE

Culture clash does not automatically lead to language death. One major factor that does is a negative attitude toward the language both in government policy and in local communities. Lack of prestige can kill a language even when a large number of speakers remain. Such situations tend to occur if a community comes into contact with another community speaking a different language that is economically stronger and more advanced, or culturally aggressive or politically more powerful (Wurm, 1991).

Prestige, the level of respect accorded to a language, is difficult to measure for several reasons. How is respect measured? Prestige may be communicated through words or actions. Much literature exists on strengths and weaknesses of MARC, but all information is not created equal. When people are deciding whether to accept or reject a statement, they take into consideration the source of the information. People are more likely to believe someone they consider to be an expert (Nass, 2010). Well-known people in the field of librarianship pronouncing MARC useless may not be offset by 10 unknown catalogers who praise it. Negative information is remembered for a much longer period of time than positive information (Hanson & Mendius, 2009). Thus experts saying negative remarks or respected organizations taking actions that lessen prestige have an enormous impact on a language.

MARC PRESTIGE

When new, MARC was credited with enabling online catalogs and automation; however, as the number of digital resources skyrocketed, new methods were developed to describe them. The Dublin Core Metadata Initiative (DCMI) came out of a joint workshop held by OCLC and the National Center for Supercomputing Applications. It promotes the widespread adoption of interoperable metadata standards and develops specialized metadata vocabularies for describing resources. The Visual Resources Association (VRA) worked to create metadata standards for images description, with the first VRA standards published in 1996, with many later revisions. MODS, an XML-based bibliographic schema, was developed by the Library of Congress as a compromise between MARC and Dublin Core. MODS trial use began in 2002. METS uses XML for descriptive, administrative, and structural metadata for objects in a digital library. This standard is maintained by the Library of Congress and was developed as an initiative of the digital library federation, with a beta version released in 2001.

It was in this environment that the ALA held the panel discussion "Is MARC Dead?" Tennant stated that MARC no longer rules and that one metadata standard is not inadequate. In "MARC Must Die," Tennant continued the disparagement saying, "There are only two kinds of people who believe themselves able to read a MARC record without referring to a stack of manuals: a handful of our top catalogers and those on serious drugs" (Tennant, 2002). Diane Hillman continued the death imagery when she remarked that the Library of Congress Working Group on the Future of Bibliographic Control "drove the final nails into MARC's coffin" by recognizing that Z39.2/MARC are no longer fit for the purpose (Hillmann, 2008).

CATALOGER PRESTIGE

There is a strong correlation between the prestige of a group of people and the prestige accorded to the language they speak, as language is intertwined with cultural identity (Kahane, 1986). Catalogers have never had tremendously high prestige. As early as 1904, Cutter remarked that implementing the Library of Congress Card service for libraries would bring an end to the golden age of cataloging (Cutter, 1904). In 1975, Michael Gorman wrote that we have moved from a crisis in cataloging to a crisis in cataloging and catalogers. Gorman used stereotypes, accompanied by caricatures, to describe catalogers. He divided the profession into the Decadents, the Stern Mechanics, the Pious, and the Functionalists. (Gorman, 1975). Continuing the negativity, Dowell noted catalog departments were considered to be "an employer of last resort—a quiet haven for those unable to make it in other areas of the library and/or academic world" (Kreiger, 1976). Cataloging staff felt equally misunderstood. Maria Uttii, when interviewed in "Will Cataloging go the Way of the Wooly Mammoth?" stated:

> Administrators treat catalogers as precocious and misguided children. We don't get any recognition for the work we do nor do we have much opportunity to advance from one level to another and financial rewards are minimal ... I'm afraid you can't be a cataloger forever unless you are willing to accept a ceiling on earnings and the suspicion that many career catalogers are loonies ... I would find it difficult to encourage anyone to come into cataloging at the present time (Crockford, 1976).

Sanford Berman blamed technological advances for less creative and autonomous catalogers and expressed alarm at catalogers' passivity (Berman, 1981, p. xi). The idea of catalogers not being creative is repeated by Michael Gorman with an additional attribution of blame. He found catalogers plagued by a continuing crisis caused by a lack of imagination, the need for prescriptiveness, the inability to make judgments, and a partly self-imposed feeling of defensiveness and isolation (Gorman, 1981–1982). In 1994, Wright State University outsourced cataloging and fired its catalogers. Arnold Hirshon of Wright State defended the action by defining cataloging as a noncore activity (Hirshon, 1994). In 2005, Deanna Marcum, associate librarian for Library Services at the Library of Congress, addressed the future of cataloging. She noted that libraries should be working with vendors to provide descriptions rather than having this work done internally. The advance of information technology and automation should allow for a different workflow. (Marcum, 2005). The 2006 Indiana University white paper on the future of cataloging specifically noted the prediction that increasingly powerful tools will eliminate the need for library catalogs and the MARC record. They recommended that the library actively seek ways to expand catalogers' work into non-MARC formats (Byrd et al., 2006). A 2010 Library Director Summit on the Future of Cataloging found that the long-term need for catalogers is still being defined. New librarians were seen as having a greater understanding of how users interact with the catalog and have a more user centered view than previous generations. (Hirshon, 2010)

INTERGENERATIONAL LANGUAGE TRANSMISSION

Another aspect of language death is lack of intergenerational language transmission. A language is more likely to be learned when it is valued by employers. To evaluate these issues published studies on graduate education and employment were assessed. When MARC began, most schools required a cataloging course to graduate with a library science degree, but by 1978 cataloging was no longer a required course for graduation from many MLS programs (Marcum, 1997). A study in 1988 replicated that over the last decades cataloging courses have shifted from required to elective. In 1989 it was suggested that large university research libraries should contribute to post graduate education of catalogers because smaller institutions lack an adequate flow of material for advanced learning. (Higginbotham, 1989). That idea acknowledges the fact that graduate education has not been the primary source of MARC knowledge. The Library of Congress maintains a website that provides access to MARC documentation. OCLC provides similar information online in its customized Bibliographic Formats and Standards. The opportunity to learn MARC exists much as it always has, though encouragement to learn it has diminished.

NUMBER OF SPEAKERS

The number of opportunities to learn a language impacts the size of the speaking population. The lack of a cataloging requirement also reflects a decreased need for that skill in the job market. In the mid 1990s a study found that 54% of U.S. cataloging job descriptions mentioned MARC, and only 1% mentioned metadata cataloging. The study found that the overall demand for catalogers in the United States had decreased (Towsey, 1997). A study of cataloging positions from 2000–2001 found that MARC was required in 48% of job postings and desired in 59%. Metadata skills was desired in 26% and required in 15% (Lussky, 2008). A study of cataloging jobs advertised on the cataloging listserv AUTOCAT from 2005 to 2006 agreed that competencies and skills of traditional cataloging were still in demand. It identified emergent areas of job growth as metadata creation, electronic resources management, digital library project management, and web development. These emerging knowledge skill sets were increasingly being integrated into traditional cataloging practices. With new responsibilities come new job titles. New titles include metadata librarian, electronic resources cataloger, and digital resources cataloger (Park, Lu, & Mario, 2009). The 2010 ARL Metadata SPEC Kit found that MARC was still the most frequently used metadata standard in ARL member libraries and continued to be required knowledge for metadata librarians, while 62% of libraries surveyed had simply refined responsibilities of existing positions to carry out metadata work (Ma, 2007). MARC and Dublin Core are the most frequently cited metadata standards in job requirements for metadata librarians. Multiple studies have found that job openings for metadata positions increased, while job openings for catalogers decreased. The title "metadata librarian" may be replacing the title "cataloging librarian" (Han & Hswe, 2010). While MARC remains important to employers, other languages are growing in importance.

UNHEALTHY CHANGE

In addition to examining people's actions and attitudes, it is also important to look at the language itself. Languages must change to remain successful and viable. As the world changes, a language must be able to continually prove itself able to signify what is in the mind of the speaker. If it cannot, then it no longer serves its purpose. In a healthy language individual speakers invent structure and words, while new ideas are communicated through the creative use of language, sometimes through the addition of vocabulary. Artificial languages appear more reluctant to accommodate new ideas because their official method of change requires committees rather than the rapidity of innovation allowed by a natural language (Dalby, 2003). The changes that occur in an endangered language are likely to be different than those in a healthy language. Languages can seem to commit suicide by bringing in more and more forms from the prestige language, until it destroys its own identity. (Aitchison, 2001). In a declining language far more features should be affected simultaneously; they should belong to more areas of language including different aspects of grammar and different lexical fields. Sometimes the speed of change can be dramatic, resulting in an abrupt shift that has been called a catastrophic or radical shift. This phenomenon has been noted in some African situations where ethnicity is weak and where external pressure to shift is high. (Crystal, 2000)

Measuring change is easier than prestige. Because AACR2 and MARC are so interconnected, it was necessary to evaluate both potential sources of change. MARBI's MARC proposals indicate what changes were proposed, the status of the proposal and who initiated the proposal. The JSC site contains documentation pertaining to earlier changes and RDA proposed changes. To assess language health, noting the exact change is not as important as determining the general nature of the change.

MARC CHANGES

Throughout its life, MARC changes have seemed to come in waves as they take time to implement and understand. Early MARC development involved evolution from LC MARC to US MARC and later MARC21. Format integration was also a large change. This study of MARC proposals started with proposals issued in the year 2000, the year the ALA panel suggested MARC was dead, and limited its scope to proposals involving the bibliographic, authority, and holdings formats. The rate of change has been relatively consistent as the number of accepted proposals has remained steady. The accepted changes are also spread over the fields, subfields, and indicators (Table 1).

On the agenda for MARBI's 2012 midwinter meeting, MARBI is scheduled to discuss what MARBI's role will be in a possible transition from MARC. Should MARBI review its charge? How will MARBI balance the needs of communities moving from MARC and communities still actively using it?

AACR2 AND RDA

Cataloging rules have always been revised, and through its history AACR2 has changed regularly. Changes went through the Joint Steering Committee, with revisions adopted in 1982, 1983, and 1985 resulting in the 1988 revision of AACR2. A 1998 edition incorporated changes from 1993 and revisions approved between 1992 and 1996. A 2002 revision incorporated the 1999 and 2001 amendments, with changes approved in 2001, including complete revisions of the Cartographic Materials and Continuing Resources chapter. Regular work on the then titled AACR3 began in 2004. After public displeasure of early drafts, the JSC decided that the code needed to be completely rethought and more, resulting in the name change to RDA in 2005. The RDA/MARC working group to coordinate development of proposals for changes to MARC to accommodate RDA was created in 2008. RDA contains many different types of changes. For example, its approach to structuring data is partly based on the conceptual model outlined in the Functional Requirements for Bibliographic Records (FRBR). It relies less on transcription and cataloger notes. Title information may come from anywhere in the resource and the use of brackets to signify information added by the cataloger is no longer required. The long used general material designator (GMD) has been replaced by Carrier, Media, and Content types. A parallel title can be made if found from anywhere in the resource. RDA also eliminates the long-standing rule of three, allowing the transcribing of all authors, regardless of number. Latin is no longer used to signify missing information in the publication field and abbreviations are no longer used.

TABLE 1 Summary of accepted MARC proposals

Year	# accepted	Changes proposed	Example of Proposal Source(s)
2000	6	URI and subfield j were added to many fields	LC, CONSER, ALCTS, Art Librarians
2001	11	changes for Unicode mapping. The 007 code was added for DVDs. Changes to 007 and 008 coding. The 260 is made repeatable.	LC, CORC, ALCTS, CONSER, and Russian State Library
2002	13	Added 065, 365 and 366 fields. Added FAST subject Headings. More changes for Unicode. Defined a subfield u in various fields. Various indicator changes.	Russian State Library, British Library, OCLC, LC, McGill University, CONSER, and CORC
2003	5	Changes to the 352. Addition of 024 add subfield for URI.	OCLC, California Digital Library, Digital Library Federation
2004	8	Unicode changes. Fields 662, 031, 258 added. Indicators were defined. Some subfields were made repeatable.	RLG, ALA, MLA and ACRL
2005	6	Unicode changes. Codes added to 008, 047 and 048. Subfield e was added to 630, 650 and 651.	MLA, OLAC, Art Libraries, RLG. MAGERT, OCLC and LC
2006	9	Unicode changes. Subfield u added to various fields and subfield r to 865. Terminology standardized for access restrictions	LC, University of Florida, DLF, MARBI and MLA
2007	6	Definitions of various subfields.	German National Library, CONSER, PCC, OLAC
2008	10	Defined Blu-ray in 007. 440 made obsolete. More new subfields defined and new indicators.	OLAC, Spanish National Library, PCC, CONSER, British National Library, California Digital Library
2009	13	More subfields added. RDA changes	RDA/MARC Committee, National Library of Spain, CONSER and OLAC
2010	8	Subfield u was added to additional fields. RDA changes. More subfield changes	OCLC, PCC, German National Library, LC and RDA/MARC Committee
2011	12	More RDA changes. Added source of thematic index number. Defining more subfields	RDA/MARC Committee, OLAC, LC, Dewey and German National Library

ANALYSIS

Did language planning impact the language death factors? There is no doubt that the environment MARC was created for involved published material, primarily books, but expanded to other physical formats. Digital information came later in overwhelming amounts. Cultures react to confrontation differently. How well did MARC face this adversity?

Did MARC experience a loss of prestige? Yes. Loss of prestige was expressed in action and in words. When created, MARC was an only child. Once digitization went mainstream, institutions which had been advocates of MARC (LC and OCLC), created new better languages. Tennant's influential negativity only reinforced this impression.

Did catalogers, the speakers of MARC, experience a loss in prestige? This is unclear. The prestige of catalogers was low and remains so. Articles after 2000 advise catalogers to update their skill sets. This generic advice could be given to almost anyone in any profession facing fast-paced technological changes. Articles seemed to hold out the carrot of prestige or the stick of unemployment as incentive to advance beyond MARC metadata.

Library Science is a relatively small field and there a limited number of professional publications. Tennant's anti-MARC articles were published in *Library Journal*, the most widely read professional magazine. The initial mention of MARC death occurred at an ALA panel. This could be interpreted as another way of establishing an invisible policy. Lack of prestige alone is enough to kill a language, especially if the death is supported by the government and official policies.

Is there less intergenerational transferal? There are fewer fluent speakers. Even though it is not required for a graduate degree, MARC is still needed for most cataloging jobs. More jobs require knowledge of MARC and additional schemes. Cataloging jobs are combining old and new responsibilities. Rather than simply requiring one or the other, there is a need to be multilingual. This will almost surely result in people who have a less thorough understanding of MARC. Educational opportunities for MARC remain available and MARC documentation is found online at no cost. There are still economic reasons to learn MARC in addition to non-MARC standards. As metadata creation is pushed upstream, more MARC record creation is done by vendors, who were not reflected in the job-posting literature.

Is MARC exhibiting unhealthy change? Yes. In a declining language many features are affected simultaneously; they should belong to more areas of language including different aspects of grammar, different lexical fields. Sometimes the speed of change can be dramatic, resulting in an abrupt shift that has been called a catastrophic or radical shift. The RDA changes were intended to be a radical shift, which coincidently also characterize a dying language. The JSC acknowledged the degree of the intended change by altering the title from AACR3 to RDA, whether or not the rule changes embrace the size of the promised change. Outside of RDA changes, MARC proposals do not indicate rapid change. The changes exhibited have been relatively constant over the past 10 years, both in the quantity and quality of change and in the proposal sources.

Planning and developing RDA has been underway for years. Most of the recent MARC proposals have been to support RDA. This indicates very active corpus planning. At times RDA has been met with skepticism and negativity, especially on cataloging listservs, and was not immediately implemented after the test phase. Some libraries are afraid of the financial impact of a major change. Language planners should be aware of the negative consequences of their decisions. These impacts could lead to a decline of loyalty to the state in times of inappropriate intervention.

WHERE ARE WE AND WHAT DECISIONS NEED TO BE MADE?

It seems that after the culture clash we are in a stage of bilingualism, as people become proficient in the new language while still retaining competency in the old one. Crystal notes that this is the short vital window where decisions must be made that will determine the future of the language. MARC records are being created; people are still actively learning it. What steps to take next depend on the language policy pertaining to MARC.

- What are the status plan, corpus plan, and acquisitions plan currently in place for MARC?
- What are the status, corpus, and acquisitions plan for MARC's replacement?

Within language policy and planning there is an enduring debate with the competing ideologies of one nation/one language versus the value of individual and society multilingualism. Tennant stated that one metadata standard in not adequate for the task. Many governments function with multiple languages. Canada has English and French and South Africa has 11 official languages. Can multiple, cultural- or format-specific options work more effectively?

CONCLUSION

Languages have been living and dying for thousands of years. Within the world of libraries, MARC has been a method of communicating for decades. Large languages are becoming larger and small ones are being replaced quickly. In the library world, MARC is a large language and yet still is finding itself being replaced, demonstrating how a lack of prestige can kill even a language in large-scale use. Governments play a large role in the success or failure of languages. By understanding of overt and covert language planning we can understand how power is being used. In U.S. libraries the power is held by large organizations such as ALA and the Library of Congress. Sometimes power is delegated to large committees such as the JSC and MARBI. It is not just what the powerful do that determines the course of a language, but also what they don't do. Inaction and failure to plan have consequences.

MARC is exhibiting several signs of a dying language. Today we are in the bilingual stage, which is where the opportunity resides to alter its course. Though still spoken and understood and desired by employers, the decline in prestige may be enough to kill it. The process is complicated by the interplay between the politics of Librarianship, the culture of catalogers, and the inherent strengths and weaknesses of the language.

The United States, where many of these organizations are based, has no official language, though the majority of the population speaks only English. The dominance of a single language culture may have influenced the thinking that MARC could be used for every format on all occasions. This policy seems to have shifted as other schemes were developed specifically for digital material. As we have shifted to a society with many languages, it becomes more necessary to develop a language policy and plan for each of these languages. The development of an overarching metadata language plan, including MARC and the MARC replacement, covering the topics of status, corpus and acquisitions, would facilitate future policy planning. In order to create an optimally effective plan further study is needed.

RECOMMENDATIONS FOR FURTHER STUDY

1. What are the components of effective status, corpus, and acquisition plans?
2. What are the shared features of successful global languages? To what degree is variation, dialect building allowed?
3. How can we allow organic growth in a MARC replacement to replicate strengths of languages when adapting to change?
4. Some theorize that language impacts how people think. How has MARC impacted the way catalogers think about and see the world?
5. There has been discussion about how the electronic communications uses such as Twitter and texting are changing written language competencies. How are these changes also impacting the way users search? How would that impact metadata?

REFERENCES

Aitchison, J. (2001). *Language change: Process or decay?* Cambridge, UK: Cambridge University Press.
Berman, S. (1981). *Joy of cataloging: Essays, letters reviews and other explosion.* Phoenix, AZ: Oryx Press.
Byrd, J., Charbonneau, G., Charbonneau, M., Courtney, A., Johnson, E., Leonard, K., & Turchyn, S. (2006, January 15). *A white paper on the future of cataloging at Indiana University.* Retrieved from http://www.iub.edu/~libtserv/pub/Future_of_Cataloging_White_Paper.pdf
Coyle, K. (2011, June). *Will RDA kill MARC.* Retrieved from http://www.kcoyle.net/presentations/ALAMARCsig_kc.pdf

Crockford, S. (1976). Will cataloging go the way of the Wooly Mammoth? *American Libraries*, 7(6), 338–339.

Cronin, C. (2011, January 8). *Will RDA mean the death of MARC? The need for transformation change to our metadata infrastructures*. Retrieved from http://chicago.academia.edu/ChristopherCronin/Talks/33602/Will_RDA_Mean_the_Death_of_MARC_The_Need_for_Transformational_Change_to_our_Metadata_Infrastructures

Crystal, D. (2000). *Language death*. Cambridge, UK: Cambridge University Press.

Cutter, C. A. (1904). *Rules for a dictionary catalog*. Washington, DC: GPO.

Dalby, A. (2003). *Language in danger: The loss of linguistic diversity and the threat to our future*. New York, NY: Columbia University Press.

De Rosa, C., Cantrell, J., Cellentani, D., Hawk, J., Jenkins, L., & Wilson, A. (2005). *Perceptions of libraries and information resources*. Dublin, Ohio: OCLC.

Giri, R. A. (2011). Languages and language politics: How invisible language politics produces visible results in Nepal. *Language Problems and Language Planning*, 35(3), 197–221.

Gorman, M. (1975). Osborn revisited; or the catalog in crisis; or four catalogers, only one of whom shall save us. *American Libraries*, 6(10), 599–601.

Gorman, M. (1981–1982). 1941: An analysis and appreciation of Andrew Osborn's The Crisis in Cataloging." *The Serials Librarian*, 6(2–3), 127–131.

Han, M. J., & Hswe, P. (2010). The evolving role of the metadata librarian: Compentencies found in job descriptions. *Library Resources & Technical Services*, 54(3), 129–141.

Hanson, R., & Mendius, R. (2009). *Buddha's brain: The practical neuroscience of happiness, love, and wisdom*. Oakland, CA: New Harbinger.

Higginbotham, B. (1989). Standards, volume and trust in the shared cataloging environment: training approaches for the smaller library. In S. S. Intner & J. Swan Hill (Eds.), *Recruiting, educating, and training cataloging librarians* (pp. 355–366). Westport, CT: Greenwood Press.

Harrison, K. D. (2007). *When languages die: The extinction of the world's languages and the erosion of human knowledge*. New York, NY: Oxford University Press.

Hillmann, D. (2008, January/February). Getting there. *Technicalities*, 29(1), 6–9.

Hirshon, A. (1994). The lobster quadrille: The future of technical services in a re-engineering world. The future is now: The changing face of technical services. *Proceedings of the OCLC Symposium, ALA MidWinter Conference* (pp. 14–20). Dublin, Ohio: OCLC.

Hirshon, A. (2010, May 26). *Library director summit on the future of cataloging*. Retrieved from http://www.lyrasis.org/Resources/~/media/Files/Lyrasis/Resources/cataloging summit report distrib.ashx

Kahane, H. (1986). Standards and prestige language: A problem in Arabic sociolinguistics. *Anthropological Linguistics*, 28(1), 115–126.

Kreiger, T. (1976). Catalogs and catalogers: Evolution through revolution. *Journal of Academic Librarianship*, 2(4), 173–180.

Library of Congress. (2011, October 31). *A bibliographic framework for the digital age*. Retrieved from http://www.loc.gov/marc/transition/news/framework-103111.html

Lussky, J. P. (2008). Employer demands for cataloger and cataloguer-like librarians and implications for LIS. *Journal for Library and Information Science, 49*(2), 116–127.

Lynch, C. (2000, January/February). From automation to transformation: Forty years of library and information technology in higher education. *EDUCAUSE Review, 35*(1), 60–66.

Ma, J. (2007). *SPEC kit 298: Metadata*. Chicago, IL: ARL.

Marcum, D. B. (2005, January 16). *The future of cataloging: Address to the EBSCO leadership seminar, Boston, Massachusetts*. Retrieved from http://loc.gov/library/reports/CatalogingSpeech.pdf

Marcum, D. (1997). Transforming the curriculum, transforming the profession. *American Libraries, 28*(1), 35–38.

Nass, C. (2010). *The man who lied to his laptop: What machines teach us about human relationships*. New York, NY: Penguin.

OCLC. (2012). *WorldCat facts and statistics*. Retrieved from http://www.oclc.org/worldcat/statistics/default.htm

Park, J., Lu, C., & Marion, L. (2009). Cataloging professionals in the digital environment: A content analysis of job descriptions. *Journal of the American Society for Information Science & Technology, 60*, 844–857.

Saye, J. D. (2002). Where are we and how did we get here? Or the changing place of cataloging in the library and information science curriculum: Causes and consequences. In J. S. Hill (Ed.), *Education for cataloging and the organization of information: Pitfalls and the Pendulum* (pp. 121–138). Binghamton: NY: Haworth Press.

Tennant, R. (2002). MARC must die. *Library Journal, 127*(17), 26–27.

Towsey, M. (1997). Nice work if you can get it? A study of patterns and trends in cataloguing employment in the U.S.A. and the U.K. in the mid 1990s. *Cataloging and Classification Quarterly, 24*(1–2), 61–79.

Wiggins, B. (2012). Library of Congress announces its long-range RDA training plan. Retrieved from http://www.loc.gov/catdir/cpso/news_rda_implementation_date.html

Wikipedia. (2011). *Metadata*. Retrieved from http://en.wikipedia.org/wiki/Metadata

Wilford, J. N. (2007, September 18). World's languages dying off rapidly. *New York Times*. Retrieved from http://www.newyorktimes.com/2007/09/18/world/18cnd-language.html

Wurm, S. A. (1991). Language death and disappearance: Causes and circumstances. *Diogenes*, 1–18.

The Possibility of the Infinite Library: Exploring the Conceptual Boundaries of Works and Texts of Bibliographic Description

STACY ALLISON-CASSIN

Bibliographic Services, Scott Library, York University, Toronto, Canada

The frictions present in the philosophical underpinnings of bibliographic control in libraries are discussed by examining the treatment of the concepts of works and texts in the literature of bibliographic control against the theories of works and texts as developed by critical theorists such as Barthes, Deleuze and Guattari, and Hayles. A radical rethinking of traditional conceptions of the work, text, and information is required if we are to have a new vision of "the library," especially one that truly approaches a "universe of knowledge."

In the hallway there is a mirror which faithfully duplicates all appearances. Men usually infer from this mirror that the Library is not infinite (if it really were, why this illusory duplication?); I prefer to dream that its polished surfaces represent and promise the infinite ..." (Borges, 2007, p. 51)

INTRODUCTION

Borges' short story "The Library of Babel," first published in 1941, is often cited as a prophetic vision of the seemingly information-rich yet wildly chaotic Internet. In the story a narrator recounts his life as a resident of a seemingly endless library of books. In the library, the galleries, the staircases, the shelves, the number of books on the shelves in each gallery, and even the design of the books are replicated seemingly endlessly. The inhabitants/librarians can glean no sense from the words contained in the books. They spend their lives attempting to find the key book, the catalog, in order to make sense of the library. It is never discovered. Borges' description of the universe in terms of a library of books resonates strongly with the term "bibliographic universe" as used in the professional and academic literature of library and information science. The International Federation of Library Association's (IFLA Study Group on the Functional Requirements for Bibliographic Records and International Federation of Library Associations and Institutions. Section on cataloging. Standing Committee, 1998) influential report, *Functional Requirements of Bibliographic Records*, utilizes the term extensively but does not define it further than "... the totality of available information resources, within the published output of a particular country, within the holdings of a particular library or group of libraries, etc." (p. 16). In this definition "universe" implies an openness that is not fully illustrated or accounted for by the idea of "totality." The friction between the idea of a constantly expanding bibliographic universe and the need for fixedness as enforced through the development and application of cataloging codes and standards is an issue that has not been suitably addressed by current literature, codes, and practices. Substantive change needs to be made in response to a perceived threat of obsolescence due to declining funding for cataloging departments, library services and collections, and the proliferation of online content. In an effort to affirm their position as a necessary institution in society, libraries are launching new online catalogs with slick interfaces, revising cataloging rules with the intent of making them applicable to a wider community, and offering new "user-centered" services. A number of influential recent reports such as The Library of Congress Working Group on the Future of Bibliographic Control (2011, 2008), Calhoun (2006), and University of California Libraries Bibliographic Services Task Force (2005) point to increasing pressure to change current practices of bibliographic control. These initiatives lack substantial and critical engagement with the foundations and principles of the library and librarianship and, perhaps most importantly, with the roots of Western epistemology. A radical rethinking of traditional conceptions of the bibliographic universe, work, text, and information is required if we are to truly have a new vision of "the library," one that truly approaches and approximates a "universe of knowledge."

This exploration will examine the conceptual frictions present in the underpinnings of bibliographic description in libraries with particular attention to the concept of "the work" versus the concrete object. The theories of works and texts as developed by critical theorists such as Barthes, Deleuze and Guattari, and Hayles will be used as a way to open up new pathways and demonstrate the need for play within our theories of bibliographic control. The first section demonstrates the centrality of the concept of "the work" to libraries as shown through the development of cataloging codes and practices, as well as how the dichotomous nature of the texts collides with the material nature of library collections. The second section demonstrates how the standardization and enforcement of "root-tree" hierarchies and attributions have forced library information into closed systems and limited the ability of libraries to develop different models for their catalogs. The last section questions the long-held and perhaps sacred ideal of bringing order to chaos by suggesting we might better incorporate what could be termed "noise" into our cataloging processes, as well as raising questions for future discussions.

DISCONNECTING CONNECTIONS

> "Hypertext is about connection—promiscuous, pervasive, and polymorphously perverse connection." (Moulthrop, 2003, p. 699)

Library collections are not promiscuous. They can only travel along approved paths, can only have approved relations and must keep to themselves. Library collections only travel along approved paths that are not random, indiscriminate or unsystematic (Oxford English Dictionary, 2012) and are constrained through numerous means such as selection methods, bibliographic control policies, catalog display systems, and in the case of material collections, physical space. The catalog is the area most tightly controlled by traditional concepts of "the book" and, consequently, most affected by a shift away from physical mediation. As libraries move more and more of their collections away from accessible shelving, and as digital collections grow, the role of catalogs, databases, and so-called discovery layers only grows in importance as they become the only contact point between library users and the bibliographic universe. In the quote opening this section, theorist Stuart Moulthrop (2003) expresses the hope many felt the Internet promised, the unending possibilities and connections without bounds, when he wrote about the promiscuous and perverse nature of hypertext. Hypertext, as defined by the World Wide Web Consortium, is: "text which is not constrained to be linear. Hypertext is text which contains links to other texts." (n.d.) Hypertext has existed for more than twenty years; however, library systems, and in particular bibliographic databases, do not meet the basic functions and promise of hypertext due in part to an adherence to conceptual systems bound to linear connections that result in a lack of sufficient and varied connections. The question is how to respond to the promise and challenge of interacting in online environments and in an ever-expanding bibliographic universe. Adopting an interdisciplinary approach to bibliographic control should figure into a functional future. As Barthes (1977b) writes

> Interdisciplinarity is not the calm of an easy security; it begins *effectively* ... when the solidarity of the old disciplines breaks down—perhaps even violently ... in the interests of a new object and a new language neither of which has a place in the field of the sciences that were brought peacefully together, this unease in classification being precisely the point from which it is possible to diagnose a certain mutation" (p. 155).

Looking to other disciplines can inspire us to break out long-held ideals of knowledge representation and control, ideas we perhaps take as immovable.

The book is a representation of traditional binary logic of Western knowledge systems (Deleuze & Guattari, 1987), and the legacy of the library, built to house books, is this system on a meta-level. It is a system enforced through the physical arrangement of library collections, the virtual space of the library and the catalog. The overarching model of knowledge organization in library bibliographic systems is that of a tree. This model must be rethought as the need for a physical library dissolves and if we hope to leverage the powerful possibilities of the Internet. Deleuze and Guattari's (1987) model of the rhizome, a botanical term for plants able to sprout growth anywhere along its length, as developed in their *A Thousand Plateaus: Capitalism and Schizophrenia* as a means to break the hegemonic power of the root/tree hierarchies of Western knowledge systems, is a potentially rich approach to the entrenchment of traditional knowledge structures in bibliographic control. The root-tree has never reached a point of multiplicity and neither have libraries. Bibliographic control, like Deleuze and Guattari's (1987) criticism of linguistics, requires a "strong principal unity" (p. 5) in order to operate. Binary logic continues to dominate information science long after they first criticized information science, amongst other disciplines, in 1980. To assess the promise or peril of the future of bibliographic control we must closely examine the governing structure to see if binary logic, as a conceptual ordering structure, can be thrown off in favor of the multiplicity and promiscuity of online texts, to open up the library to performance and play, to embrace what Svenonius (2000) might term "the idiosyncratic."

FROM CHAOS INTO ORDER

Professional librarianship as is practiced in the Anglo-American world has its roots in England and the United States in the Victorian period (Garrison, 2003) and is a product of a number of forces, the primary one being the Industrial Revolution. The profession is closely tied to the legislated beginnings of public education, public libraries, the education of women and the resulting entrance of women into the professional workforce, and the rise of the bureaucratized office. During this period, library collections rapidly grew in size in keeping with the increased availability of printed materials and coupled with larger and more varied user populations. Pressure grew to enable better access to the expanded bibliographic universe over title lists. The development of "Panizzi's Rules" for the British Museum by Anthony Panizzi in the early 1830s marked the beginning of modern cataloging (Coyle, 2010). Before the 19th-century library catalogs were title lists of what the library contained and did not seek to make connections between the names of authors, titles, or editions. One of the earliest means to achieve improved access was to collate different editions of the same title. Grouping different editions of the same title requires one to agree that there is a concept called "the work" uniting all the objects together. The work is not something that can be seen physically or even in an online environment and comprises abstract, ideational content. The creation of relationships based on works in library catalogs also required the creation of links between authors. The shift from simply listing the objects collected by the library to the collation of works based on edition represented a major change in the way libraries were organized and understood—one we perhaps take for granted today.

The most widely used set of descriptive cataloguing rules in the English-speaking world is the *Anglo-American Cataloguing Rules* (AACR). It was first published in 1967, went through two major revisions in 1988 and 1998 as well as various smaller updates. AACR was undergoing a third revision, when a major shift in structure resulted in a change in title to *Resource Description and Access* (Joint Steering Committee for Development of RDA, & American Library Association [JSC/RDA], 2010). RDA (2010) has not yet been widely adopted. Both AACR and RDA are founded on the "Paris Principles" of 1966 that "clearly embraced the importance of the work, explicitly identified components of a definition of "work" and began to classify components of what were considered to be related works" (Smiraglia, 2003, p. 25), codifying the primacy of the work in libraries. In the latest, and final, update of Joint Steering Committee for Revision of AACR, American Library Association & Canadian Library Association (JSC, 2004) the term *work* does not appear in the glossary, does not appear on its own in the index, and is not clarified or defined anywhere else in the volume despite the fact that the rules are peppered with the term. In the index the only reference to "work" is listed as "Work (uniform title)" thus a "work," in AACR terms, is connected to the idea of a "conventional collective title" or a "particular title" that is needed in catalogs for the purpose of collocation, implying that there was an ideal abstract work in existence (JSC AACR, 2004). The ubiquitous use of the term work and the glaring omission of definitions or clarification of this term reveals a serious disjunct between the creation of the physical description of the "item in hand" and the creation of "access points," the link between the abstract ideational content and the physical attributions of that content. This is particularly evident in the introduction to Part II of AACR, where catalogers are instructed: "The rules in part II apply to works and not to physical manifestations of those works, though the characteristics of an individual item are taken into account in some instances." (JSC AACR, 2004, p. 305) RDA attempts to address this problem.

Central to the organization to RDA is the *Functional Requirements for Bibliographic Records* (FRBR) and the *Functional Requirements for Authority Data* (FRAD). FRBR and FRAD are conceptual data models released in 1998 that define and exploit bibliographic relationships to aid information retrieval. As FRBR and FRAD begin to shape and affect the intellectual and technical systems underpinning the organization of library collections, it is important to acknowledge that embrace of the "work" as the central organizing function in library catalogs is significant. Previous models of bibliographic control were primarily concerned with the recording of the physical properties of objects, while RDA, with its emphasis on intellectual content over physical carrier, has the potential to shift the focus more fully to ideational abstract content, binding bibliographic description to a concrete conception of the mechanics of the bibliographic universe.

While there are a number of components of FRBR, what is most pertinent to this discussion are the Group One Entities, those of *work, expression, manifestation,* and *item*. These four terms designate a hierarchy to be defined in a bibliographic database, the hierarchy at the heart of RDA. The top level is the work: "a distinct intellectual or artistic creation ..." and is held in the abstract, while the item stands for an actual physical or virtual entity at the bottom of the hierarchy (IFLA Study Group, 1998, p. 13). The primacy of the work as a governing structure is without question. A further FRBR component that has been incorporated into RDA is the model for determining bibliographic relationships. These relationships forge the connections between works within the bibliographic database, and they are more tightly controlled than previous AACR models. In FRBR, "Relationships serve as the vehicle for depicting the link between one entity and another, and thus as the means of assisting the user to navigate the universe that is represented in a bibliography, catalog, or bibliographic database" (IFLA Study Group, 1998, p. 56). Although the FRBR model opens up the possibility of increasing the relationship linking between entities in the "bibliographic universe," many of the most intriguing possibilities, such as Section 10, "Recording relationships between concepts, objects, events & places," remain undefined within RDA at this time. Furthermore the Group One entities and bibliographic relationships continue to follow the traditional structure of a root-tree hierarchy, made explicit through the ordering of the entities in diagrams, with "work" at the top through to "item" at the bottom. As the FRBR/RDA model becomes increasingly visible in library cataloging systems, it is clear that the library community continues to attempt to define a universe of knowledge through the use of hierarchy and attribution. Hierarchical structures impose a system within which certain kinds of data are privileged over others, increasing the need for vigilance to ensure that aspects of the bibliographic universe do not become invisible.

A further problem with the centrality of "the work" as a means of imposing order on the bibliographic universe is its abstract nature. It has no material existence and is imaginary. "The work" is highly Platonic in that it assumes the existence of an ideal form with an essence that can be used to produce a stable representation in the catalog. Svenonius (2000) has pointed out that "critical as it is in organizing information, the concept of *work* has never been satisfactorily defined" (p. 35). Furthermore, "The concept of a work as an intellectual or artistic creation—a Platonic object consisting of disembodied information content—is intuitively satisfactory. However, it is less satisfactory in actual practice, where the problem to be faced is how to determine what work a given document represents" (p. 35). Thus fully operationalizing "the work" in bibliographic description may prove a slippery exercise. A radical, and perhaps unintuitive, idea is the materialist troubling of the existence of the ideal work. Hayles (2003) argues that a theory of works is not useful in the digital age, suggesting, "There is no Platonic reality of texts. There are physical objects such as books and computers, foci of attention, and codes that entrain attention and organize material operations" (p. 270). For theorists such as Kittler (1999) the shift from concrete material objects to digital objects results in a total breakdown of the idea of a medium at all. He writes, "With numbers, anything goes. Modulation, transformation, synchronization, delay, storage, transposition, scanning, mapping—a total media link on a digital base will erase the very concept of medium. Instead of wiring people and technologies, absolute knowledge will run as an endless loop" (p. 2). The *1*s and *0*s of binary code erase any real or material difference between objects. This view is completely at odds with the current direction of bibliographic control, and the potential alternative views expressed by theorists such as Hayles and Kittler are worthy of further exploration. By enshrining the work as the central organizing principle of RDA we have subscribed to a view of texts and information that tightly follows a Western Platonic ideal, and while this may aid retrieval in libraries built around this epistemological system, it begs the question: What are we missing?

BODIES AND SURFACES

Attempts to reconceptualize bibliographic control and catalogs for the seemingly boundless online environment have for the most part created an online version of a print card catalog of books, with all the restrictions of and trappings of physical text resulting in what Diane Hillman (2010) has termed the "tyranny of the record." Current practices of bibliographic control, including RDA, continue to be centered on the creation of closed linguistic surrogates. Hayles (2003), writing specifically about the translation of print media to online media, provides some interesting thoughts on what is neglected, ignored, or, even worse, taken for granted in the migration process. She draws particular attention to how the neglect of certain aspects of the physical object, such as "the lovely feeling of old leather" (p. 269), become so "naturalized" that we fail to recognize the limiting nature of these choices. Hayles writes: "*Choices* have been made about which aspects of the book to encode, and these choices are heavily weighted toward the linguistic rather than the bibliographic" (Hayles, 2003, p. 270). We have come to expect bibliographic description to take linguistic form rather than, for example, visual or audio. Moulthrop (2003) claims, "Textuality is our most powerful way of shaping information" in online environments (p. 697). This continues to be true of information systems, such as software code and modes of display, and most certainly applies to the creation of bibliographic data. All media, not only print books, are forced through a bottleneck of linguistic representation in the act of bibliographic description. Moreover as we move further toward the acceptance of FRBR as the conceptual model of choice for bibliographic description with an idealized work at the top of a hierarchy, we will continue to replicate systems that ignore the importance of materiality. Despite the proliferation of other kinds of media on the Internet, most systems remain dependent on linguistic representation and linguistic metadata. Linguistic representation has become naturalized, and adherence to a text-based, book-based, or index card-based vision of libraries restricts our ability to envision bibliographic data in a different way.

An additional challenge to expanding a future vision of library catalogs is the static nature of bibliographic data. Coyle (2010), writing a brief history of library metadata concludes, "It also was designed to basically stay the same throughout its existence, not to be recombined with other data" (p. 10). To aid the user in finding and identifying resources, the act of cataloging requires the creation of bibliographic surrogates. However, these surrogates, in essence, stop time. It is like taking a snapshot that fixes the object at a particular point. Svenonius (2000) uses the term "space-time embodiments of information" (p. 107) to refer to the concrete existence of documents. Bibliographic records also become a particular "space-time embodiment." Conceptual friction arises with current FRBR-based models of bibliographic description such as RDA, as "the work" must be recorded and fixed in order to function. The "work" concept both fixes and stabilizes the whole of the bibliographic universe, thus creating objects that become a "signifying totality" (Deleuze & Guattari, 1987) with an essence that can be described and documented. Bibliographic description requires the practice of what some literary and cultural critics might refer to as clinical methods, meaning objects to be cataloged become like dead bodies that can be dissected and analyzed, dependent on ideas related to a Platonic reality of works. While it may indeed be true that the work concept is optimal for information retrieval (Hayles, 2003), it is at the same time restrictive and like certain aspects emphasized in the conversion of physical objects to electronic objects, it is perhaps in danger of becoming a naturalized assumption regarding the organization of the bibliographic universe. The dominance of the work concept and need for a stabilized object within the practice of bibliographic control forms a normative matrix, making it challenging and perhaps even impossible to conceive of forming bibliographic data differently.

THE TYRANNY OF ATTRIBUTION

As demonstrated, the centrality of the idea of the work and the (vital) need for attribution bind library systems to replicating traditional systems of control. Barthes (1977a) found that the "image of literature to be found in ordinary culture is tyrannically centred on the author" (p. 143). The model of bibliographic control as developed in AACR (2004), and further amplified in RDA (2010), stresses attribution of authorship, or those considered "responsible for the creation of, or contributing to the realization of, the intellectual or artistic content of a resource" (section 2.4.1.1). Barthes (1977a, 1977b), Deleuze and Guattari (1987), and Hayles (2003) all suggest an emphasis on determining attribution, to the exclusion of potential creators, places limits on creativity. Instead of "works" Barthes promotes and idea of "texts" and though this quote is lengthy, it is a particularly useful definition of the text. According to Barthes (1977b) the text:

> [is] woven entirely with citations, references, echoes, cultural languages (what language is not?), antecedent or contemporary, which cut across it through and through in a vast stereophony. The intertextual in which every text is held, it itself being the text-between of another text, is not to be confused with some origin of the text: to try to find the "sources," the "influences" of a work, is to fall in with the myth of filiation; the citations which go to make up a text are anonymous, untraceable, and yet *already read*: they are quotations without inverted commas. (p. 160)

Deleuze and Guattari (1987) take this idea further, suggesting that multiplicity can only exist in the absence of attribution, writing a "book has neither object nor subject, it is made up of variously formed matters, and very different dates and speeds. To attribute the book to a subject is to overlook this working of matters, and to the exteriority of their relations" and further, "A book is an assemblage ... and as such is unattributable" (p. 4). The act of attribution is a myth even in the simplest of cases, given that objects in the bibliographic universe are never the result of completely original thought. Moreover Barthes (1977a) suggests:

> We know now that a text is not a line of words releasing a single "theological" meaning (the "message" of the Author-God) but a multi-dimensional space in which a variety of writings, none of them original, blend and clash. The text is a tissue of quotations drawn from innumerable centres of culture (p. 146).

Thus, according to these theorists, a text, when taken out of the constraints of the need for attribution, can exist as multiplicity, as assemblage, as performance. Hayles (2003) offers, "To bring the Work as Assemblage into sight at all—requires a fundamentally different view of authorship than that which undergirds the idea of the works as an immaterial verbal construction" (p. 279). How might allowing the text to operate affect bibliographic control? What kind of space might the text inhabit if the need is for a "multi-dimensional space"? Does the online network offer the necessary multiplicity within which the object as assemblage can operate? According to Barthes (1977b), the "text ... decants the work ... from its consumption and gathers it up as play, activity, production and practice. This means that the Text requires that one try to abolish (or at the very least to diminish) the distance between writing and reading, in no way by intensifying the projection of the reader into the work but by joining them in a single signifying practice" (p. 162). The distance between writer and reader has been abolished. Could libraries diminish the distance between writer and reader and open up a new space, one that could enable a shift from order and gatekeeping into a new relationship and understanding of information?

THE INTOLERABILITY OF COMMUNICATION PROBLEMS

> When it was proclaimed that the Library contained all books, the first impression was one of extravagant happiness. All men felt themselves to be the masters of an intact and secret treasure. There was no personal or world problem whose eloquent solution did not exist in some hexagon. The universe was justified, the universe suddenly usurped the unlimited dimensions of hope ... As was natural, this inordinate hope was followed by an excessive depression. The certitude that some shelf in some hexagon held precious books and that these precious books were inaccessible, seemed almost intolerable (Borges, 2007, p. 55).

The quote above could be taken as an allegory of the "famed information overload" (Coyle, 2010, p. 11) being faced by today's users. We in the cataloging community have perhaps been guilty of an overemphasis on finding an "eloquent solution," rather like the librarians in Borges' story, to the perceived problem of information chaos. We seek to create a bibliographic universe where messages are received with perfect clarity, with the minimal amount of "noise." However to aim for a meeting of the FRBR (1998), user tasks of "find, select, identify, obtain" through absolute precision in the creation of bibliographic records is perhaps to miss out on the vital role serendipity plays in human activities. What limits are we placing on our data by only connecting users via the "approved" pathways as set out in our cataloging standards? For example Powers (2011) noted this issue in writing on a user study at Mississippi State University of the EBSCO Discovery Services (EDS). EDS is a federated search product and they had expected users to be overwhelmed by the number of unrelated search results. Instead,

> The biggest surprise ... came from doctoral students and faculty. Dissertation writers get increasingly familiar and focused with their research as they compile a literature review, and the tighter the focus, the better EDS served their needs. Serendipity returned as cross-disciplinary searches became a reality with extremely narrow topics. (para. 5)

Highly structured library metadata is often contrasted with the messy Web and couched in terms of being preferable as it better aids users in refining their results (Coyle, 2010); however, Power's findings challenge this assumption. She (2011) found graduate students and faculty appreciated the interdisciplinary nature of the search results and felt it "stretched a professor's expertise" (para. 6). We think of one of the chief functions of knowledge organization as bringing together like things, but what if there was value to bringing together *unlike* things? It is sometimes the unexpected encounter or the unexpected result that is the most productive. This is part of the pleasure of serendipity. How can we move toward the performative nature of the text and the spontaneous possibility of the rhizome within the practice of bibliographic control? Opening our catalogs up to the possibility of serendipity is perhaps even more important now that most of the initial work of searching is done online. We need our catalogs to expose the constellation of possible meanings, to recognize the possibility of the "object as assemblage," not just "people who borrowed this also borrowed" and vetted reviews.

THE TECHNOSOCIAL FABRIC OF THE NETWORKED TEXT

One of the most attractive threads in Barthes' (1977b) writings on the text is the idea that "the metaphor of the Text is that of the *network*" (p. 161). And further, the text is "that *social* space which leaves no language safe, outside, nor any subject of the enunciation in position as judge, master, analyst, confessor, decoder" (p. 164). The idea of a text within a networked social space (a social network?) most certainly aligns with current online environments. Here also are opportunities for libraries to expand thinking around collections and the control of those collections. Would it be possible to capture and expand the social network around online texts in an academic setting? Can the work-as-assemblage be exposed? Or would any attempt at fixing these relationships just be a return to the "work problem"? Thinking about the "building blocks of knowledge" may be a way to bring out a more performative method of bibliographic control. One that recognizes not only the complete "products of knowledge," objects we expect to find in the bibliographic universe, but also the in-between objects, the unknown unknowns. We must get beyond the idea of what we conceive as a standard and even desirable bibliographic record and attempt to surface the "stereographic weave of signifiers" (Barthes, 1977b, p. 159) at play within our collections.

One could think of this way of cataloging as weaving a part of the "technosocial fabric." I first noticed this term in a blog post on *Online Fandom*, written by social networking and popular culture theorist Nancy Baym. Baym (2008) recounted a story where she credited the "technosocial fabric" of her life with allowing her to find a band she liked through a recommendation of a friend she had reconnected with on Facebook. This recommendation had come in the form of a photo of the band, which prompted her to seek out more information and ultimately purchase the music. Thought-provoking aspects of this anecdote are the use of personal recommendation to find information and in particular, the use of an image as a point for starting a search. While many current library discovery systems allow for social tagging, reviews, and display cover images, these enhancements remain outside the bibliographic record and in most cases are not searchable. Baym (2008) admonishes those of us in the business of creating discovery systems to do better, writing:

> It is very important to remember the serendipitous ways that we stumble across music through our connections with friends and the need to enable that kind of discovery by making the kinds of things fans want to promote easy to pitch and find. Too often music discovery sites foreground the parts that can be done by machines forgetting that the most meaningful music recommendations emerge unpredictably when the technosocial fabric is woven well enough and across sites to let interpersonal surprises occur. (para 12)

A reminder perhaps that, like the users in Power's study, the idea of a perfectly constructed search retrieving a perfectly matched set of results may not be what generates the most useful results. In monitoring my own online activities, I have realized that I do not think of online activities as being separate, but move from one site to another through the social links of applications like Facebook, blogs, chat, and social bookmarking. My online activities take place along the threads of my technosocial fabric and the image of this fabric is the rhizome. It is spontaneous and uninhibited by hierarchy. The idea of technosocial fabric also resonates in the context of Barthes' text in that he stresses the social aspect of the text and a breakdown between the perceived barriers between author and reader. The weave of online activities for many people is tight and loose, multitudinous and confined. The promise of the infinite library is not in one particular system or web site, or through the control of relationships, but in social connections and in the messy, serendipitous ways in which our everyday interactions with information build human culture. How can we develop a functional model of a more performative way of cataloging?

THE FUNCTIONAL FUTURE

Hope for the functional future of bibliographic control most certainly lies with the adoption of a Linked Data model, the most likely candidate being Resource Description Framework (RDF) with eXtensible Mark-up Language (XML) as the encoding mechanism (Library of Congress, 2011). Linked Data would allow bibliographic data to move beyond the confines of a single space, and it is the method through which other conceptual models could be in play alongside models such as FRBR. Linked bibliographic data is rhizomatic in the extreme. Many of the reports and papers cited at the beginning of this article have focused on increasing the ease of bibliographic data exchange, making bibliographic data more accessible to outside web services and systems and on making better use of existing structured data such as that offered by publishers. This would result in cost savings for libraries, optimistically freeing catalogers to concentrate on areas such as special collections and as a means for greater community involvement in integrating library bibliographic data with the data from other cultural institutions such as museums and archives (Library of Congress, 2008, 2011). In the context of this paper a Linked Data future for bibliographic description follows the model of the network and the rhizome, exploding the confines of the hierarchical limitations of the relational database and any particular set of cataloging rules or conceptual models. It would become "of the Web" rather than "on the Web" (Singer, as cited by Knight, 2011). Library data must shift to a fully networked environment, one that allows for the multiplicity of human social interaction to take place and become part of the weave of the "technosocial fabric" of people's lives. With actionable and dynamic linked data, connections could be made anywhere, in and outside the perceived confines of the library, and unlike current forms of bibliographic control, it is not static. Links are not confined to preset hyperlinks. Barthes (1977b) writes, "The Text is not a co-existence of meanings but a passage, an overcrossing; thus it answers not to an interpretation, even a liberal one, but to an explosion, a dissemination" (p. 159). Bibliographic data in the Linked Data environment exemplifies this model. Data would not just exist in different bibliographic containers, but a more open, machine-readable format would enable this "overcrossing" and, hopefully, disseminate library data in the widest possible way, scattering it to not only the most fertile ground, but also to places not normally cultivated by libraries.

Additionally a Linked Data environment could possibly also allow catalogers greater freedom to add what might be perceived as subjective data or data that resides outside the purview of current rules in ways that are useful beyond local systems. This could be the most valuable means to increasing the visibility of neglected names, subjects and physical aspects of objects within our collections. As Baym (2008) reminds us, it is the aspects of information retrieval not solved by machine intervention that require the most attention. A model of cataloging could also be developed that could be less concerned with creating records deemed either "brief" or "full" but rather always in progress, always on the way to becoming, and never complete. An example from my particular area of music cataloging could be the adding of individual performer names for larger ensemble recordings when we do not have a complete list of names. In such an environment, if bibliographic data could exist within a Linked Data cloud, it might be hoped that other community members could add additional names and information, building a network of connections.

CONCLUSION

Does the seemingly infinite flow of information represented by the Internet bring the promise of the "Universal library" or does the seeming lack of boundaries mean it is the "Library of Babel," a place where there are infinite amounts of information but no understanding? We need a new conception of "library," one that has nothing to do with branches, or genres of libraries, or physical spaces at all. It is everything and nothing. In online environments there is only the constant flow of information, which occasionally takes the form of a work container, or a text container, and is only bound at any one time by the conception of the user. As the Age of the Card Catalog begins to wind down, nuanced analysis of the implications of this shift may aid us in finding the future of bibliographic control. The truth remains that effective information retrieval does depend on highly organized data, making the continued use of the work-ideal and attribution likely and even desirable. My aim is not to suggest that all previous work on bibliographic control need be thrown away, or that RDA and FRBR are not enormous steps forward in improving the functionality of bibliographic databases, but rather to demonstrate how the work-based underpinnings of bibliographic control may reinforce a particular view of the bibliographic universe. The question is not whether we should be concerned only with the material nature of library collections or with the abstract concepts of works, or even how to perfectly reconcile the two, but whether we can recognize the philosophical issues that arise out of the friction between the two and how these inform future directions. The future might well lie with a more performative mode of bibliographic description, one concerned less with creating "surrogates" and more with the weave of the network and the play of the text. The question for the future may be what kind of organism are we cultivating? Root or rhizome?

REFERENCES

Barthes, R. (1977a). The death of the author. In S. Heath (Ed.), *Image, music, text* (pp. 142–148). New York, NY: Hill and Wang.

Barthes, R. (1977b). From work to text. In S. Heath (Ed.), *Image, music, text* (pp. 155–164). New York, NY: Hill and Wang.

Baym, N. (2008, August 3). Online music discovery in action [Web log post]. Retrieved from http://www.onlinefandom.com/archives/online-music-discovery-in-action/

Borges, J. L. (2007; 1964). The library of Babel. In D. A. Yates & J. E. Irby (Eds.), *Labyrinths: Selected stories & other writings* [Selections.] (pp. 51–58). New York, NY: New Directions.

Calhoun, K. (2006). *The changing nature of the catalog and its integration with other discovery tools.* Washington, DC: Library of Congress.

Coyle, K. (2010). *Understanding the semantic web: Bibliographic data and metadata.* Chicago, IL: ALA TechSource.

Deleuze, G., & Guattari, F. (1987). *A thousand plateaus: Capitalism and schizophrenia* [B. Massumi, Trans.]. Minneapolis: University of Minnesota Press.

Garrison, D. (2003; 1979). *Apostles of culture: The public librarian and American society, 1876–1920.* Madison: University of Wisconsin Press.

Hayles, N. K. (2003). Translating media: Why we should rethink textuality. *The Yale Journal of Criticism, 16*(2), 263–290.

Hillmann, D. (2010). *RDA vocabularies in the semantic web: What they are, how they work.* Retrieved from http://www.slideshare.net/ALATechSource/diane-hillmann-rda-vocabularies-in-the-semantic-web

IFLA Study Group on the Functional Requirements for Bibliographic Records and International Federation of Library Associations and Institutions. Section on Cataloguing. Standing Committee. (1998). *Functional requirements for bibliographic records.* München, Germany: K. G. Saur.

Joint Steering Committee for Development of RDA and American Library Association. (2010). *RDA toolkit.* Chicago, IL: American Library Association.

Joint Steering Committee for Revision of AACR, American Library Association and Canadian Library Association. (2004). *Anglo-American cataloguing rules: 2004 update* (2nd ed.). Chicago, IL: American Library Association; Canadian Library Association.

Kittler, F. (1999). *Gramophone, film, typewriter* (G. Winthrop-Young, Trans.). Stanford, CA: Stanford University Press.

Knight, F. T. (2011). Break on through to the other side: The library and linked data. *TALL Quarterly, 30*(1).

Library of Congress Working Group of the Future of Bibliographic Control. (2011). *A bibliographic framework for the digital age.* DC: Library of Congress.

Library of Congress Working Group on the Future of Bibliographic Control. (2008). *On the record.* Washington, DC: Library of Congress.

Moulthrop, S. (2003). You say you want a revolution? Hypertext and the laws of media. In N. Wardrip-Fruin & N. Montfort (Eds.), *New media reader* (pp. 691–704). Cambridge, MA: MIT Press.

Oxford English Dictionary. (2012). *"Promiscuous, adj. and adv.".* Retrieved from http://www.oed.com.ezproxy.library.yorku.ca/view/Entry/152429.

Powers, A. C. (2011, December 7). EBSCO's EDS: Relying on patron data to show the way. *Library Journal,* Retrieved from http://reviews.libraryjournal.com/2011/12/reference/discovering-what-works-librarians-compare-discovery-interface-experiences/

Smiraglia, R. P. (2003). The history of the work in the modern catalog. *Cataloging & Classification Quarterly, 35*(3–4), 553–567. doi:10.1300/J104v35n03_13

Svenonius, E. (2000) *The intellectual foundation of information organization*. Cambridge, MA: MIT Press.

University of California Libraries Bibliographic Services Task Force. (2005). *Rethinking how we provide bibliographic services for the University of California.*

World Wide Web Consortium. (n.d.). *What is HyperText?* Retrieved from http://www.w3.org/WhatIs

Index

AACR and AACR2 (Anglo American Cataloging Rules) 79, 81, 191; hybrid environment 200, 201–2, 205; implementation of AACR2 163–4; inadvertent RDA: new catalogers' errors in AACR2 *see separate entry*; Joint Steering Committee for Revision of AACR2 229, 235, 246; NOMAP (Natives of Montana Archival Project) 147, 156, 157; RDA training 137; subject access 92; tyranny of attribution 250

Abbott's system of the professions 59–62, 71–2; cataloging work, how technology has changed 62–7; could functional future change cataloging work 67–71

Access database 152–3, 154, 157

Adams, K. 130

adult learners and workplace learning 138–40, 141–3

Africa 234, 238

Aitchison, J. 234

Albitz, R.S. 65

Allen, B. 90

Allen, M. 140

Allen, R.B. 16

American Library Association (ALA) 199, 200; AACR2 229; ALA Connect service 141; international members 193; MARC 227–8, 229, 231, 235, 237, 238

Ananiadou, S. 13

Anderson, R.C. 139

ANSI (American National Standards Institute) 37

Antelman, K. 130

Archambault, J. 148

Arens, E. 201

Atkins, D. 10

authority control: beyond library catalogue 68–9; interface design and 84–5; RDA: more work for catalogers 68

authority control in molecular biology 9–13, 25–6; bio-ontologies 15–16, 20, 22, 25; discussion 23–5; dynamic quality problems 21–2; entities and relationships: central dogma theory 13–14, 23; entity identification system 17; genenames.org website 14; incomplete mapping 20–1; inconsistent mapping 19–20; issues 18–22; metadata schemas 17–18; named entity recognition, disambiguation and unification 12–13, 23–4; nomenclatures 14–15, 23, 25; problem statement 11–12; reference sequences 15; research questions and methodology 12; tools 14–18

awareness and training needs of UK catalogers: RDA 190–1, 192–4, 206–7; access to toolkit 203–4; analysis of emails from CIG e-forum 194–206; current actions and sharing 197–9; hybrid catalog 199–202, 205; methodology 194; overview of emails 194–7; productivity 204–5; RDA and future of bibliographic control 191–2; topics covered by emails 197; training 205–6

Ayers, L. 64, 65, 67

Baer, W. 126
Baker, B.B. 63
Baker, T. 128
Banush, D. 66
Bard, J.B.L. 16, 22
Barthes, R. 243, 244, 250, 251, 252, 253, 254
Bates, M. 90, 91, 101
Bauer, J. 139, 142
Baym, N. 253, 254–5
Beck, D. 148
Beck, M. 143
Beghtol, C. 90
Beitzel, S. 101
Berners-Lee, T. 46
Biella, J. 220, 224
bilingualism 230, 238, 239
biology, molecular *see* authority control in molecular biology
biomedicine 16
Blake, K. 32
Blanksby, M. 162

INDEX

Blaschke, C. 13, 14, 16
Bloss, M. 214
Bodenreider, O. 16
Boock, M. 64, 65
Borges, J.L. 242–3, 251
Borgman, C. 90
Bowen, J. 149
Bowker, G. 91
Boydston, J.M.K. 66
British Library 193, 201–2, 206, 229
British Museum 191, 245
Broughton, V. 90
Buckland, M. 90
Buizza, P. 93
Bush, V. 32
Buttlar, L. 63
Byrd, J. 233

Calhoun, K. 243
Canada 193, 198, 229, 238
Carlyle, A. 1
Carpenter, T. 32
Carty, C. 194, 197, 198, 199
Chamberlain, C. 32, 44, 50
Chapman, J.W. 67, 151
Clair, K. 66
Clark, T. 17
Cochrane, P. 89, 90
Cohen, A.M. 13
Collins, M. 32
communities of practice 139–40, 143, 145
competition for new work *see* Abbott's system of the professions
computer: and changes to cataloging work 62–4; skills 157, 158; *see also* internet
conceptual boundaries of works and texts of bibliographic description 242–4, 255; bodies and surfaces 248–9; disconnecting connections 244–5; from chaos into order 245–8; functional future 254–5; intolerability of communication problems 251–2; serendipity 251–2, 253; technosocial fabric of networked text 252–3, 254; tyranny of attribution 250–1
Condron, L. 140
Connaway, L.S. 42
continuing education *see* training/teaching
contract catalogers 63
Coyle, K. 37, 94, 114, 115–16, 123, 149, 228, 245, 249, 251, 252
Crick, F. 13
Crockford, S. 232
Cronin, C. 228
crosswalks 133
Crystal, D. 230, 234, 238
culture clash 230
Cunningham, A. 40

Curran, M. 130, 138
customization 63
Cutter, C.A. 92, 191, 232

Dalby, A. 234
Dalgleish, R. 17, 20
Danskin, A. 192, 201–2, 204–5
data structure 158
databases, authority control for library 68–9
de Bruijn, L. 13
De Rosa, C. 228, 230
death *see* language death and language planning: MARC and RDA
definitions: bibliographic control 33–5, 124; functionality 35; learning 139
Deleuze, G. 243, 245, 249, 250
Delsey, T. 94
den Dunnen, J.T. 14
DeZelar-Tiedman, C. 66
digital collections, authority control for library 68–9
digitization projects 64–5, 233; Natives of Montana Archival Project (NOMAP) *see separate entry*
DNA *see* authority control in molecular biology
Dowell, A.T. 163
Dublin Core (DC) 37, 38, 49, 64, 101, 128, 191, 192, 231, 234; NOMAP (Natives of Montana Archival Project) 151, 152, 153, 154, 155, 156–7; Semantic Web 116, 120–2, 123
Dunsire, G. 116

editions 245–6
Eisenman, R. 45
electronic discussion lists/bulletin boards 141
electronic resources librarian/cataloger 64–5, 234
Elmasri, R. 10
Eskoz, P.A. 63
Everett Allgood, J. 130

Facebook 253
Farb, S.E. 43
Farradine, J.E.L. 90
Feltner-Reichert, M. 149
Field, D. 17, 18, 21
FRAD (Functional Requirements for Authority Data) 23–4, 25, 60, 67–8, 93, 246–7; subject access *see separate entry*; training 179, 214
Francis, E. 199, 205
FRBR (Functional Requirements for Bibliographic Records) 23, 24, 25, 35, 60, 202, 235; characteristics of FRBR-ized catalog interface 78–9; conceptual boundaries of works and texts of

INDEX

bibliographic description 246–7, 249, 251, 254, 255; new work for catalogers 67–8, 69; philosophy 76–8, 85; Semantic Web 116, 117; serials, library linked data and 125–34; subject access *see separate entry*; teaching/training 142, 168, 174, 175, 176, 177, 179, 206, 214; user tasks 76; viability of FRBR-ized catalog interface 79, 85–6
Fritz, D.A. 78
FRSAD (Functional Requirements for Subject Authority Data) 60, 67–8, 93; subject access *see separate entry*
Fundel, K. 19–20

Garrison, D. 245
Gatti, T.H. 63
Gelber, N. 140
Gemberling, T. 94
genes *see* authority control in molecular biology
Giesecke, J. 64
Giri, R.A. 228
Glazer, N. 139
Go, K. 12
Goll, J. 19, 21, 22
Google 230
Gorman, M. 24, 44, 66, 232
Graham, C. 126–7
graphic design 158
Greenberg, J. 20, 21, 89
Guattari, F. 243
Guerrini, M. 92
Gulley, M.L. 15

Hall, S.E. 218
Han, M.J. 64–5, 66, 67, 234
Hanson, R. 231
Harris, R. 64
Harrison, K.D. 227, 230
Hartig, O. 149
Hartley, J. 45
Hawkins, L. 138
Hayles, N.K. 243, 248, 249, 250–1
Hazen, D. 32
Hebraica 224
Higginbotham, B. 233
Higgs, P.G. 11, 24
Hill, J.S. 213, 214
Hillmann, D. 117, 118, 130, 164, 231, 248
Hirons, J. 137
Hirshon, A. 232, 233
Hitchens, A. 163, 164, 165, 178, 214
Hjørland, B. 89, 90, 91
Hodge, G. 16
Hoffman, G.L. 65–6
Hopkins, J. 163
Howard, J. 215

Howarth, L. 34
HTML (Hyper-Text Markup Language) 49, 148
HTTP (Hypertext Transfer Protocol) 128
Hudgins, J. 149
Hutchens, C. 41
hypertext 244

inadvertent RDA: new catalogers' errors in AACR2 212–13, 225; bracketed data 221–2; capitalization 218–19; gift-scores cataloging project at UNT 215–23; identifying information given with a name 220; implications 223–5; literature review 213–15; noun phrases 219–20; personnel on project 216; publisher 220–1; relationships 222–3; summary 223; training of student workers 216–18
information overload 251
interface design 75–6, 85–6; current trends: review of recent literature 79–81; FRBR philosophy 76–8, 85; FRBR-ized catalog interface 78–9, 85–6; keyword searching 80, 81, 82–3, 85; proposed cataloging adaptations in response to selected trends 81–5
International Standard Name Identifier (ISNI) 113
internet 242, 243, 244–5, 249, 254–5; and changes to cataloging work 64–5; MARC's culture clash 230; technosocial fabric of networked text 252–3, 254
Intner, S. 213, 214
introverts 141, 144
ISBD (International Standard Bibliographic Description) 92, 128, 213, 216, 221, 223; Semantic Web 116, 119–22; training 179
ISO (International Standards Organization) 37, 38–40; writing reviews 44–6, 55–6

Jackson, S. 89
Jansen, B. 101
Jansen, L. 63
Jardine, H. 198
Jeng, L.H. 64
Jizba, L. 140
Juran, J. 18

Kahane, H. 232
Khatri, P. 19, 22
Kiorgaard, D. 191
Kittler, F. 248
Knight, F.T. 149, 198, 254
Knowles, M. 138
Krallinger, M. 13, 14
Kreiger, T. 232
Krikelas, J. 89

INDEX

Lambe, P. 16
Langridge, D. 90
language death and language planning: MARC and RDA 227–8, 238–9; AACR2 and RDA 235–6; analysis 236–8; bilingualism 230, 238, 239; cataloger prestige 232–4; decisions needing to be made 238; further study 239; intergenerational language transmission 233; language death 230; language policy and planning 228–9; MARC changes 235; MARC prestige 231, 239; MARC's culture clash 230; negative information 231; number of speakers 233–4; prestige 230–1; unhealthy change 234
Larson, R. 89, 90
learning *see* training/teaching
LeBlanc, J. 199
Lee, H. 89
Library of Congress (LC) 91, 191, 206, 207, 232, 238, 243; AACR and AACR2 163, 200, 229; capitalization 219; communities of practice 145; geographic subdivisions 84; hybrid 199–200; MARC 60, 70, 71, 79, 200, 202–3, 206, 228–9, 231, 233, 237; METS 231; MODS 200, 231; name authority file 21; new bibliographic framework 60, 70–1, 72, 133–4; Program for Cooperative Cataloging (PCC) 142, 145, 199–200; publisher 220–1; RDA 60, 79, 164, 172, 177, 178, 193, 198, 200, 206, 229; Rule Interpretations (LCRIs) 220–1, 222; standards 37; subject headings (LCSH) 21, 80, 83, 128–9, 227
library vendors 63, 65, 66, 70, 126, 133, 232
lifelong learning 213
Linker, T. 203
Lipetz, B. 89
Liu, H. 19
Lopatin, L. 64
Lorimer, N. 219
Lubetzky, S. 92
Lussky, J.P. 233
Lynch, C. 42–3, 64, 230

Ma, J. 32, 65, 191, 234
Machovec, G. 32
MacMullen, W.J. 12, 17
Manola, F. 114, 127, 128
MARC (Machine Readable Cataloging) formats 72, 81, 123, 136, 137, 138, 148, 149, 213, 216; computers 62; language death and language planning: MARC and RDA *see separate entry*; Library of Congress (LC) 60, 70, 71, 79, 200, 202–3, 206, 228–9, 231, 233, 237; library vendors 64, 65; NOMAP (Natives of Montana Archival Project) 155–7; RDF approach and MARC 21 114; relationship designators 222; serials 127, 131–2, 133; surveys: use of 191–2; training 179; UK 191–2, 202–3, 204, 206
Marcum, D. 134, 232, 233
Mariner, L. 215
Markey, K. 90
Martin, S. 17
Matthews, J. 89
Maxwell, R.L. 94, 98
Mayfield, M.K. 140
Medical Library Association's Technical Services Standards Committee (MLA/TSSC) *see* serials: metadata and standards
metadata librarians 64–5, 66, 67, 71, 234; NOMAP (Natives of Montana Archival Project) 151, 152, 153–4
metadata workflow integration into traditional cataloging unit: NOMAP 147–9, 157–9; hurdles and solutions 155–7; Phase I 148, 150–2; Phase II 148, 152–4, 155; Phase III 148, 154–5, 158; setting 150
Miksa, S. 193
Millsap, L. 62
molecular biology *see* authority control in molecular biology
Montana *see* Natives of Montana Archival Project (NOMAP)
Morgan, E.L. 93
Morrissey, S.M. 35
Moulthrop, S. 244, 249
Murphy, S.A. 35
music cataloging 255; musical scores *see* inadvertent RDA: new catalogers' errors in AACR2; sound recordings 82–3, 84

Nass, C. 231
Natives of Montana Archival Project (NOMAP) 147–9, 157–9; hurdles and solutions 155–7; integrating data and 150–5; setting 150
Naun, C.C. 80, 81
Needleman, M.H. 32, 138
Neidorf, R. 142
networked text, technosocial fabric of 252–3, 254
Nielsen, J. 195
NISO (National Information Standards Organization) standards *see* serials: metadata and standards

OCLC (Online Computer Library Center, Inc.) 37, 44, 62, 66–7, 133, 164, 200, 216, 222, 224; Dublin Core Metadata Initiative (DCMI) 231; MARC 228, 229, 233, 237
O'Connor, L. 62
Oliver, C. 68, 98, 127, 198
O'Neill, A.L. 140
ontologies 13, 14, 16; bio- 15–16, 20, 22, 25

INDEX

open access 10, 22, 32, 125
O'Reilly, B. 198
outsourcing 63, 232

Panizzi, A. 191, 201, 245
paraprofessional catalogers 63–4, 67, 69–70; NOMAP (Natives of Montana Archival Project) 152, 153, 154, 155; training 140, 142, 152, 153
Paris Principles 92, 246
Park, J.-R. 67, 151, 234
Patton, G. 23
Paul, K. 140
Perry, J.-C. 199, 201
personality 141, 144
Pesch, O. 40, 42
Peters, T. 101
Pitts, S. 140
poetry library 215
Power, G. 140
Powers, A.C. 251–2
preliminary training for RDA: survey of cataloging department heads 161–2, 178–9; content included in training sessions 174–6; helpful content 176–7; helpful types of training sessions 173–4; informed consent fact sheet 180–3; literature review 162–4; methodology 165–6; perceptions 177–8; research question 165; response rate 166–7; results 166–78; survey questions 166, 183–9; types of training sessions 167–73
prestige 230–1; cataloger 232–3; MARC 231, 239
productivity and introduction of RDA 204–5
professions *see* Abbott's system of the professions
Program for Co-operative Cataloging (PCC) 142, 145, 199–200
Pruitt, K.D. 15

Ransom, N. 201
RDA (Resource Description and Access) 25, 60, 67–8, 79, 229; awareness and training needs of UK catalogers *see separate entry*; conceptual boundaries of works and texts of bibliographic description 246–8, 250, 255; inadvertent RDA: new catalogers' errors in AACR2 *see separate entry*; language death and language planning: MARC and *see separate entry*; Library of Congress (LC) 60, 79, 164, 172, 177, 178, 193, 198, 200, 206, 229; preliminary training for RDA: survey of cataloging department heads *see separate entry*; Semantic Web 116–22, 123; showing relationships and expanding authority control work 68; subject access *see separate entry*; teaching and effective learning of *see separate entry*
RDF (Resource Description Framework) 71, 123–4, 148, 254; functional futures 122–3; linked data: interoperability from bottom-up 116–22; Semantic Web and 114–16; serials, FRBR and library linked data 127, 128–9, 131, 134
recommended practices 40–1
reflective practitioner 139, 142
relational databases 158
review of draft standards *see* standards development
Riemer, J.J. 66, 149
Riesthuis, G. 100
Riva, P. 127, 130, 132
Robu, I. 49
Rosenberg, Frieda 130

San Gil, I. 17
Sanchez, E.R. 164
Šauperl, A. 90–1
Scherdin, M.J. 141
Scheschy, V.M. 63
Schön, D. 139
Schottlaender, B.E.C. 66
Schreier, A.A. 39
scientific data 26; authority control in molecular biology *see separate entry*
Seal, R.L. 14
search engines 230
Semantic Web 10, 46, 49, 113, 123–4, 149, 201; functional futures 122–3; linked data: interoperability from bottom-up 116–22; Resource Description Framework (RDF) and 114–16; *see also* serials, FRBR and library linked data
serendipity 251–2, 253
serials: metadata and standards 31–3, 49–50; guidelines for reviewing standards 53–5; guidelines for writing reviews 55–6; intersection of standards and professional work 48–9; key definitions 33–5; literature review 35–6; MLA/TSSC experience 33, 44–8, 56–8; recent trends in standards development 37–41; standards: acquisitions perspective 41–4; standards primer 36–7
serials: training 142; RDA Test Report 137–8; Serials Cataloging Cooperative Training Program (SCCTP) 142
serials, FRBR and library linked data 125–34; significant difference between traditional and linked data model 129
set-theoretic approach 94
Shera, J.H. 3
El-Sherbini, M. 63, 138
Siemaszkiewicz, W. 164

INDEX

Simpson, B. 63
Smalheiser, N. 10
small- to medium-sized organizations 149, 179, 204, 215, 233
Smiraglia, R.P. 246
Smith, B. 20, 22
South Africa 238
Spink, A. 101
spreadsheets 122, 151, 152–4; tracking workflow 48–9
standards development 31–5, 49–50; guidelines for reviewing 53–5; guidelines for writing reviews 55–6; intersection of standards and professional work 48–9; literature review 35–6; MLA/TSSC Survey 46–8, 56–8; recent trends in 37–41; serials: acquisitions perspective 41–4; standards primer 36–7; writing reviews 44–6, 55–6
Stenson, R. 203, 205
student assistants 63; inadvertent RDA: new catalogers' errors in AACR2 *se separate entry*
Stvilia, B. 10, 18
subject access 88–9, 106–7; empirical study: subject entities and relationships in user search queries 100–6; FRBR family of models and RDA: modelling 92–101; future research 107; information professionals creating subject metadata: problems 90–2; iterative process of 91; problems 89–92; subject attributes 95–7; subject entities 93–5, 101–3, 106–7, 247; subject relationships 98–100, 103–6, 107, 247; users of information systems: problems 89–90
Svenonius, E. 24, 89, 91, 93, 94, 245, 247–8, 249

Tagliacozzo, R. 89
Taube, M. 90
Taylor, A.G. 61, 90
Taylor, H. 199, 201
Taylor, W. 193
teaching and effective learning of RDA 136–7, 145; adult learners and workplace learning 138–40, 141–3; attitudinal support for workplace learning 144–5; communities of practice 139–40, 143, 145; examining RDA and RDA Test Report 137–8, 142, 144; implications for training 141–3; interactive workshop model 140; knowing your audience 141; reflective practitioner 139, 142; using technology to best advantage 143–4; workplace learning in library literature 140; *see also* awareness and training needs of UK catalogers: RDA; inadvertent RDA: new catalogers' errors in AACR2; preliminary training for RDA: survey of cataloging department heads
technology and changes to cataloging work 62–7, 123–4, 155–6, 158; cataloger prestige 232–3; could functional future change cataloging work 67–71; MARC's culture clash 230; number of MARC speakers 233–4
technosocial fabric of networked text 252–3, 254
Tennant, R. 228, 231
thesaurus 13, 14, 16, 19
Thomas, T. 80
Tillett, B. 24, 79, 94, 95, 99, 100, 113, 198
Towsey, M. 233
training/teaching 70; awareness and training needs of UK catalogers: RDA *see separate entry*; evaluation of 162; graduate education 233; identification of needs 162; inadvertent RDA: new catalogers' errors in AACR2 *see separate entry*; literature review 162–4, 213–15; NOMAP (Natives of Montana Archival Project) 152, 153, 156–7, 158; preliminary training for RDA: survey of cataloging department heads *see separate entry*; standard of performance 162; teaching and effective learning of RDA *see separate entry*; training methods, choice of 162
transaction log analysis: empirical study: subject entities and relationships in user search queries 100–7
Trickey, Keith 193, 194
Trosow, S.E. 62
Turner, P. 12

Uniform Resource Identifiers (URIs) 70, 114–15, 116, 117, 118–19, 128
United Kingdom *see* awareness and training needs of UK catalogers: RDA
universal bibliographic control (UBC): Semantic Web *see separate entry*
universe of knowledge *see* conceptual boundaries of works and texts of bibliographic description
University of California Libraries Bibliographic Services Task Force (2005) 243
Urban, R. 101
Uttii, Maria 232

Valentino, M.L. 67, 149, 152
vendors, library 63, 65, 66, 70, 126, 133, 232
Veve, M. 66, 149
VIAF (Virtual International Authority File) 113
video-recording records 83, 84
Vogh, B.S. 67

Wain, H.M. 14, 21
Wand, Y. 18

Wang, R. 18
Watson, F. 202
webcasts or webinars 143–4, 158, 167, 168, 172, 173, 179, 192
Webster, P. 32, 37, 40, 44
Weinberg, B.H. 90
Weinheimer, J. 35
Wells, K.L. 63
Wells, M.R. 162–3, 167
Welsh, A. 193, 198, 205, 214
Wenger, E. 139–40
Westbrook, L. 142
Wiggins, B. 193, 199, 202–3, 229
Wilder, S.J. 63
Wilford, J.N. 227
Williams, H. 198, 201, 205
Wilson, P. 90, 91
Wilson, T.D. 89
World Wide Web *see* internet

Wu, M. 195
Wurm, S.A. 231
Wynne, S.C. 79–80, 81

XML (eXtensible Markup Language) 18, 49, 118, 148, 191, 231, 254

Yasser, C.M. 42
Yee, M.M. 80, 81, 84, 85
Yilmaz, P. 17–18, 21
Younker, J.T. 148

Zavalina, O. 102
Zeng, M.L. 94, 149
Zhang, Y. 5, 100
Zhu, J. 43
Zhu, L. 67

www.routledge.com/9780415623568

Related titles from Routledge

Designing and Developing Library Intranets

Edited by Nina McHale

The book covers, among other topics, third-party hosting; the use of freely available blog and wiki software for internal staff communication; and developing library intranets in ColdFusion, Microsoft SharePoint, and the open source Drupal content management system (CMS). More importantly, the authors examine in detail the human factors, which, when not thoroughly addressed, are more often the cause for a failed intranet than the technology platform.

This book was published as a special issue of the *Journal of Web Librarianship*.

Nina McHale is Assistant Systems Administrator at the Arapahoe Library District, USA.

August 2012: 246 x 174: 176pp
Hb: 978-0-415-62356-8
£85 / $140

For more information and to order a copy visit
www.routledge.com/9780415623568

Available from all good bookshops

www.routledge.com/9780415689694

Related titles from Routledge

Twenty-first Century Metadata Operations
Challenges, Opportunities, Directions
Edited by Bradford Lee Eden

It has long been apparent to academic library administrators that the current technical services operations within libraries need to be redirected and refocused in terms of both format priorities and human resources. This book details the aspects of technical services reorganization due to downsizing and/or reallocation of human resources, retooling professional and support staff in higher level duties and/or non-MARC metadata, "value-added" metadata opportunities, outsourcing redundant activities, and shifting resources from analog to digital object organization and description.

This book will assist both catalogers and library administrators with concrete examples of moving technical services operations and personnel from the analog to the digital environment.

This book was published as a special double issue of *Cataloging & Classification Quarterly*.

Bradford Lee Eden is Associate University Librarian for Technical Services and Scholarly Communication at the University of California, Santa Barbara.

September 2011: 246 x 174: 160pp
Hb: 978-0-415-68969-4
£95 / $155

For more information and to order a copy visit
www.routledge.com/9780415689694

Available from all good bookshops

For Product Safety Concerns and Information please contact our EU
representative GPSR@taylorandfrancis.com
Taylor & Francis Verlag GmbH, Kaufingerstraße 24, 80331 München, Germany

www.ingramcontent.com/pod-product-compliance
Lightning Source LLC
Chambersburg PA
CBHW081803300426
44116CB00014B/2220